D1120995

These are uncorrected pages. All quotes should be checked against the finished book.

For more information, contact:

David Olsen, Publicity Assistant | (510) 883-8280 | dolsen@ucpress.edu
155 Grand Avenue, Suite 400 | Oakland CA 94612-3758 | www.ucpress.edu

Maps for Time Travelers

The publisher and the University of California Press Foundation gratefully acknowledge the generous support of the Ahmanson Foundation Endowment Fund in Humanities.

Maps for Time Travelers

HOW ARCHAEOLOGISTS USE TECHNOLOGY TO BRING US CLOSER TO THE PAST

Mark D. McCoy

UNIVERSITY OF CALIFORNIA PRESS

University of California Press
Oakland, California

© 2020 by Mark D. McCoy

Library of Congress Cataloging-in-Publication Data

Names: McCoy, Mark D., 1975– author.
Title: Maps for time travelers : how archaeologists use technology to bring us closer
  to the past / Mark D. McCoy.
Description: Oakland, California : University of California Press, [2020] | Includes
  bibliographical references and index.
Identifiers: LCCN 2019041034 (print) | LCCN 2019041035 (ebook) |
  ISBN 9780520303164 (cloth) | ISBN 9780520972650 (ebook)
Subjects: LCSH: Archaeology—Remote sensing. | Aerial photography in archaeology. |
  Remote-sensing images. | Archaeology—Data processing. | Geographic information
  systems.
Classification: LCC CC76.4 .M38 2020 (print) | LCC CC76.4 (ebook) |
  DDC 930.1—dc23
LC record available at https://lccn.loc.gov/2019041034
LC ebook record available at https://lccn.loc.gov/2019041035

Manufactured in the United States of America

29 28 27 26 25 24 23 22 21 20
10 9 8 7 6 5 4 3 2 1

For Ann, Elsie, and Sam

Contents

Conclusion

Preface

What do archaeology and time travel stories have to do with one another? Quite a lot actually. Both are ways that we satisfy our curiosity about the past. Time travel is a fiction genre that we all know well. But archaeology is less familiar: it is not always clear what is going on, or why.

I am an archaeologist and I wrote this book to introduce you to how geospatial technologies are changing the way we investigate the past. These technologies include GPS, satellite imagery, digital maps, and other instruments that are becoming more common, like drones and 3-D laser scanners. Here you will find a crash course, with minimal jargon, on how we employ these tools to create a better, more complete picture of the ancient world.

I have a deep respect for my colleagues who have dedicated their careers to working out how to make specific technologies better serve archaeology. I, however, am a technology omnivore. Over the years I have used every geospatial technology described in this book in the pursuit of knowledge about life on Pacific islands in the era before contact with the outside world. I started down this road by learning how to use digital mapping software called geographic information systems (GIS).

I started using GIS in archaeology in the late 1990s. It was especially handy when, as a PhD student at the University of California, Berkeley, I was interested in how changes in the landscape reflected trends in the ancient economy and society of the Hawaiian Islands. The tiny island of Molokaʻi, the setting for my research, had largely been bypassed by modern urban development. This means that today you can hike around and see thousands upon thousands of stone walls and foundations of houses temples, and other structures abandoned centuries ago. I might still be wandering around there if not for GIS. It not only gave me a way to organize and explore the vast and continuous landscape of features, it also allowed me to do spatial analyses that would have been almost impossible to calculate by hand. These analyses showed how changes in small communities fit into the bigger history of the island, a history that had been passed down through oral traditions for generations.

My research in the Hawaiian Islands, and other Pacific islands, forms just a small part of what has been called a geospatial revolution in archaeology. Back in 2006, when I landed my first academic job, archaeology was well on its way to dealing with the teething problems that came with adopting GIS into our discipline, and you could see a shift toward investigating whole landscapes rather than individual sites. That first job was teaching at San José State University in Silicon Valley. Elsewhere in Silicon Valley at the same time, Google was bringing GIS to the masses. They had launched their digital globe, Google Earth, and a web-based GIS, Google Maps. While not built with archaeology in mind, web-based GIS made it easier than ever to connect people in the modern day with the physical remains of the ancient world.

The developments that really got the geospatial revolution rolling were new remote sensing and high-resolution survey techniques that brought with them a flood of new data. Within the past decade, the resolution of satellite images improved dramatically, making it more feasible to find and map archaeological sites using satellites. Archaeologists' use of 3-D models and of incredible imagery from drones has exploded. Lasers mounted on aircraft have allowed us to map things otherwise hidden under thick tree canopy—something I have found especially useful in my own research—and have been hailed as an innovation on par with the invention of radiocarbon dating in terms of their impact on archaeology.

This revolution was in full swing by the time I moved to Dallas to teach at Southern Methodist University in 2014, but one extraordinarily important element was still missing. We forgot to explain to the public what exactly these leaps meant for archaeology. The consequence has been a resurgence of the popular image of archaeology as a treasure hunt, rather than as the pursuit of knowledge. I have read news coverage of archaeology so sensationalized, so deeply misguided by the treasure hunter trope, that it no longer bears any resemblance to what contemporary archaeology really does.

I sat down and thought hard about how to explain things in a new way. In a way that would speak to that part of everyone that wonders about the distant past. Then it came to me: time travel. We are not using these technologies to make treasure maps. We are using them to make maps for time travelers. Not literally, of course. We are not making maps so that future time travelers can program their onboard navigation systems and set off for the ancient world. But we do expend so much effort determining precisely where and when things happened, I can't think of anything we would be doing differently if we really were writing directions for time travelers.

If you want to see a good example of how this technology is creating maps suitable for time travelers, take a minute and check out

ORBIS, Stanford's geospatial network model of the Roman world. It was created to put the costs of communication across the Roman Empire in more relatable terms than distance; specifically, in terms of time and money. It can tell you how long it will take, and how expensive it will be, to travel between Rome and London by oxcart. It is basically Expedia for Europe, the Middle East, and North Africa in AD 200.

I love time travel. But fictional time travelers almost never go to the time that I am most interested in: the time before writing was invented. Strangely, most of us hardly even notice. That is frustrating to me because most of the human past happened before writing. And it is why I felt it was important in this book to represent a cross-section of research on different times and places, not just my own research.

This is not a guide to what happened, but to how we know what happened. How to tell fact from fiction. I start with a brief introduction to how archaeologists think about location and what instruments we use to create digital worlds. These technologies have become pervasive across archaeology, but there are a few topics that they have proved especially helpful for, including retracing movement and mobility, working out how our ancestors fed themselves, and reconstructing the kinds of societies they built. In the end, I discuss some of the challenges of applying geospatial technologies more broadly, beyond the few places that have thus far received most of our attention, to expand and deepen our picture of the ancient world.

There are outstanding books, chapters, and articles on geospatial archaeology. When I did a search at the start of writing this book I found three thousand references to archaeological studies using geospatial technology over just the past decade. That search led me to the unusual map on the cover of this book. At first glance, it looks like a long, deep canyon. It is in fact a shallow footprint preserved in volcanic ash. It was recently uncovered at Laetoli in Tanzania and is more than three million years old. It is based on a 3-D model that was made by taking many pictures from different angles—a process called photogrammetry. It is estimated that the archaic human who left that footprint behind was a great deal larger than others whose footprints had been uncovered earlier, and so the excavators nicknamed them Chewie, as in Chewbacca. Most of the references I found, like the paper on Chewie's footprint, were written for other researchers to read. They are often so specialized that they would be difficult to decipher even for scholars in aligned disciplines.

We aren't trying to be opaque. Archaeologists want to share the work we are doing. For me, I especially love sharing my research with the descendants of the people whose lives I study. We may not share immediate ancestors but for a time we are joined in our common historical curiosity. Vestiges of the past are precious but not rare; archaeologists have recorded them at millions of locations around the world. I don't know if that kind of shared curiosity is replicable on a global scale but I would like to believe it is. And so, if you have never read a book about archaeology, but you love time travel and want to see where this is going, buckle up.

Mark D. McCoy
Dallas, Texas
June 2019

Acknowledgments

I can tell you with absolute certainty that time travel will not be invented in my lifetime. I know this because if it were going to be, my future self would have posted a completed copy of *Maps for Time Travelers* back to myself when the manuscript was still in its infancy. Sadly, I had no writing help from the future. Thankfully, there have been plenty of people in the present willing to lend a hand, and without whom I could never have finished this immensely nerdy book.

The first people I want to recognize are the people in the present, and in the distant past, who contributed to the archaeology that I describe here. I decided early on that to appreciate the geospatial revolution requires thinking about how the technology has been applied in the Maya area, the Middle East, and so many other places, not just the islands of the Pacific familiar to me. That meant writing about places I have never been and time periods in which I am not an expert. I tried my best and I apologize for any mistakes or mistranslations.

I am indebted to the scholars who kindly read and extensively commented on an early version of the book: David G. Anderson, Jesse Casana, Mark Gillings, K. Ann Horsburgh, Meghan C.L.

Howey, Thegn N. Ladefoged, Rachel Opitz, and Kisha Supernant. They helped me see the big picture and pushed me to present a realistic, rather than idealized, portrayal of what we have done with these technologies, and to discuss what we must do to realize the benefits of using these tools more broadly. I would also like to thank Marieka Brouwer Burg, Andrew Dufton, Meghan C. L. Howey, John Kantner, and Parker VanValkenburgh for their work on recent conference sessions for the Society for American Archaeology meeting that put the academic spotlight on topics covered here.

This book started out as a rather dry, academic review of the geospatial revolution in archaeology that was fated to adorn the bookshelves of a few experts. It took some time to figure out how I might translate those ideas for a wider audience, and it took even longer to actually do it. I had a lot of help over the years from people who shared their thoughts on archaeology, or time travel, or both. I want to thank them all, especially Mike Adler, Michael Aiuvalasit, Helen Alderson, Melinda Allen, Andrea Barreiro, Nick Belluzzo, Simon Bickler, Michael Callaghan, Bill Christopher, Bonnie Clark, Maria Codlin, David Cohan, Douglas C. Comer, Karisa Cloward, Jon Daehnke, Jeff Dean, Carolyn Dillian, Sunday Eiselt, Kelly Esh, Shawn Fehrenbach, Julie S. Field, James L. Flexner, Esteban Gómez, Josh Goode, Michael W. Graves, Regina Hilo, Kacy Hollenback, K. Ann Horsburgh, Adam Johnson, Fiona Jordan, Alex Jorgensen, Ian Jorgeson, Jill Kelly, Brigitte Kovacevich, Spencer Lambert, Jason E. Lewis, Ryan Lockard, Stace Maples, Peter Mills, Matt McCoy, David J. Meltzer, Mara A. Mulrooney, Lee Panich, Seth Quintus, Allison Ralston, Leslie Reeder-Myers, Andy Roddick, Chris Roos, Libby Russ, Jesse Stephen, Jillian Swift, Tracy Tam-Sing, Nico Tripcevich, Joshua Wells, Steve Wernke, and Charmaine Wong.

Southern Methodist University supported this work not only by granting me research leave for the Fall 2017 semester, but also more broadly, by creating an academic environment where I can interact with scholars who help me think outside the narrow confines of my specialty. I am especially grateful to my co-organizers of the interdisciplinary research cluster GIS@SMU, Klaus Desmet and Jesse Zarazaga, and to a working group on Big Data organized by Monnie McGee and Daniel Engels that included Jeff Kahn, Justin Fisher, Jennifer Dworak, Dave Matula, and Eli Olinick.

Thank you to my editor, Kate Marshall, for her help with so many things, and for squashing the rumor that the University of California Press is no longer publishing books about archaeology. An enormous thank-you to my developmental editor, Megan Pugh, who keenly drew out the nonfiction message, reined in my digressions into science fiction, and helped with the book's title. Thanks to copyeditor extraordinaire Caroline Knapp, who cleared the minefield of errors that I left behind with grace and humor. Thank you to Enrique Ochoa-Kaup, Tom Sullivan, and the rest of the team at the press for their invaluable help with the book's production.

I know from personal experience that a book about archaeology can be transformative. The book that changed my life, that set me on my career path, was one of the first published by Patrick V. Kirch, the dean of Pacific archaeology. He has since followed up by writing so many more books that I have lost count. His flair for storytelling has been on display in more recent scholarly books written for the public. I do not have his gift but those later books gave me the confidence to write this one. For that, I say to him, *mahalo nui loa*.

I am not sure how far back my obsession with maps goes. I do, however, remember exactly when I was introduced to the world of digital maps. For that, I have one person to thank: Thegn N.

Ladefoged. He is a leader in geospatial archaeology. We have known each other for more than twenty years now and he deserves credit for the best parts of this book. He is also my friend, which I sometimes feel the need to point out to other people, because productively engaging in scholarship sometimes looks a lot like arguing. He's often right, but don't tell him I said so.

My parents, who left us too soon, let my siblings and me watch way too much television when we were growing up. Today, my brother, Matt McCoy, is my science fiction guru. He read early drafts of the book and contributed to this more than he knows. My sister, Erin Lockard, will forever be a lot cooler than me. As I wrote, they were my imagined target audience; smart, fans of a good story, but not experts in geospatial technology or archaeology.

The premise for this book—that archaeology is more like a time travel story than an adventure story—was something that I feel was staring me in the face for a long time but came into focus all at once. When it did, I found my wife and pitched her the idea. For context, her name is Dr. K. Ann Horsburgh. She is a biological anthropologist, a professor, and expert in ancient DNA, with a PhD from Stanford. Even if she did not have those qualifications and credentials, she would still be the brains of the operation in our house. She saw it right away, and I knew I was on to something. Ann has suffered through every page of this book. For that, and so many other reasons, I have dedicated the book to her, and to our two tiny time travelers, Elsie and Sam, whom we are sending on their way to the future.

Part I

1 *Historical Curiosity*

We are the only creatures on the planet, as far as we know, who can imagine what the world was like before we were born. The picture that each of us forms in our minds when asked to think about what it would have been like to live hundreds or thousands of years ago is distinctive. Even when considering the same object in a museum, or visiting the same ruins of an ancient city, no two people imagine the same thing. And if we are honest, lots of what we picture is pure speculation.

As it turns out, speculating about the past is something we humans have been doing for a long time. The world's earliest examples of art preserved on cave walls provide a vivid image of a landscape full of strange animals, many now extinct. It is a safe bet that if our ancestors were capable of creating and comprehending art—a process estimated to have begun about fifty thousand years ago—then origin stories, myths, and legends describing the past were already being passed down from generation to generation.[1]

In popular fictions, archaeologists take risks and track down relics from the past. Indiana Jones, Lara Croft: these are adventure stories. But modern archeologists are not out to raid tombs or hunt for treasure. We are engaged in the science of reconstructing humanity's past. So as a fiction genre analogue, adventure stories are, at best, a bad fit. Archaeologists are more like the people who create and devour stories about time travel: we are intensely curious about history. We are interested in artifacts not for their own sake, but because they can help us understand the societies that produced them.

Humanity has made massive technological leaps that have given us the evidence necessary to separate fact from fiction about what the world was like in the past. Written records, maps, and calendars, the earliest examples of which go back five thousand years, have captured certain times and places in incredible detail. Within the past two centuries, the technology to faithfully preserve images and sounds lets us experience the past through historic photographs, recordings, and films. And since the 1950s, the discovery of radiocarbon dating has allowed archaeology to take fragmented physical evidence from around the world—artifacts and architecture—and piece it together into an increasingly coherent picture of our shared history.

There has also been a leap forward in the pursuit of the distant past thanks to a host of technologies that fall under the larger category of geospatial technologies. The term *geospatial* refers to the relative location of things on the planet. Devices and applications that use locational data include technology with which we are well acquainted. Need a ride somewhere? The GPS inside your phone uses your location to connect you with rideshare drivers and a digital map plots the route to your destination. Want a preview of the place you are going? You have a lot of options—digital maps, satellite and street view images, and 3-D models of buildings and the landscape around them. This blending of the real world and the digital world will only continue as augmented and virtual reality become more common.

Tech companies like Google make a lot of money from geospatial technologies. But the origins of many of them are far outside Silicon Valley. GPS, for example, has a fascinating history. Developed during the Cold War, the Global Positioning System was for many years a closely guarded military secret. Even more bizarre, GPS works only thanks to advances in theoretical physics that predated the first satellite by fifty years. To be able to triangulate your location using the swarm of satellites above us requires precise synchronization of your device and the satellites. On Earth, synchronization is trivial since we have atomic clocks everywhere keeping perfect time with one another. But on GPS satellites, time moves differently. In orbit, weaker gravity and the crafts' incredible speed mean every GPS satellite experiences a day that is thirty-eight microseconds (one millionth of a second) shorter than ours. Not spectacular time travel, but enough to put your Earth-bound device and the satellites out of sync without accounting for Einstein's theories of special and general relativity.

Archaeologists have a track record of being early adopters of geospatial technologies to improve how we study, interpret, and represent evidence of the ancient world—and the lives of the people who lived in it (McCoy and Ladefoged 2009). Some have used lasers mounted on aircraft to reveal ruins of cities below the jungle canopy. Others have come together to create digital atlases and indices to document hundreds of thousands of places where archaeology has been found. (In this book I use the term *archaeology* to refer to "the scientific study of material remains (such as tools, pottery, jewelry, stone walls, and monuments) of past human life and activities," as well as to the "remains of the culture of a people" (merriam-webster.com).) Still others have applied 3-D scanning—using images from drones and ground-based laser scanning—as a powerful tool not only for preserving sites, but also for giving virtual tourists a look inside the world's most incredible monuments.

As the technology has evolved, geospatial tools have gone from being used for a fairly narrow scope of activities to being incorporated into almost everything we archaeologists do. The ancient world may be receding further and further into the past, but with the help of geospatial technology, archeologists are bringing us closer to it than we have ever been. At no point in human history have we been able to create a better, more complete, and more accessible rendering of the past. It is a geospatial revolution. It is still up to us as individuals to try to tell fact from fiction, but now we have an additional problem: How do we make sense of such a massive amount of information and use it to form a clear picture of the past?

·   ·   ·

Fictional time travel and the science of archaeology are almost never talked about side by side, so before we go too far down the road, I want to clear up a few things about their histories.

To begin, it is important to remember that for many years, before archaeology came along, the Bible was thought of as a history book. For example, in 1650, an Irish archbishop went as far as to calculate the specific year when the Earth was created by counting the generations of families mentioned in the Bible. He estimated our planet had been created six thousand years ago, in 4004 BC. When Europeans traveled to North and South America, some accounted for the existence of Native Americans, unmentioned in the Bible, by declaring them the lost tribes of Israel. Over the years, it became increasingly clear that such explanations could not accommodate the hard evidence that history had unfolded differently. By the nineteenth century, the young science of geology was showing that natural features like the Grand Canyon resulted from millions of years of erosion. Scientists made it clear that Earth must be many, many times older than six thousand years.

Around the same time, Christian Thomsen, tasked with displaying finds at the National Museum in Copenhagen, developed a new system for categorizing antiquities, as objects from the distant past were then called. Thomsen reasoned that stone tools found deep underground must be from a time before metallurgy. Based on the locations where other tools had been discovered, he discerned that bronze preceded iron—and thus the classifications Stone Age, Bronze Age, and Iron Age were established.[2] This nineteenth century antiquarian was not working in isolation. Other natural philosophers, as they called themselves, observed Stone Age deposits that included the bones of extinct animals. This was independent confirmation of what cave paintings, like the famous ones at Lascaux, taught us: people were around tens of thousands of years ago during the last Ice Age, at the same time as long-extinct animals.

This rudimentary way to tell time was quickly joined by something that would make room for the new science of archaeology to grow: Charles Darwin's theory of evolution by natural selection. When *On the Origin of Species* was published in 1859, it gave us a mechanism to understand how new life could form through random chance and circumstance. The giraffe did not will itself to grow a long neck: conditions over many generations favored the success of individuals born with a slightly longer neck. Humanity had not been designed, or magically brought to life from clay: like giraffes, we too have an evolutionary history.

In Darwin's day, the details of our evolution were poorly known. Over the years we would come to appreciate that humans, as we are today, are relative newcomers to the Earth. We never walked with dinosaurs, unless you count the scurrying of our distant mammalian ancestors as walking. We only became biologically distinct from the common ancestor we share with chimpanzees about seven million years ago; the first stone tools were chipped into existence two to three million years ago; and the first people with our current body form came on the scene a mere 250,000 years ago. And evidence suggests that our cognitive evolution reached the point it is today only fifty thousand years ago, when we were able to conceive, among other things, of earlier eras.

At the start of the twentieth century, universities began awarding degrees in anthropology.[3] Fueled by the knowledge that there were thousands of years of human life and culture before our own, early archaeologists endeavored to reconstruct the "culture histories" of people who lived long ago. When did these cultures come about? Where were they located? Did they die out, or slowly transform? The idea that there were cultures like the ones we know from the contemporary world that lay waiting to be discovered through careful study of the physical evidence left behind (artifacts, art, architecture, human remains) was now cutting-edge science. Early scholars went forth and created new long timelines for everywhere.

It was no coincidence that time travel stories became popular around the same time. Western society as a whole was so taken by new discoveries about the past that its historical imagination clicked into high gear, spawning a new market for speculative fiction. But even as archeologists plunged into the ancient past, time travel stories have tended to take place in more recent eras that authors could at least partially access through written, historical records. Perhaps authors found it easier to imagine a time in the past they could read about themselves, or, to take another tactic and send characters into a future unconstrained by historical reality.

While both time travel fiction and archaeology exhibit a concern for other eras, time travel stories have other functions as well—entertainment and social commentary chief among them.[4] The other times that travelers encounter serve as mirrors of the present day. In 1889, for example, Mark Twain sent the fictional Hank Morgan back to medieval England in *A Connecticut Yankee in King Arthur's Court*. The book came out when the myth of the antebellum South as a land of Arthurian nobility and romance had gained national traction. Twain set out to ridicule that myth. Hank Morgan uses his knowledge of science and technology to create miracles that earn the esteem of King Arthur's court, but he does not content himself with a position of power. Instead, he fights for equity for an oppressed underclass. Americans, Twain suggests, needed to do the same.

The contemporaneous novels *Looking Backwards,* by Edward Bellamy (1887), and *The Time Machine,* by H. G. Wells (1895), comment upon present-day conditions by sending time travelers to the future.[5] Both backward and forward time travel continue as literary conventions in the perennial BBC television favorite *Doctor Who,* about an alien Time Lord whose machine, the Tardis, can go anywhere in space and time. In practice, the Tardis often goes to familiar historic eras and the far distant future.[6] I am a big fan of the show but I do worry that this aspect of time travel fiction unintentionally dampens our historical curiosity about the era before writing; something that archaeologists have been trying to stoke in the broader public since the early days of archaeology.

· · ·

Earlier generations of professional archaeologists had far fewer tools at their disposal—an unenviable position, but one that makes their accomplishments all the more impressive. Take, for example, V. Gordon Childe. In the 1920s, Childe, a young, bespectacled, Oxford-educated Australian, started to study Stone Age Europe. He read reports of excavations, examined first-hand the bits and pieces from the past collected in museums, and conducted his own investigations. He was especially interested in the transition from what had come to be known as the Old Stone Age, or Paleolithic, to the New Stone Age, or Neolithic.[7]

Childe was fascinated by the Neolithic because it marked the start of agriculture, the creation of villages, and eventually, the birth of new societies.[8] He described these changes with intense, time-space charts showing the shift in regions from one style of artifacts to another. Population movements were illustrated in maps by arrows darting out of modern day Turkey into Eastern, and then Western, Europe. Ultimately, the evidence suggested that the "origins of civilization"—as this fundamental cultural change was then known—had been catalyzed by migrants from the Middle East (see figure 1). Childe published his research in a book he called *The Aryans: A Study of Indo-European Origins* in 1926. That same year Adolf Hitler wrote *Mein Kampf,* and forever coopted the term *Aryan* to refer to racial purity. Childe was no Nazi. He came to the term by drawing on historical linguistics, not nationalism, and far

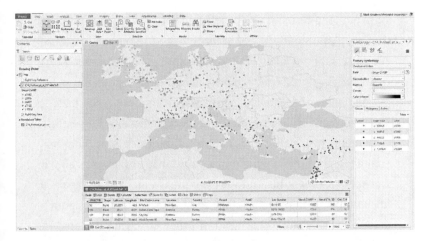

FIGURE 1. The spread of farming from the Middle East to Europe (about five thousand to ten thousand years ago). Dots represent the earliest signs of farming in each location. Earlier radiocarbon dates are dark, later dates are light. Data source: Pinhasi, Fort, and Ammerman (2005). Data displayed in ArcGIS Pro 2.2.3.

from advocating racial purity, the point of his culture history was to show the Asiatic roots of many of the defining characteristics of Europe before writing.

Childe argued that a process he called the Neolithic Revolution, which included the domestication of plants and animals, had caused a ripple effect across the world. In another well-known, but poorly titled, book, *Man Makes Himself*, he suggested that not just evolution, but also free will leads us to shape our own destiny (Childe 1936). The title may have neglected women and children, but the overall idea is a good one. His work, along with that of his peers, meant that by the 1930s, scholars were writing about prehistory in the same way that historians had long been writing about the recent past.[9]

It is remarkable to me that just as archaeology was making headway in showing the public how we could make sense of the ways our long-term history has shaped the present, the first novel that couples time travel and archaeology—L. Sprague de Camp's (1939) *Lest Darkness Fall*—falls disappointingly into the stereotype of archaeologist as self-interested adventurer. Its protagonist, the fictional American archaeologist Martin Padway, goes back to Rome in the sixth century AD, and through his knowledge of the past, steers history to avoid the start of the Dark Ages. That may sound like the kind of enlightened move made by Twain's hero in *Connecticut Yankee*, but Padway (who's really more of an expert on ancient history than archaeology anyway), sets Rome on a path to colonize the New World ahead of other European nations. He seeks personal power for himself and imperial glory for Rome.

After World War II, the technical advances that were born of the Cold War had completely unforeseen results for the field of archaeology. The biggest one was the discovery by Willard Libby that all living things incorporate into themselves a small amount of a naturally occurring isotope of carbon and that by measuring this isotope we could work out how long ago something died. Libby, a chemist who had helped in the American effort to build the first atomic bomb, showed that carbon-14, unlike most carbon, was unstable and decayed away, but at an extremely slow rate. A bone from an animal or the wood from a tree that died today has 100 percent of its radiocarbon (the term for radioactive carbon) but 5,730 years in the future it will only have half that amount. In another 5,730 years, half of the remaining amount will have disappeared, leaving just 25 percent of the original quantity. With the basics of this natural process worked out, it becomes possible, if you have bone or burned wood, to figure out when the animal or plant died based on how much radiocarbon is left. Of course, the carbon isotope would eventual decay entirely away, but that takes more than fifty thousand years, a point when other radiometric methods can be used to work out how old something is.

Carbon dating unshackled archaeologists. Before radiocarbon, working out how old a deposit or ruin was depended a great deal on luck. If you happened to find pottery made in a style that you recognized from a local sequence, you might be able to work out its age relative to other places. Fail to find that critical evidence and you were stuck. Radiocarbon gave us a tool to create chronologies using almost any biological material that we might find.

By the 1960s, radiocarbon dating was applied globally, and archaeologists started to ask questions that involved more than writing culture histories. What motivated the new generation of archaeologists was something of a return to the intellectual space created by Darwin's theory a century beforehand. What was our place in the natural world? How did the distinctive things humans can do help us survive and thrive? Much closer ties to the natural and earth sciences led to even more challenging questions: Were we responsible for the extinctions of animals in the Ice Age? This is also when aerial photographs started to become standard in large-scale field surveys aimed at working out how people used different ecosystems.

The 1960s also saw a return to the idea that our ancestors were responsible for their own destiny. Archaeology set its sights on economics, politics, and why different kinds of societies formed. Borrowing from geography, we began looking at how the distribution of artifacts could reveal how people made and distributed all kinds of goods. To do this, it became increasingly important to know where in the natural world people got their raw materials—for example, for making stone tools or fine goods—as these could be read as clues about how the larger economic system worked and changed over time. At this time, large monuments, which had always been of interest to archaeologists, were understood as more than ruins. They represented how much labor a leader could amass for construction, a proxy measure for hierarchy that, ideally speaking, could be applied to lots of different places. Modern archaeology built on the work of Childe and his peers, but the old methods were no longer adequate. Instead of piecing together evidence from the past in isolation, archaeologists connected with other sciences and stayed on top of the latest technical advances that might unlock some hidden aspect of the past.

.   .   .

Satirists like Twain approach the past with a specific aim, but archaeologists are supposed to remain unbiased, taking care not to let their views cloud their reckoning. We have not always succeeded. Take, for example, the hard-to-shake stereotype of "man the hunter." Just think about how many times you have seen artists' reconstructions of ancient scenes of heroic men wielding spears. The problem with the "man the hunter" image is not that men did not hunt: the problem is other activities defined men's lives, and women and children's lives mattered too.

Time travel fiction on television today is a great example of expanding the stories we tell about the past.[10] As shows have begun to include a more diverse cast of travelers we see new narrative depth centered on dueling impulses: to preserve the past or to correct it.[11] The character Rufus Carlin, played by Malcolm Barrett, on the show *Timeless,* for example, shines a spotlight on the fact that America's past, no matter the era, is dangerous for an African American like him. By giving characters like Carlin the power to travel backwards in time, the stories must deal with the inherent contradiction: Why should any time traveler work to preserve a past that was unjust toward people who look like them?[12]

These new narratives speak to important facets of telling non-fiction stories. For the same reason that the identity of the time traveler matters, we need archaeology written from diverse perspectives. In the United States, my generation of archaeologists is the first to have started out our careers at sex parity, an equal male to female ratio (Zedar 1994); but parity in participation in key aspects of the discipline, like publication in peer-reviewed scientific journals, remains woefully unbalanced (Bardolph 2014). This is true not just for women but for so many others who have in effect been barred from full and equal participation in archaeology because of their identity. One result is that many fewer stories are being told than should be.

And just as there are many stories to tell, there is much more archaeology to tell them about than you might think. In 1972 the United Nations began identifying places as World Heritage sites, affording them international recognition that, it was hoped, would give sites some degree of protection that might supplement the laws and regulations of individual nations.[13] Today there are 878 sites with World Heritage status. A few hundred more sites are well known enough that they have their own Wikipedia pages. But these numbers are misleading about the prevalence of archaeological sites: archaeologists have found millions upon millions of them. And those are just the sites we know about. So, while they are precious, sites are not rare, and in many respects we struggle with having too many to care for given the resources we have to investigate and protect them.

Some archaeologists have suggested that, if you think about it, we already time travel. Bodil Petersson and Cornelius Holtorf, of

Linnaeus University, write that time travel is best understood as "an experience and social practice," and might be as common as when historical reenactors recreate a bygone era (Petersson and Holtorf 2016; Holtorf 2016). Eugene Ch'ng, a professor of cultural computing at the University of Nottingham in Ningbo, China, follows a similar line of reasoning when he proposes that an immersive experience in virtual reality designed to mimic the past is "virtual time travel" (Ch'ng 2009). Any time we imagine the past, psychologists say, we are engaging in "chronesthesia," drawing on what we know to take journeys in our minds (Tulving 2002).[14] Even if you find this a bit too abstract, there is an important kernel of truth in this view of time travel: all archaeology requires, to varying degrees, imagining the past from the perspective of the present.

Archaeologists must balance our impulse to create a detailed picture of the past—like the kind required to create a virtual time travel experience—and our job as scientists, concerned with cause and effect, and the fundamental forces that drive changes in history. Over the past fifty years, we have been able to write the first detailed global history of our species founded on good empirical evidence thanks in large part to the technological advance of radiocarbon dating. Over the next fifty years, we will be writing the second draft thanks to geospatial technologies; but before we can, we need to talk more about the difference between "finding things" and "finding things out."

2 Finding Things Out

Would time machines, if they were available to us today, make archaeology redundant? Gavin Lucas, a professor of archaeology at the University of Iceland, posed exactly this question. His answer: yes. If we could step out of a time machine and find a perfectly intact previous time period where we could talk to people in real time, as it were, then we would be in the domain of ethnography, not archaeology (Lucas 2005, 118).[1] Lucas notes that, like all ethnographers, the time-traveling sort would bring with them their biases. James Gleick, the author of *Time Travel: A History*, observed the same thing in fiction: the time traveler is always a product of the time in which the story was written (Gleick 2016). The characters created by Isaac Asimov and other writers from science fiction's golden age of the 1950s and 1960s are products of that era, no matter where in time they may travel.

While humans have had the capacity to imagine the past for a long time, we have our limits, and thinking about time itself can get confusing quickly. That's why we have come up with so many different metaphors. None of them are perfect, but an enduring one is the notion of time's arrow. Imagine watching an archer loose an arrow. It may fly on any of one of a nearly infinite number of spatial pathways but there is only one way we can observe it. We see the arrow released from the bow, fly, then come to rest. We cannot watch it in reverse, or pause it midflight, or see its journey out of order. The way we travel through time is fixed and, also, time is not optional. All of us will experience time's arrow.

The metaphor of time's arrow is useful but it does not capture all the special properties of time. One property of time, in the way that we experience it, is that without intervention things do not become more ordered as time moves forward, only less ordered. Imagine two adjoining boxes, one filled purely with oxygen, the other purely with nitrogen. If you create an opening so the gases can move freely between boxes, the oxygen and nitrogen atoms will randomly bounce around, and over enough time, they will eventually become equally mixed in both boxes. They will not spontaneously order themselves back to their original, separated states. The principle that describes the two gases mixing with each other over time in a closed system is called entropy.[2]

Entropy is the enemy of archaeology. As much as we might wish to talk to the people we study, archaeologists are not time-traveling ethnographers: our data and methods are focused on things left behind, lost, broken, built, modified, and buried. And so all of our tricks to wrap our hands around what happened must revolve around those ancient things. The mixing and degrading of objects from long ago, while inevitable, makes our job go from difficult to nearly impossible.

The fundamental way that archaeologists fight entropy is through recording the location where something is discovered. Our shorthand for this is *context*. Context in the common usage of the word describes the broader circumstances in which something happened, the circumstances that give it meaning. Just as words can be understood only if we know their context, physical evidence of the past can be read correctly only if we know precisely where in the world it was found. It is one of the reasons we dig so slowly and carefully.

Lewis Binford, a leading American archaeologist, was once accused of making the erroneous assumption that all the artifacts we find are lying exactly where they were first dropped, cemented in place as the poor city of Pompeii was by the eruption of Mount Vesuvius (Schiffer 1972). Binford was not so naive. He saw all archaeology as having been "ravaged" by time's arrow, but asserted that that was only problematic if the goal was the reconstruction of a single moment in time (Binford 1981, 196). In his view, the point of archaeology is to look at the big picture, beyond a single time period or place. Change in human history, like an archaeological deposit, accumulates over a long, long period of time. This raises a fundamental question: Is the goal of archaeology to reconstruct life at one given moment—which is made difficult by the fact that most sites have not been sealed by volcanic ash—or should we instead focus on finding grander patterns beyond people's experiences? This matters for how we think about mapping because it shapes a host of decisions about what we think locational data are telling us.[3]

The fundamental way we talk about location in archaeology is in terms of sites. But, if you think about it long enough, you'll realize that entropy erodes even the idea of an archaeological site. In fact for a long time archaeologists have considered what it would be like to abandon the notion of the site. It is not as crazy an idea as it sounds.

As a unit of scientific study, "site" is ambiguous to the point of meaninglessness. Ancient people were not making sites for us to discover. They were just going about their lives making things,

dropping and losing things, building things, and sometimes bury-
ing things. The physical indications of these activities are found in
discrete locations, true, but that probably has as much to do with
current conditions, and what has happened since things were lost
or left behind, as it does with the activities that happened there
long ago.

It is not uncommon for different archaeologists to use completely different criteria to identify the boundaries of sites, and it is
surprisingly difficult, and sometimes impossible, to have field surveys replicate one another. The reason is that what is visible on the
ground will change over time. The scatter of artifacts and foundations of buildings that we call a site may be easily seen on the day
we visit, but covered by vegetation on the next visit. Natural erosion can both cover sites, hiding things once exposed or washing
away artifacts, deposits, and eventually, whole buildings.[4]

The alternative to looking for sites would be a siteless survey—
mapping everything without the expectation of labeling points or
areas as individualized sites (Dunnell and Dancey 1983). Strangely,
one of the voices that leapt to the defense of the seemingly inde-
fensible idea of sites was Binford (1992). The logic behind his
defense was, at the end of the day, rooted in pragmatism. He
argued that if one can go out and find discrete locations in the
world today where there is archaeology, then sites do exist. He did
not deny they are a problematic category but pointed out they are
a useful abstraction for archaeology, one that allows us to get on
with what we need to do.[5]

And so, we continue both to use the term site and to recognize
that entropy makes the notion of a site almost meaningless, in
somewhat the same way that Newton and Einstein both gave us
ways to think about time that are useful in different ways. Newton

gave us a rigid view of time as constant; seconds, hours, days, years ticking way. Thanks to Einstein, we also know that time is relative. That is why a GPS satellite experiences a day that is ever so slightly shorter than ours; Einstein's view is a better description of how time actually works. We nonetheless continue to use a Newtonian view of time as constant when we go about our day because it is useful as a way to organize how we experience time.

I am going to occasionally use *site* throughout the book because I find it useful, but when I do, think of it like the way you might refer to places by their street addresses. A street address is a useful way to give the location of something without describing the building or other things at that location. Or to put that another way, the site is not the archaeology, it is where the archaeology is.

. • .

The archaeologist David Hurst Thomas said that archaeology is not about "finding things," it is about "finding things out." It is true. Our commitment to knowledge distinguishes archaeology from treasure hunting. In fact, to an archaeologist, there is only a loose relationship between "finding things" and "finding things out."

There are two things that all archaeologists know about discovery that we rarely talk about, because when you put them down on paper they sound completely counterintuitive. The first is that it is possible to find artifacts and sites without really finding out anything new about the past. Take King Tut. In 1922, the headline of the *New York Times* read in part "SPLENDORS OF TOMB OF TUTANKHAMEN; Howard Carter's Discovery in Upper Egypt Reveals Glory of the 18th Dynasty." The story of this find has been repeated too many times to count in places like *National Geographic* magazine.[6]

There is nothing wrong with appreciating the beauty of the famous golden death mask buried with King Tut. But it is worth asking: What did we learn about ancient Egypt from the discovery of the intact tomb of the Pharaoh Tutankhamen? There is a valid argument to be made that learning the details of a single pharaoh's tomb is more knowledge for knowledge's sake, but at the end of the day, the find told us nothing we didn't already know. It didn't help us confirm or reject a hypothesis about happened in the past. It didn't tell us much of anything. Howard Carter had an adventure finding King Tut—fortune and glory—but did nothing much for the larger project of archaeology.

The second completely counterintuitive thing about discovery is that it is possible to learn a great deal about the past without finding new artifacts or sites. In the early 1920s, nerdy V. Gordon Childe spent a lot of time in museum collections across Europe. He knew that retracing the roots of modern Indo-European language speakers was going to require putting together puzzle pieces from over a massive area. The answer was never going to be found in a single site or in a single artifact, no matter how fun it is to find things. The result was a time-space chart in which prehistory started to take on the level of organization that already existed for history.

One of the reasons that it is possible to learn a lot without finding things is that archaeology is not as rare as you would think. Where I live, in Texas, we keep a close eye on how many active oil wells there are at any one time. Right now, there are about 186,000. Yet you might be surprised to learn there are probably more locations with archaeology then there are oil wells in Texas.[7] That is wild, but makes sense given that people have been living here for about twenty thousand years. To give you an idea of the scale of known archaeology: when Houston was hit by Hurricane Harvey in

2016, about one thousand recorded locations with archeology were flooded, and that was just a fraction of the three thousand known to archaeologists at the time of the storm (Reeder-Myers and McCoy 2019). That's why taking care of known archaeology and turning the large amount of physical evidence of the past into knowledge about the past can be more pressing problems than finding locations with intact archaeology.

In the excitement over what archaeologists can do with new geospatial technologies, it is easy to lose sight of the fact that recording the location of things is just the first step. There is a great deal more work necessary to turn that into knowledge. To unpack the different ways archaeologists use location to create knowledge a good place to start is by breaking down three closely interrelated aspects of location: data, information, and evidence.

.   .   .

Locational data can be thought of as answering the question: Where is it? Geospatial technologies and modern survey techniques have given us a buffet of options when it comes to recording where something is found. We can walk around the foundation of a piece of architecture with a GPS and it is mapped instantly. We can rapidly record the locations of thousands of individual artifacts with a machine called a total station, a standard piece of equipment on a construction site.[8] We can use a laser scanner mounted on top of a tripod, or fire up a drone and fly around taking pictures. But, if you have ever struggled with a remote control with too many buttons you know that, even though pressing a button is easy, having too many choices can be problematic. To get a sense of how we got to this point let's start at the beginning, with GPS.

I have used GPS for surveying for more than twenty years now and in a range of different jobs. The kind of work I do now, academic archaeology, is what produced most of the research you will read about in this book. Academics tend to be employed by universities but can also be attached to institutes and museums. Field surveys for academic projects are designed to address blue-sky research questions as well as to achieve a set of educational or cultural heritage goals. The two other major types of jobs in archaeology are part of the larger field of cultural resource management. There are private companies that conduct surveys on a project by project basis, usually tied to land development, an industry that goes by the shorthand title of contract archaeology, or salvage archaeology. Other archaeologists are employed across government positions that spend a great deal of their time either regulating the private sector or caring for, and interpreting, archaeology on public land. Field surveys for contract or government archaeology tend to be narrowly defined by the task at hand. Nonetheless, all field surveys are expected to follow the same professional standards, and so, in my experience, if there are differences between how GPS is used in the field, they are regional, rather than specific to the type of job.

In the 1990s, when hardly anyone had a mobile phone and the miniature computers that we think of now as phones were still the stuff of science fiction, I was introduced to this new thing called GPS. This was when I was an undergraduate at the University of New Mexico; before I found my way to the islands of the Pacific. I had a friend who had recently graduated and gotten a job with the US Forest Service assessing damage to archaeology in an area that had been burned by an intense wildfire. I volunteered to go along and help. One day the two of us piled into my truck and drove out to a trailhead in an isolated section of the Jemez Mountains of New Mexico. With nearly all of the vegetation burned away, well-preserved ancient houses tucked up against hillsides, which on another day we would have walked right by without seeing, were exposed. We abandoned the backcountry trails many times that day to look over the houses and take notes. Even twenty years later, it hurts my pride to admit that in our excitement we got lost in the scorched landscape. At sunset there was a vigorous debate about our location that in the end was impartially settled by the GPS pointing us back to the road where I had parked my truck.

In the early days of GPS, satellite navigation remained a closely guarded military technology. The bulky US government-issued GPS that I carried around the mountains of New Mexico even had a so-called kill button on it, so you could quickly delete all previous locations before it fell into enemy hands. For a while there were two different sets of navigation satellites. The United States had GPS satellites; the USSR had its own navigation satellite system, known as the Globalnaya Navigazionnaya Sputnikovaya Sistema (GLONASS). Both the American and Russian systems worked on the same principle: a ground-based device received radio signals from orbiting satellites to triangulate coordinates on Earth. For a time, the United States even went as far as intentionally introducing error to reduce the usefulness of GPS readings on unauthorized receivers.

The navigation satellites put into orbit during the last days of the Cold War are now integrated into one global navigation satellite system (GNSS) along with several other satellite constellations. GNSS is now the standard industry term for satellite navigation, but we will probably continue to casually use *GPS* in English. Smartphones now come equipped with a tiny GPS receiver chip that uses ground-based cellular towers to further improve readings when possible.

The invention of GPS by itself did not make things more complicated. In fact, back in the awkward early days the receiver would tell you your coordinates and you would have to do the low-tech job of plotting onto a paper map to work out where you were. That's what my friend and I were doing as the sun set in the Jemez Mountains. If you have never done it, it is actually not as hard as it sounds.

If you find yourself confronting an old printed map you will find latitude and longitude are either drawn as intersecting lines or marked along the sides. Latitude is your position relative to the equator, given as degrees. For example, if you could draw a straight line from the center of the Earth to the equator (the equator is 0°) and then a second straight line from the Earth's center to San Francisco, the angle made by the two lines would be about 38°. If you did the same measurement for the city of Auckland, you would get 37°, which is why all latitude measurements have to specify if they are north or south (in this case, 38°N and 37°S). Longitude is your position relative to an arbitrary line through Greenwich in the United Kingdom. If you again could draw a line from the center of the Earth, but this time one through Greenwich and the other through Washington, DC, you would find the angle to be 77°. For Hyderabad, on the opposite side of Greenwich, the angle is 78°, which is why longitude must indicate west or east (in this example, 77°W and 78°E).

Degrees of latitude and longitude must be cut up into finer units to give an exact position. On the surface of the Earth, a single degree is about 111 kilometers, or about the distance between the Bronx, New York and New Haven, Connecticut. That's a big area.

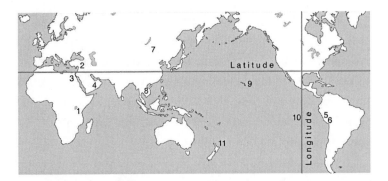

FIGURE 2. Latitude and longitude. In this example of how coordinates are plotted onto a world map, the location shown is latitude 32.846666 (N 32°50′48″) and longitude -96.785000 (W 96°47′6″). Approximate locations of some of the places mentioned in the book are shown: (1) Laetoli, Tanzania; (2) Hamoukar, Syria; (3) Karnak, Egypt; (4) Ubar, Oman; (5) Viru Valley, Peru; (6) Mawcha Llacta, Peru; (7) Valley of the Khans, Mongolia; (8) Angkor Wat, Cambodia; (9) the Hawaiian Islands; (10) Rapa Nui (Easter Island), Chile; and (11) Aotearoa (New Zealand).

The traditional way to cut up degrees is into sixty equal parts, called minutes (′), and then to cut each minute into sixty parts, called seconds (″). A single second on the ground is about twenty-five or thirty meters, which was just fine for the old days of physically plotting a location on a paper map.

My office at Southern Methodist University in Dallas is located near N 32°50′48″ , W 96°47′6″. To make that more manageable for computers, we now often use decimal degrees, with negative numbers to indicate south and west. In that system, my office is near 32.846666, -96.785000. A single millionth of a degree is equal to about eleven centimeters on the ground, so you can be quite precise about location (see figure 2).[9]

Geographic information systems (GIS) software allows us to level up from plotting GPS coordinates on paper maps.[10] It was specialized and high-tech at the time when I first learned how to use it. There are many more casual users now, and a lot more GIS applications. We even teach it to elementary school kids. Digital mapping is so pervasive it is easy to lose sight of what makes GIS a special category.

If I had to describe GIS in just a couple of words I would say it is a smart map. There are several core things that set it apart from other applications. At the minimum it should be able to display geographic data in a real-world coordinate system (e.g., latitude and longitude), to bring in new layers of geographic data, to store attributes linked to geographic data, and to query and analyze data by location. Those are a lot of technical specifications, so let me explain in terms of the world's most used GIS: Google Maps.

Google Maps is a web-based GIS rather than a standalone piece of software on your computer, and because we interact with it in a browser, lots of how it works is not obvious.[11] For example, everything you see on the map is being displayed in real-world coordinates. If you want to test that out, right-click a location and choose "What's here?" The program will display the address and coordinates in latitude and longitude decimal degrees. If you have used "My Places" to store locations then you know Google Maps can also add new layers of information (this feature is migrating to something called "My Maps").

Behind the scenes, points representing businesses are being kept somewhere on Google's servers, or in the cloud, in a massive spreadsheet where each individual record has a number of attributes that are automatically displayed when you click on them:

address, website, phone number, hours, and so on. Google Maps is built for spatial queries—that is what you are doing when you ask for businesses "Near Me." The GIS makes geography part of the calculation by only looking within a set search radius around you. It is also built to do spatial analysis, specifically, to find a path between you and any other location. Its algorithm takes into consideration things like current traffic conditions and if you are walking, driving, or taking public transportation, when it suggests a route and estimates the time it will take.

If the only thing that archaeologists ever wanted to do with GIS was to make attractive maps of the things we found, choosing how to record archaeology would be fairly uncomplicated and hardly worth mentioning. But, as a discipline, we were already obsessed with location well before GIS came along, and this has naturally led to some confusion over what location tells us.

Archaeology only starts with the question: Where is it? We also must answer the question: How did it get there? For me, when we move beyond the question of where something is, we are moving into the realm of locational information. Locational information requires interpretation or inference based on factors other than just where a thing was found. This is what we mean by *context* in archaeology and at minimum it involves an estimation of the age of the deposit or settlement, the likely activities there, and the different ways that nature and the actions of people impacted what we find. It is something that we get better at inferring with experience, and it helps to have good independent lines of evidence to work with. Locational information is nonetheless an awkward category, since so many of these factors may be unknown, vaguely known, revised by new data, or just unknowable without a time machine.

Even as we declare a partial victory over entropy through imposing order via locational data and information, another danger lurks in the shadows: equifinality.

. • .

In fiction, there are a lot of ways to travel through time. The traveler might instantaneously jump through time, travel faster than light, or move through different dimensions. Remarkably, one of the least popular is the method devised by H. G. Wells for *The Time Machine:* traveling by staying in one place.[12] The things archaeologists find travel through time slowly by staying in one place, with time moving forward around them. Of course, things do not stay in the same place. They are ravaged by time's arrow—moved by nature, moved by people—and many things have their journey to the present day cut short by being destroyed by decay. H. G. Wells explained how his time machine could move forward in time and avoid rusting away into a heap—or violating the problem of more than one thing occupying the same space—with some literary hand-waving. What happened to the time machine along the way from the present to the future was not relevant to his story. But what about the archaeological record? How much do we need to know about the life histories of things?

I have already mentioned one powerful tool for working out the life history of an object: radiocarbon dating. Radiocarbon dating is like nature's coroner; it gives us an approximate time of death for things that died within the last fifty thousand years. There are a host of other cunning ways to date things by means of natural decay or some other process that can be calibrated to give us an idea of how long a particular artifact has been time traveling.

We have a myriad of forensic methods that are put to work in creating a story about an artifact or the place where we found it. But what if you have a lot of different stories that all produce the same outcome? That is what we call equifinality. Here's an example.

In 2003, excavations at an old wharf recovered a Roman coin minted way back in 7 BC. That would not be news, but this copper coin was found in New Zealand, more than eighteen thousand kilometers from Rome.

The first people to settle the islands of New Zealand, also known as Aotearoa, did so more than one thousand years after the coin was made, around AD 1250. How did the coin get there? Was a Roman ship wrecked in the far Southern Pacific? Or sometime in the last two hundred years was the coin brought from Europe and dropped or thrown into the water? Both have the same outcome— the coin found in New Zealand in 2003—but the latter is much more likely.

If you were hoping to read about the existence of a hitherto unknown Roman shipwreck, that is perfectly natural. Lots of us, myself included, want our historical curiosity satiated by a cracking good tale, and by that measure the Roman Robinson Crusoe story beats the lost coin story by a mile. That's part of why equifinality is rhetorically tricky. It requires a degree of dispassion in the review of facts and probabilities. The interpretation that the Roman coin was thrown away or lost sometime in the last two hundred years is based on a number of sound tenets. There are records of thousands of Europeans going to New Zealand in that time period and bringing with them things from their homelands. Also, the practice of throwing coins into water for luck, or as votive offerings, is a well-documented tradition practiced by Europeans. And coins are small and get lost by accident all the time.[13]

There is a scientifically valid approach to considering several hypotheses at once, known by the shorthand "multiple working hypotheses" (Chamberlin 1965 [1890]). The idea is that if you cannot defeat equifinality, then best embrace it. But how can we decide between competing explanations when they are a closer call than the Roman coin example? Here is where independent lines of evidence are important. The coin is not the only archaeological find in New Zealand, nor is it the only Roman coin found in the world. Comparing the artifacts previously found independently of that specific coin gives us the confidence to choose one explanation over another.

Locational data and information do not speak for themselves. That's why you can find things without necessarily finding things out, and learn things from existing data and information without pinpointing the locations of unknown archaeology. To make them speak we must answer the question: What does it mean that these things were found there? Even if it is not spoken, this requires a theory about how the ancient world worked. When location is used to support, or to discredit, a claim about what happened in the past, then we are talking about locational evidence.

.   .   .

Let's recap. Archaeology is big on knowing exactly where things are found. Good locational data are important because we must make a series of inferences about how these objects, deposits, and architecture got there. We presume that since these things were thrown away, lost, or abandoned, that they, to varying degrees, have been randomly strewn around the place thanks to entropy. This mixing around, with help from nature and from people, destroys patterns we might find useful in our efforts. (And sometimes it even makes new spatial patterns that are misleading when working out what happened in the past.) We also must contend with the fact that completely different activities may leave behind nearly identical spatial patterns.

To turn locational data and information into something useful for learning more about the past requires epistemology. Epistemology refers to a way of thinking, a logical framework that defines variables and relationships between variables, and directs how to make sound arguments and discern between correct and incorrect inferences.

There are two fundamentally different ways of thinking about locational evidence that are relevant to archaeology—one grounded in science, the other in the humanities. Each centers on the analysis of spatial relationships between things to learn more about the past, and has its own intellectual history. Many archaeologists, myself included, are comfortable with using either depending upon the goal of the research.[14]

Let's start with how we can use science to learn something new about the past based on good locational information. For this we go back to between AD 750 and 1050 in what is now southern Mexico and its neighbors, Guatemala, Belize, Honduras, and El Salvador. We call this the Terminal Classic era in the history of Maya civilization. To be clear, when we say "terminal" we do not mean that this is when all the Maya died. There are about seven million Maya living today. The Terminal Classic is part of the longer Classic Period, defined by the era when society was ruled by monarchs who vied for control beyond the land around their capital. The "terminal" part is as in *terminus*, the end of that period. It is a time when things changed so dramatically it is better known today as the Maya collapse.[15]

The Maya collapse is a topic that receives a head-spinning amount of attention. One review of recent literature estimated that there had been more than four hundred academic publications about it in the previous decade (Aimers 2007). That's a new one about every ten days. You might draw the conclusion that that is because we have been finding lots and lots of new Classic Maya centers, but we have not. Another recent study shows that the rate of the discovery of new centers has dropped dramatically since the 1980s, and even before that it hovered around two per decade (Surovell et al. 2017). All that research has generated a consensus on a couple of things: there was no single cause for the changes in society seen at this time; and collapse is a misleading shorthand for what occurred, since we see both continuity and new centers emerging afterwards. And so while archaeologists have been trying to throw away the term "collapse" since the 1970s, I am going to continue using it here, but with the caveat that it is complicated.

One of the ways that archaeologists have come to eliminate incorrect theories about the Maya collapse, and develop a more subtle picture of what happened, is through spatial analyses of centers, the cities where people lived. Thankfully for us in the modern day, Maya rulers carved the date of construction on their large stone monuments—on stelae, lintels, and staircases—and we can translate those dates to the Western calendar. An archaeologist at the University of California, Los Angeles named Fredrick J. Bove used that information to make a map of the Maya collapse (Bove 1981). He reasoned that the dates of the latest constructions across the region would make a spatial pattern that should match one of the going theories for what had happened. For example, if people abandoned monument construction first in the west and then the

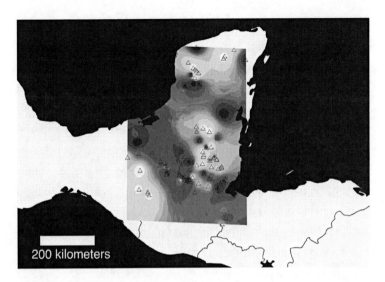

FIGURE 3. The last monuments of the Classic Maya period. This map shows where and when people stopped building monuments between AD 730 and 910; earlier dates are dark, later dates are light. Locations of centers are marked by triangles. Data source: Ebert, Prufer, and Kennett (2012).

east, then the map should show the collapse sweeping in an orderly way from west to east.

What does the Maya collapse look like on a single map? As it turns out, the end of monument building was kind of blotchy (see figure 3). It occurred earlier in some places, later in others, not at all what one would expect for centers falling like dominos from an external invading army sweeping across the land. More importantly, the visual comparison was backed up with statistics that took the proposed scenarios and showed how closely they fit the geospatial pattern. The best fit in this case is the hypothesis that internal competition between centers was to blame.

What if the blotchy pattern on the map is just random? This "what if" was the center of an intense back and forth after Bove published his study (Kvamme 1990; Whitley and Clark 1985). There is a kind of spatial math built around this particular problem, and it is called Moran's Index, or Moran's I for short. I could go on about the wonderfully nerdy way this particular index works and how it was applied to the Maya, but the important thing for now is that it answers three questions. First, is there structure in the geospatial data? Meaning, are values related to each other in space or just random? Then, is that structure positive or negative? That is, are values more likely to be neighbors with a similar value, or are close neighbors more likely to be dissimilar, as on a checkerboard? Finally, how confident can we be that this isn't just random? In the end, when the correct statistical method was applied to the Maya collapse data, it turned out that no, these were not just random blotches.

The original study by Bove showed how external forces were a poor explanation for the collapse, and that finding shrank the geographic scale in which it was necessary to look for underlying causes. There have been more spatial statistics thrown at this same dataset that show that the timing of when monument building ceased tends to be similar within groups of centers (Ebert, Prufer, and Kennett 2012; Premo 2004). There is also the suggestion that the blotches could be explained by erosion hitting some centers harder than others (Neiman 1997).

I am attracted to spatial puzzles like this. Part of it is being able to apply the tool kit of geospatial science—testing hypotheses, leveraging statistics to quantify confidence in statements, and then tasting the satisfaction of winning a battle in the war against entropy and equifinality. Working on these puzzles also implies something about human history—that it is knowable, that not all of it was random, and that we can discover new things about it. And as in all science, that we are never finished: everything we think we know is provisional and could be revisited because there is always more to learn.

. . .

Science gives us some remarkable details about the past. We are however not purely analytical creatures. We have empathy for those who have gone before, and that informs our historical curiosity. We wonder what their lives were like and how they saw the world. Today, we connect with how the past was lived through the humanities, including history, literature, and art. But what about the distant past, from which we have no writings, no paintings? How do we connect to people from these eras?

Let's look at how a humanities perspective can be used to learn something new about the past based on good locational information. In Neolithic Britain, around 3100 BC, at a location near the River Avon, an unnamed group of people got together and dug out a massive ditch defining a circle with the diameter of football field (figure 4). This monument was added to over time. Some five hundred years after that ring ditch was created, people would drag twenty-five-ton stones from forty kilometers away and erect one of the most iconic pieces of architecture on the planet: Stonehenge.

One way that archaeology can help us understand what went on at Stonehenge is by considering the notion of a sense of place. As individuals and as larger groups, we make emotional connections to locations. A sense of place can be intimate and personal, like calling a place home; or it be can public and shared, like recognizing that a natural feature or built monument holds historical or spiritual value. It stands to reason that we can use our faculties to some degree to intuit what places meant to people in the past.

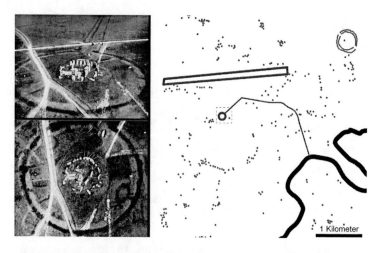

FIGURE 4. Stonehenge. These two 1906 air photos on the left show a crop mark encircling Stonehenge's megalithic stones. Remarkably, it wasn't until the 1990s that the broader landscape was mapped. The map on the right shows Stonehenge, the Avenue that connects it to the River Avon, the Cursus, Durrington Walls, and locations where barrows have been reported. Sources: Cleal, Walker, Montague (1995); Tilley (2010).

Christopher Tilley is an archaeologist at University College London and he has spent a long time walking over the countryside, thinking about places like Stonehenge and what they meant to his ancestors. We have already talked about how archaeologists are obsessed with location, especially with context. When it comes to monuments, Tilley considers their context relative to a geographic scale that takes into consideration how we humans experience the world. After all, these were not built by aliens or elephants: they are meant for us.

Tilley posed a straightforward question: "Why is Stonehenge located where it is in the landscape? Why here? Why *this* place?" (Tilley 2010, 64; italics in original). Remarkably, until the 1990s, we could not begin to answer this question. Investigations by dilettantes called "antiquarians" and early archaeological studies centered on the large stones to the exclusion of the immediate surroundings. That began to change twenty years ago with surveys around the monument, filling in the map with the locations of barrows (small artificial hills) and other monuments, as well as the topography (natural ridges, hills, shallow valleys) along the western banks of the River Avon. The area around Stonehenge that has been walked, mapped, and scanned with geophysical instruments is 180 square kilometers, almost twice the size of Disney World.[16] Large sections have been opened up with excavations to expose previously unknown architecture and a much tighter radiocarbon-based chronology has developed. That has allowed a fuller picture of how people might have thought about the place.

The decision to build Stonehenge—which is just one of the many pieces of architecture in the complex—can be traced back to almost a millennium before the first of the massive stones were imported, when a three kilometer long, narrow enclosure was created. Today it is called the Cursus. On the map it looks like a west-east-oriented racetrack, or a landing strip. It was not used for either of those purposes. Rather it is thought to have been for ritual pilgrimages and processions. From this point forward the area accumulated ritual structures, including the ring ditch that represented the first version of Stonehenge, or Stonehenge before the stones.

Much later, around the same time as the iconic stones were put into place, a village comprised of thousands of people was founded nearby. Tilley (2010) notes that it was the placement of these stones that gave what was otherwise a rather boring location, topographically speaking, its "drama and theatrical power." He observes that the stones sit within a slight basin that makes a kind of "visual envelope" that includes a portion of the Cursus to the north, but excludes the river and the village, neither of which are far away. If one begins connecting the dots representing barrows, the pattern of where one can view Stonehenge may explain why the map shows barrows located in clusters or arcs.

The landscape around Stonehenge has something in common with the Disney theme parks: both incorporate a distinctive formal path designed to connect places. At Disneyland, it is Main Street USA, which starts at the main entrance and leads to a statue of Walt Disney and Mickey Mouse. At Stonehenge, this path is called the Avenue. The Avenue makes a wide arc from the River Avon, the same river that abuts the village upstream, to the nine-meter tall stones of Stonehenge. The numerous burials that have been found within Stonehenge itself suggest to some archaeologists a symbolic connection between a place for the living, the village, and a place for the dead, the standing stones (Parker Pearson and Ramilisonina 1998).

This question of why Stonehenge was built is another great spatial puzzle. In this case finding an answer is less about testing alternative hypotheses and more about generating a synthesis that appeals to common human experiences: the creation of burial monuments to honor the dead, in places that already carry meaning to people, and that symbolically connect the living and the dead. There are additional interpretations for the use of Stonehenge as a kind of calendar that tracked the movement of the sun throughout the year, or as a place where oral traditions were recounted and passed down. The main point is this: we can only understand these places because we are also humans. And the same things can be said of the humanities as of the sciences: we are never finished, everything we think we know is provisional and could be revisited, and there is always more to learn.

I love watching my children run around looking for hidden plastic eggs on Easter. It is pure fun. The thrill of finding things lost and left behind from long ago is part of archaeology. But unlike an Easter egg hunt, the goal is not to find things—the goal is to find things out. In archaeology that means thinking really, really hard about how things got to where they are and what that means.

Here I have outlined how the location where we find things can be thought of in three closely interrelated ways: as data, information, and evidence. Turning locational data into locational information in archaeology requires strong inference, and in the end, while this is what constitutes expertise, it is worth knowing for anyone interested in the past. Turning locational information into evidence requires thinking through an intellectual framework as illustrated above with simple examples of how spatial analysis can be done through scientific and humanities lenses.

In the next several chapters we will look at how geospatial technologies are making it easier to find lots of things, before we get back to the bigger question—how are they helping us find things out?

Part II

3 Views from Above

Our first picture of the Earth from above came from the happy coincidence of early aviation and the invention of photography. The picture—the world's earliest air photo—was taken from a hot air balloon hovering over Paris in 1858. That image did not survive, but others from that era did, like figure 5. The Arc de Triomphe, at the center, had only been completed about thirty years before this picture was taken. How spectacular this new technology must have been to people 150 years ago. As striking as this image was, and still is, photos of archaeology from above remained simply a novelty for many, many years. The bread-and-butter of archaeology remained excavation and mapping ruins with wonderfully detailed hand-drawn maps.

The story of how archaeologists have learned to use images taken from aircraft, and then by satellites, is not a heroic tale. It is not a story of advances in technology leading scientists into hitherto unknown levels of understanding in a straightforward way. There were some false starts, like in the 1980s and 1990s, when satellite imagery was used on an absurd adventure to find the so-called "lost city of Ubar." In contrast, when the pieces have come together well—the right tool, the right place, the right research

FIGURE 5. The evolution of air photography. These two images of the Arc de Triomphe in Paris were created 150 years apart from one another. On the left is a picture taken from a hot air balloon by Gaspard-Félix Tournachon (also known by the name Nadar) in 1868; on the right, one from Google Earth, 2018. Photo source: Wikimedia Commons. Data source: Data SIO, NOAA, US Navy, NGA, GEBCO Landsat / Copernicus.

goals—the results have been truly outstanding. That's what happened just after World War II, when air photos helped a young American archaeologist named Gordon Willey efficiently map what he found in Peru as part of an imaginative look at the ways history played out at the level of an individual community. We begin this chapter with the story of Gordon Willey.

.   .   .

Gordon Willey grew up during the Great Depression in a middle-class household, and excelled in his studies in high school and college. But, in 1936, all his applications to graduate schools were rejected. Undeterred, he joined digs around the country and a few years later was admitted to Columbia University. Archaeology at this time was all about chronology: digging places rich in artifacts and using their changing styles to build up a culture history. And Willey did just that for his dissertation research in Peru, which he completed shortly before America entered World War II.

Next, Willey took a big, big risk. After the war he returned to Peru as part of a Smithsonian research team to undertake something that no one had done before. The target was Viru Valley, a place with a climate not unlike Southern California. The idea was to look for the foundations of ruins representing settlement across an entire coastal valley and reconstruct the pattern of where people lived in different periods (see figure 6).

Mapping during the 1946 survey required walking over what Willey later called, the "stony and seemingly endless remains of Viru's prehistoric settlements" (1974, 154). He was accustomed to fieldwork in Peru so that didn't worry him. His real worry stemmed from the fact that by spending nearly the whole time hiking around instead of digging up some deposit rich with artifacts, he was wasting his time, and to some degree putting his future professional career in question.

The success of the survey was thanks in large part to contributions by James A. Ford. Jim Ford, a self-described overgrown country boy from Mississippi, was just a couple of years older than Willey and today is best known for his work with artifacts in North America. It was Ford who had the idea that they could use air photos to map the valley efficiently. At the start of the season, before heading to Viru, the team stopped off in Lima. There they bought twenty-two air photos, each about half the size of a movie poster. The survey had been flown by the Peruvian Air Force and printed

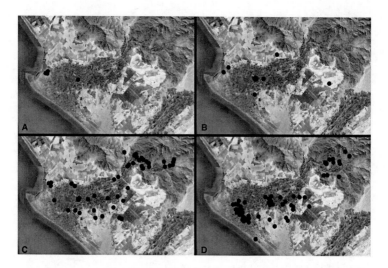

FIGURE 6. Settlement patterns in the Viru Valley, Peru. Gordon Willey's first attempt to reconstruct settlement patterns shows four time periods. From upper left, clockwise: (A) a time when few people lived in the valley (Cerro Prieto Period); (B) the first period when we find houses and community buildings (Guañape Period); (C) the time when fortification were added (Puerto Moorin Period); (D) and the period when people moved into a dense concentration near the coast (Gallinazo Period). Source: Willey (1953). The length of the valley, from the ocean to the uplands, is just over thirty kilometers, or about a seven-hour hike.

at a 1:10,000 scale. It is hard to see anything at that scale. Two football fields set end-to-end would be just two centimeters long so things like the foundations of houses were too small to see.

To make the photos useful, they used a type of projector that let them blow up each picture and then make maps at a 1:700 scale by tracing the projected image. At that scale two football fields would be more like thirty centimeters. Viru Valley's ancient architectural features—walls, mounds, and pyramids made of earth and stone—stood out from the surrounding natural landscape on air photos because, for lack of a better description, they looked like weird shadows. Having traced the shadows to create maps revealing the locations of architecture, the crew not only had a good idea how to navigate but also an idea of what was there before they arrived.

Viru Valley has its share of big stunning architecture. But Willey and the Smithsonian team wanted to locate and map all kinds of different places, including places where people lived, farmed, and worshipped. After four months of chasing down weird shadows on air photos the team came back with results that exceeded expectations. They had recorded archaeology in three hundred locations. That is a lot, but the number was not as important as the picture that emerged when they put them in order of construction. In those days, the order was based on the artistic styles and types of artifacts observed on the ground surface, especially pottery.

Broadly speaking, they found the earliest farmers who settled in the valley had built "no mounds or special buildings" (Willey 1953, 400). As time passed, villages marked by small houses emerged, with buildings that might have been temples or had some other use to the community. Later, the first pyramids, fortifications, and palaces were built. Importantly, Willey and his team also traced the history of a massive investment in canals to irrigate fields. Mundane, sure. But with the canals the natural environment of the valley allowed for the production of enough food to support a large and growing population. The distant past was starting to make sense, remarkably, without a massive amount of digging.[1]

A few years after the Viru Valley project, Willey was given an endowed chair at Harvard—one of the universities that had rejected him in his first attempt at graduate school—and he introduced the world to this new way of looking at archaeology like this:

The material remains of past civilizations are like shells beached by the retreating sea. The functioning organisms and the milieu in which they lived have vanished, leaving the dead and empty forms behind. An understanding of structure and function of ancient societies must be based upon these static molds which bear only the imprint of life. Of all those aspects [of prehistory] . . . which are available to the archaeologist, perhaps the most profitable for such an understanding are settlement patterns. (Willey 1953, 1)

In other words, by studying settlement patterns archaeologists could potentially see the real-world consequences of all sorts of things, such as how populations grew and societies evolved.

Interest in settlement patterns caused a boom in the use of air photos in archaeology. All around the world in the 1960s and 1970s, a whole generation of archaeologists went forth into the backcountry—no GPS, no cell phones, just marked-up air photos in their backpacks, and what they hoped was a reliable Jeep. We had finally come to appreciate that to ask and answer interesting questions it would be necessary to be able to say what was going on around a single location, or between locations, rather than limit our focus to excavations in one place. That idea—that you could read the past from looking at changes in the arrangement and types of settlements—was itself revolutionary.

. . .

The most incredibly detailed maps of ancient Europe available today are not the results of teams of archaeologists combing the backcountry, but are nonetheless also tied to the clever use of air photos. See that dark circle around Stonehenge? It is a patch of grass that grows slightly differently where a ditch stood centuries before the first large stones were placed. This phenomenon is often observed in air images of farmers' fields and has picked up the name crop mark.[2]

Crop marks come in a wide range of geometric forms and you can find them all over the world. Crop marks like Stonehenge's ring ditch come from above-average growth. The grass is a shade greener because the buried ditch holds moisture, acting like a big flowerbed. These greener marks are called positive crop marks, or dark crop marks. This is opposed to something like a buried wall that negatively impacts the health of grass because plants on top of a buried wall have shallower soil and less water. That makes the grass browner—or lighter, in black-and-white images—thus those are called negative crop marks, or light crop marks. Crop marks are more or less visible depending upon the specific environmental conditions when a picture is taken.[3] The season, the time of day, and even something as momentary as a passing cloud are all factors that will impact what archaeology will be visible, partially visible, or invisible in an air photo. But once you know these basic principles, crop marks open up a whole host of possibilities for mapping the archaeological landscape from the air.

Not long after the first air photos of Stonehenge were taken, World War I broke out and European skies became the stage of the first aerial war. Over the muddy trenches of Belgium and France airplanes were being used as bombers and dueled in air-to-air combat made famous by stories like that of the Red Baron. Reconnaissance photo surveys to map changes in the field of battle from the air gave each side information about the enemy's territory and what they were preparing to do, and became essential to military campaigns. Unbeknownst to them at the time, these military aviators were also taking pictures of thousands of locations with intact archaeology across Europe.

Archives hold hundreds of thousands, or possibly millions, of images taken over Europe during World War I and World War II, before modern development and well before the era of good satellite photos. There have been efforts recently to make archived air images useful for remote sensing. I want to highlight just two studies that are good examples of the work that is being done.

We start over Belgium. For much of World War I there was a stalemate between entrenched armies in a battlefield known as the Western Front, which extended from the Belgian coast to the French Alps. Flying over this no-man's-land one risked being shot down, but the traditional method of military intelligence gathering—soldiers on horseback scouting ahead of the main force—was simply not an option under these conditions.

Recently, a research team at the University of Ghent in Belgium wanted to use World War I images to hunt down a distinctive type of crop mark left by the moats that had once surrounded good-sized farms (Stichelbaut et al. 2013).[4] Moated farms were not castles; they were the homes of well-to-do farmers or of minor elites. They date to the medieval period, which covers about one thousand years, roughly AD 400 to AD 1500. The moats served the same purpose as they would for a castle: home security. Inside the area guarded by the moat you would have lots of room for houses, livestock, and gardens. Creating a good, complete map of these is the first step in the reconstruction of medieval settlement patterns.

The air images first needed to be organized by where they were taken. The researchers' plan was to create a digital version of the mosaics of printed air photos that archivists have used for many years as finding aids.[5] The idea was that a geospatial index of images would allow one to search by map, rather than searching by something like a place name, to find images in the collections. Next, the Ghent team used the index to identify digital versions of four thousand photos that were then put into real geographic space so they looked like one massive composite picture of a section of Belgium circa 1914 to 1918. There are a number of factors—like accounting for the angle the image was taken from, finding landmarks on the ground, et cetera—that made this no small task. And all this had to be done before looking for their target, the moated farms.

The team found five hundred farms, only a fraction of which were previously known to archaeology. And it should be said, the density at which these moated farms are now reported is incredible. If you walked across Belgium in a straight line for an hour you would come across about five. Data-driven projects like this one, meaning projects inspired by the availability of a dataset like the World War I images, are designed to guide other research.[6] Without them we might never know that a certain set of remote sensing imagery can give us a picture of settlement from a specific time.

One of my favorite findings of the Ghent study has to do with some circular patterns on the imagery that, all things being equal, look like Bronze Age earthworks that would have dated to long before the moated farms. They are not. In reality the circles were temporary pens thrown up to keep horses during the long stalemates of trench warfare. Great news for military historians who want to map out the war, and a cautionary tale, for archaeologists mapping features from the air, not to overinterpret the things we see.

Some of you are asking: How had no one noticed these crop marks before? In fact, many people had noticed crop marks; at a minimum, farmers would have taken note of the big, unnatural-looking shapes in their fields. That is why remote sensing projects are often better thought of as exercises in mapping rather than as discoveries. If you want to see what real dedication to this way of mapping looks like, look no further than the far southwest corner of the United Kingdom, in the county of Cornwall.[7]

Cornwall is about the size of Rhode Island, and like the rest of the United Kingdom, has the full English breakfast of archaeology: stone monuments, earthworks, and actual castles. Lots of these are well known, but the effort to map them all is overwhelming. For decades archaeologists have used air photos to try and put together a map of, well, everything. One recent effort, part of English Heritage's National Mapping Programme, involved thirty-three thousand photographs, many taken by the Royal Air Force (RAF). For twelve years a team of archaeologists combed through images, put them in a digital map, and checked finds against known records. They mapped thirty thousand unique features and added ten thousand new records, nearly doubling the previous total known places with archaeology in Cornwall.

The thing I really admire about this effort is the fact that even though almost three quarters of the new records were from one specific set of air images, they did not simply discard the rest in favor of the most productive images. It is cartography, not a treasure hunt. Leaving out chances to add to the map is bad archaeology. This specific type of archaeology is certainly relevant to research, and to some degree driven by data, but its underlying purpose is to document cultural heritage in order to better take care of it. These maps are critical since you cannot save things if you do know where they are or what they are.

. . .

Like that first air photo taken over Paris, the era of taking pictures of our planet from space came from innovation in flight. The first image from space was taken just after the end of World War II. In 1946, American engineers put a 35-millimeter motion picture camera in a captured German V-2 rocket and sent it more than one hundred kilometers above New Mexico. After it crashed back to Earth they found that, by some miracle, portions of the black-and-white film had survived the ordeal, giving us a grainy but nonetheless magnificent picture of our home. It took another twenty years to get good pictures from space. In 1965, both Russian cosmonauts and American astronauts began extravehicular activity—spacewalks. And they brought their cameras.

Taking pictures from space, like all the technology that came out of the space race, had its false starts and secrecy. The first spacewalker was a Russian cosmonaut who had a camera strapped to his chest. Much to his dismay, he realized only after he was outside his capsule that engineers had failed to account for how his suit would expand in the vacuum of low Earth orbit. He ballooned up like a marshmallow. Not only was he unable to reach the camera on his brief and terrifying spacewalk, he nearly failed to squeeze back into the capsule.

The Americans managed a successful spacewalk just a few months later as part of the Gemini program. If you are into film photography, which today is expensively retro, the camera they brought was a Hasselblad 500c with a 70-millimeter lens.[8] The boxy black thing shot medium-format film, a kind of film about

FIGURE 7. Spy satellite image of a tell. This image of Hamoukar in Syria was taken from the Corona satellite on December 11, 1967; Hamoukar is one of hundreds of tells in the Corona Atlas of the Middle East (Casana and Cothren 2013). Satellite imagery has been used here for mapping, among other things, ancient roads (Ur 2003, 2010). Source: corona.cast.uark.edu.

twice as wide as the film used in standard film cameras, and it took big beautiful pictures with incredible detail from a perspective that even today few people have seen firsthand.

Away from the public eye, in the guarded, smoky backrooms of the CIA, satellite pictures were being used years before the first spacewalks. By 1960, a spy program run through the CIA and US Air Force that would be known by the codename Corona had perfected a method of remotely guiding a satellite to any place they chose to conduct a covert survey, often Russia or China (see figure 7). (The Russians were not far behind with their own parallel series of spy satellites as part of the Zenit program.) At a price tag of about one billion dollars a year in modern US dollars, Corona was no small undertaking and had some remarkable technical achievements.

The V-2 rocket that took the first image from space had to come crashing back to Earth to deliver its payload. The Corona satellites however had to be able to get the pictures safely, quickly, and covertly, back to Earth in order to be effective. The solution: dropping undeveloped film from space. The satellite would take a roll of medium-format film of a target, package it up in a cardboard box, and it would be ejected from orbit. It would parachute down and a plane would scoop it up in midair.[9]

By the time the Corona program was mothballed, in 1972, replaced by new satellite systems that did not require parachuting film down from space, nearly a million black-and-white images had been taken. Twenty years later, in the mid-1990s, the Cold War was waning and the US government declassified and released the pictures to the public. On digitized versions of the best-resolution early satellite images, a pixel is less than two meters on the ground, and at that resolution is it possible to see the same kind of detail that the Viru Valley project obtained with blown-up air photos. And while, like the air photos taken by World War I aces, these pictures no longer have strategic military value, archaeologists have found a way to put them to use in a part of the world where modern conflicts have made it increasingly difficult to conduct new field surveys: the Middle East.

. . .

In the imagination of Hollywood, the Middle East is a dry, sparsely populated place. But if you wanted to send time travelers back to the world's first towns, villages, and cities, that is where they would go. Early urban life is cemented onto the Middle Eastern landscape in the form of artificial hills called tells. A tell is the byproduct of generation after generation building on the same plot of land. If a time traveler visited one of these tells during the first generation it was in use, the traveler might find a small village of simply constructed houses, all at about the same relative elevation as the flat farm land around them. Come back in a few centuries, and the descendants of those villagers are now living higher, on top of a pile of old foundations. The practice has continued; in fact, lots of people today live on tells.

Since people live on tells for generations, the sites are always being rearranged and rebuilt, especially so by modern development. In 2012, some forty years after the last Corona picture was taken, a team from the University of Arkansas led by archaeologist Jesse Casana seized on the opportunity to compile an atlas of tells over a massive area. With a grant from the National Aeronautics and Space Administration (NASA), they put about one thousand Corona images into a GIS—difficult because of all the corrections that were necessary to match the pictures to the ground—then launched it online.

Today the Corona Atlas of the Middle East shows the locations of over eight hundred tells, many of which have carried on as towns in the modern day. Further studies with Corona images have demonstrated that the atlas is only the tip of the iceberg. Casana has increased the number of sites from hundreds to thousands (Casana 2014), and others have documented the networks of ancient roads in the region—unnaturally straight lines carved across the landscape—that connected people for centuries (Menze and Ur 2012). But, what about archaeology in other places—can you see the Great Wall of China in those spy satellite pictures?

I can't remember a time when I was not fascinated by space. As a kid, I would rattle off facts about astronomy to any adult who would listen, and plenty who only pretended to. One of those facts was that the Great Wall of China is the only human-made object that you can see from space with the naked eye. You may have heard this before. Like me, you may have even repeated it to other people. It turns out, the Great-Wall-from-space "fact" is false.[10] Bizarrely, the idea goes back to 1754. An English antiquarian named William Stukeley was part of society's upper classes, and while he took a special interest in monuments, especially the rings of large stones at Avebury and Stonehenge, he certainly had no special insight into optics or astronomy or Chinese archaeology. That did not stop him from dipping his quill into a small pot of ink and asserting in a letter that the Great Wall was the only thing people had built that could be seen from the Moon.

I had a look at some of the declassified Corona images flown over Beijing and zeroed in on a place where I know a nicely preserved section of the Great Wall snakes around the mountains just north of the city.[11] More than two centuries after Stukeley's wild claim, those images debunk that notion definitively. No wall is visible. To be fair, the best resolution of the pictures I looked at were not that great; one pixel is about ten meters wide on the ground. On higher resolution images, like on Google Earth, you can clearly see the Great Wall, but at that higher resolution you also see lots and lots of other human-made things—villages, cities, roads—again debunking the myth.

The capacity to look easily from above at anywhere is something we take for granted today. And so I think it is worth taking a minute to consider all that went into making that perfect blue digital marble, and what it has done for archaeology.

·   ·   ·

Google Earth may have been born in 2001, but the underlying data that went into making it began to be gathered when NASA shifted away from the Apollo missions of the 1960s to prioritize low-orbit flight. That move would give us the iconic 1980s space shuttle program and the construction of habitable satellites, the forerunners of the current International Space Station (ISS). In 1972, NASA launched the first generation of satellites aimed at getting full-coverage images of the Earth, as well as scanning using a range of onboard sensors. This program, called Landsat, was certainly less well known than the space shuttle, but it has managed to outlive other NASA undertakings; it has now been through eight generations of satellites, each an improvement over the last, the most recent in 2013.

Landsat's first few satellites carried imaging sensors to record energy, both visible and invisible to the human eye, that is reflected off the Earth's surface. Picture an old-fashioned radio dial with a small section in the middle being the energy wavelengths of visible light. You may remember the mnemonic "Roy G. Biv" for the order of colors in a rainbow (red-orange-yellow-green-blue-indigo-violet). That is the visible light spectra ordered by low frequency (red) to high frequency (violet) and all those wavelengths were recorded by the Landsat satellite's optical sensors.

On our old-fashioned radio, the low stations (the far left-hand side of the dial, past red) represent the infrared spectra, and the frequencies just a bit too high for us to see (the right-hand side of the dial, past violet) are the ultraviolet.[12] Instruments that record wavelengths from across the electromagnetic spectrum are termed multispectral. NASA knew the value of getting information from across frequencies and so Landsat satellites have had multispectral sensors from the start.

With improved computers in the 1970s and 1980s, the Landsat satellites could simply transmit data back to NASA. But that is a lot of data to transmit—how did they do that back in the era of fax machines and brick-sized mobile phones? Several practical decisions were made that would be important for how useful the data would be to archaeology.

Humans evolved not just the ability to see a narrow range of light, but also the ability to break the continuous range of values into discrete colors. NASA engineers did the same for Landsat satellites. Instead of a spectral readout that told you how intense the energy was at every frequency at every single point on the ground, data between certain frequencies were grouped together into bands (band 1, band 2, et cetera). Each Landsat mission would improve how finely these bands were cut. For example, on the first mission there was a band called "visible orange-red" (580–680 nanometers) that in the most recent mission was cut down to just "visible red" (640–670 nanometers), a decrease of about a third in the amount of spectral bandwidth.[13]

These images were released not just for government use but also for wide public use—a factor that may help account for why Landsat has outlasted many other programs—and the data came to end-users already postprocessed. Postprocessing is a catchall term for the things you have to do to data to make them useable. A scientist could order Landsat data and they would show up already in a real-world coordinate system, just like a map.[14]

Lastly, and most importantly for archaeology, NASA had to make a compromise between how detailed and how complete a picture of our planet the satellites would aim for, and the emphasis was placed on completeness over resolution. In the first missions, each pixel represented an area of about eighty-by-eighty meters, and that was quickly shrunk to forty-by-forty meters.[15] Over time that got down to thirty-meter spatial resolution and down again to fifteen-meter resolution. Today, in everyday terms, at its finest resolution, a pixel on a Landsat image is a bit larger than the size of a standard parking space. And so, while NASA had to work incredibly hard to bring us these data and images, they have never been particularly useful to archaeologists since they are so low-resolution.

In the 1980s NASA started holding conferences to try to use the data that they were getting in a way not originally intended: to help find archaeology. And like the Kickstarter online platform today, over the years NASA backed some great ideas, as well as some bad ones.

As the Landsat satellites whizzed around scanning the planet, NASA also used the space shuttle missions to collect the data necessary to create a realistic 3-D model of the Earth. Remember, our home is not a perfect sphere, and at this time topographic information for some remote parts of the world was still pretty basic due to a lack of good-quality air images. So in the 1980s NASA started shooting the planet with radar from space.

The idea is pretty simple. Radar is standard in aviation because you can send out a signal that will bounce back and tell you the relative location of solid objects. The signal can pass right through clouds, and it works in the day and in the night. To use it in space for surveying, a radar device was loaded into a space shuttle along with the rest of its payload; once in orbit the shuttle opened its doors facing the Earth and started shooting. The technical term for this is synthetic aperture radar, to specify that it is creating the model from a moving radar platform.

At those early NASA-sponsored conferences it was the radar data that really caught everyone, archaeologists included, by

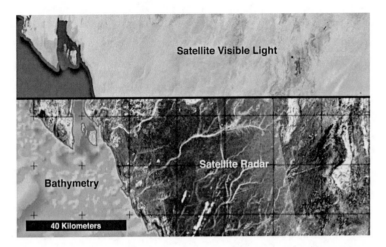

FIGURE 8. Extinct rivers of the Western Sahara. These "radar rivers"—
a nickname they picked up when they were first spotted on satellite radar
images of the Sahara in the 1980s—flowed about twenty thousand years
ago, before the Sahara was desert and when the African coastline was further
offshore. In this recent study, both satellite radar and mapping of the sea
floor (bathymetry) were used to retrace watercourses. Source: Skonieczny
et al. (2015).

surprise (see figure 8). In 1981, the first shuttle imaging radar instrument (SIR-A) was flown and the resulting images showed what
looked like rivers in the Sahara, where there simply are no rivers.
These "radar rivers" were the result of the signal passing a meter
below loose desert sands and revealing the locations of major rivers
and streams that had not flowed for thousands of years. Within a few
years archaeologists were checking these out in person, a process
called ground-truthing, and sure enough not only could you see the
physical evidence of the old river deposits under the desert sands,
there were artifacts along their banks (Wendorf, Close, and Schild
1987). Without the radar images of these deposits it would have been

a lot more difficult to flesh out the picture of what life was like in the region before it transformed into the world's largest desert.

Space radar-driven applications continued off and on in archaeology after the discovery of radar rivers. Radar was used, for example, to look for sections of our old friend the Great Wall of China. In a short paper published in 1997, scientists showed that you can see sections of the Great Wall, including parts in poor condition and buried by sand (Xinqiao, Huadong, and Yun 1997). But, it soon became clear to everyone that being able to detect things underground from space was a rarity that could only be achieved under limited conditions: basically only big things buried under loose sand.

The combination of images at too low a resolution to be useful to most archaeologists and the limited utility of radar data meant that NASA generally got a lukewarm reception by the field in the early years. This is too bad since with closer collaboration NASA might have avoided a goofy adventure looking for a lost city.

·   ·   ·

In the late 1980s, the world was introduced to the time-traveling adventures of Southern California slackers Bill and Ted. How do they get a time machine? Why are they traveling in time to meet well-known historical figures? Those questions miss the point. The point is they are out to have an excellent adventure, or in the sequel, a bogus journey.

I love NASA. But in 1983, they got conned into going along on an adventure concocted by a dude from Southern California. The dude's name was Nicholas Clapp. Clapp lived down the road from the hometown of Bill and Ted and he worked on documentary films. He wanted to go on an adventure, specifically an adventure to the Arabian Peninsula to look for the "Atlantis of the Sands," a city called Ubar.

The place-name "Ubar" appears in the Qur'an and other ancient texts. Research published after the excellent adventure suggests the name does not refer to a specific city but to a region at the edge of the Great Arabian Desert. In other words, there is no lost city of Ubar because there was never was a *city* called Ubar to begin with.

Remember, in 1983, NASA was doing its best to kick-start remote sensing for wider applications beyond the organization's primary missions. And so when Clapp picked up the phone and cold-called the Jet Propulsion Laboratory (JPL), instead of being told to buzz off, he got a sit down with Ron Blom. Blom was an expert on the application of remote sensing in geology, and had a PhD from the University of California, Santa Barbara. They met in JPL's cafeteria and Clapp sold Blom on the idea of looking for Ubar using the new satellite data. Given that professional archaeology had shown an interest in radar rivers, it made a certain sense to go looking for a specific archaeological target in the desert.

The pair started by checking out images in an area around modern-day Oman. At that time they had only data from the first couple of generations of space radar instruments (SIR-A and SIR-B), and the launch of the next generation was delayed after the Challenger accident in 1986. When they looked for Ubar using the radar imagery, they did not see anything that could be a lost city. And so they consulted Landsat. As it turned out, the longer wavelengths (near infrared) showed old tracks in the desert, which of course was a promising way to look for an ancient settlement. But the Landsat images were pretty coarse resolution, so Blom combined the data from Landsat instruments with higher-resolution data from the French space agency's new SPOT satellite. SPOT, or Satellite pour l'Observation de la Terre, had panchromatic imagery at ten-meter resolution. And voilà! Now the pair could see tracks leading to an L-shaped thing in the desert; they called it "Site L."

By the time Clapp had collected the funding and other experts for the expedition to Site L, it was 1990, just a couple of months before the start of the Gulf War. To get to this specific, remote location they used something that was super high tech at the time: GPS. And when the Royal Oman Air Force helicopter landed the team near the L-shaped thing, they found archaeology, but not what they were looking for.

Thankfully, the team included an archaeologist. He looked around and in a few minutes he had found artifacts from the Neolithic. As it turned out, the L shape was a natural depression exposed by shifting sand dunes. The team had imagined that Ubar belonged to a later period, the Bronze Age. These older—and more modest—signs of life from the Neolithic suggested that perhaps this route was not viable in the time period that they were interested in. After the Gulf War, they came back again several times, this time targeting some funny shapes that they saw on satellite images near an existing village. These turned out to be a stone fortification where most of the architecture had been covered by sand or collapsed in a sinkhole. Today, if you search for "Ubar, Oman" in Google Earth you will instantly be taken to a satellite image of the fortification the team described on their later visits.

Clapp got what he was after. In the early 1990s, the Ubar story got some news coverage and, as you would expect, he made a documentary and wrote a book along the same lines. To his credit, Blom has since has worked with professional archaeologists and he wrote the only academic-minded summary of the trips to Oman (Blom et al. 2006). Nonetheless, the whole thing was a bust from the perspective of archaeology. But then, it was never really about the archaeology. It was about the search and the promise of adventure; it was always about finding things and never about finding things out.

You might say, this all sounds like just a bit of harmless fun. But we no longer live in a world where you need an expert from NASA to access high-resolution satellite images, and a growing number of archaeologists use remote sensing in their work today. Regional maps now show archaeology over a much, much larger geographic area than ever before and with an unprecedented richness. In areas where we once knew of a handful of locations with archaeology, we now know of the possibility of tens of thousands of locations, bringing us closer to realizing the dream of understanding past societies that was first expressed through the study of settlement patterns. That is hard enough, and it is made harder when archaeology is portrayed as a treasure hunt.

·   ·   ·

We will return to satellites as one of the instruments we use to create, or recreate, digital versions of the ancient world. Next, we turn to real devices we use today that resemble something straight out of the time traveler's toolkit: scanners.

4   Scans of the Planet

Today, the archaeologist's toolkit includes a wild variety of scanners. Before scanners, looking for archaeology, documenting it through mapping and technical drawings, and sharing the results was often laborious. Scanners that use lasers to render a 3-D digital model of the real world have changed how we do each of these tasks because they are capable of producing a realistic copy of any part of the archaeological record that we can see. But, while it is getting easier and less expensive to use these, they cannot tell us what is under the surface. To get a sense for what is under the ground, or under the sea, we use a different set of scanners.

Archaeologists today drag a number of different contraptions over the ground with the aim of finding buried things without digging. The reason we do this is simple: when you dig, you have destroyed at least part, and possibly all, of the archaeology there. In much the same way that surgeons aim to be minimally invasive, we dig only when necessary, and when we do, we dig as little as possible. We use scanner data from instruments that measure different natural properties of our planet—such as the magnetic field or electric conductivity of soils—to make sensible decisions about where and how much to dig. For a number of reasons, imaging buried archaeology is a lot more difficult than making a 3-D model of something, which is why we often call it "prospecting," rather than mapping.

There are a lot of misconceptions about how these technologies work and so I think it is worth deconstructing what they can do before getting further into the kinds of datasets they produce and what we can do with those. Let's start with my personal favorite: lasers.

· · ·

Over my lifetime I will see more archaeology than did any of the generations that came before me, thanks to lasers. In archaeology, as in other disciplines that involve fieldwork, such as geology or ecology, you never expect to see more than an incredibly small portion of what you are looking for in the world. There is only so much time that you can spend hacking through jungles or digging in the desert. There will always be more just over the horizon, or in the next layer, and so we do the best that we can with the time and resources we have.

Laser scanners mounted on airplanes, set up on tripods, and shrunk down to be handheld size are being used every minute to create realistic digital models of artifacts, ruins, and entire ancient cities. Technology that produces point clouds (more on what these are later) to capture everything in three dimensions is often referred to as lidar, or LiDAR, shorthand for light detection and ranging.[1] Laser scanning has been called the key to the geospatial revolution (Chase et al. 2012). While I am skeptical when any technology is put on a pedestal, in this case the acclaim is well deserved. Not since the invention of photography allowed us to capture the world in two dimensions have we had such a leap forward in recording the environment around us.

Lasers have been used as a geospatial technology since their invention because they are so fantastic at measuring distance. Bouncing a laser off something to work out distance is a method called time-of-flight. Here's an example of how it works.

In the early 1960s, when scientists were still working out all the things we can do with lasers, they shot a laser at the Moon. Photons going forward in a single beam took 2.56 seconds to reflect off the Moon and return home. Since the speed of light is constant (about 30 centimeters per nanosecond or 300,000 kilometers per second), once you have clocked the flight time of your laser beam you have what you need to calculate distance (i.e., the time it took for a one-way trip to the Moon (1.28 seconds) × the speed of light (300,000 kilometers per second) = the distance to the Moon (384,000 kilometers).

To measure much shorter distances between things you have to be able to time the laser's flight down to the nanosecond. With modern computer processing speeds, that is not a problem and that is why you can walk into a hardware store today and find a laser tape measure that uses time-of-flight to measure distances within an accuracy of about the thickness of a coin.

While making single-distance measurements has been possible for a long time, aerial surveying with lasers—called airborne lidar or aerial laser scanning—was not broadly feasible until the 1980s. It works by taking an overwhelming number of laser measurements. The laser scanner (shooting up to one hundred thousand pulses per second) does not know ahead of time which pulses will reflect off the tops of trees and which will hit the ground and manage to make it back to the aircraft. But that is fine because it is using time-of-flight.

The first wave of beams to return to the aircraft, called the first return, is assumed to have hit treetops and the roofs of buildings, since those are closest. The last returns are assumed to be from the ground since it is the furthest solid object from the laser scanner. In an open field the first and last returns come back at nearly the same time. In a dense forest, where only a lucky few get to the ground and back, there will be a longer gap in time between the first and last returns because the last returns are traveling further.

The result of all these measurements is a point cloud. If you opened a point cloud's raw data on a computer you would find a seemingly endless list of millions or billions of spots that laser beams have bounced off of, with their longitude, latitude, and elevation. Other values can be added on the end of each line, such as code representing the color of that spot. When a program reads these coordinates and makes a visualization of them it looks like a big cloud of dots, hence *point cloud*.

.   .   .

Airborne lidar produces some of the most fantastically detailed images of archaeology imaginable. But not all lidar is equally good for all archaeology. Consider the fact that the first lidar flight over Stonehenge failed to detect some of the iconic megalithic stones.

Back in 2000 few archaeologists in the United Kingdom had even heard of lidar. Within a decade, interest in lidar had grown so widespread that English Heritage (now Historic England) put out a guide for its use under the fanciful title of *The Light Fantastic: Using Airborne LiDAR in Archaeological Survey* (Crutchley and Crow 2010; see Crutchley and Crow 2018 for an updated version). The short guide is in fact anything but fanciful. Its aim is to dispel myths about lidar and to help archaeologists to "decide first whether using lidar data will actually be beneficial in terms of their research aims and then how it can be used most effectively" (2010, 3).

That first aim of the guide, to decide if lidar will be useful, is a particularly important one. Even today archaeologists still have a hard time with this because there is an impulse to use lidar data simply because they are freely available. The widespread availability of lidar in the United Kingdom and other countries is thanks to government-funded flights aimed not at archaeology but at other contemporary needs, such as planning. The reason that researchers need to stop and consider quality and coverage of specific datasets is that one can waste a lot of time on data that are not high quality enough to identify the intended archaeological targets (Opitz and Herrman 2018).

Stonehenge is great object lesson in the importance of data quality. The first airborne lidar datasets available had only one ground point per two square meters on the ground. If you were trying to use it to map cars even the tiny Mini or VW Bug would, on average, have been reflected in four data points and thus easily detected. However, if your targets were stones that are close together and of varying sizes, it would be easy to miss one or not to be able to distinguish where one stone stopped and another stone began. And that's just what happened. Soon afterwards, higher-resolution lidar data, at one ground point per square meter, yielded much better results.

When NASA made another big push to promote remote sensing in archaeology some of that funding went to study the Maya city of Caracol.[2] A decade ago, few people outside of the field of Mesoamerican archaeology had heard of the city. Located in Belize, it was occupied for sixteen hundred years (from about

650 BC to AD 950) then was abandoned during the Maya collapse.[3] Despite being absolutely covered in jungle, it had been painstakingly documented by archaeologists Diane and Arlen Chase over twenty years. The pair, now based at the University of Nevada, Las Vegas, managed to use traditional methods to map an area about the size of a small college town (twenty-three square kilometers). The process was slow but excellent for documenting the city's epicenter with its tall monuments, plazas, and roads, called causeways, snaking out in all directions. Groups of houses dotted the area, which is typical in the sprawling cities of the region.

The Chases knew there was more beyond what they had mapped. The agricultural infrastructure in the city—fields comprised of thousands of individual terraces and other features— were too numerous to count and were locked, as it were, under thick vegetation. These fields were extremely important in a time and place in human history in which capital was nonexistent. They allowed up to one hundred thousand people to live in this one location and allowed the larger political economy to flourish. Food was the currency of the day.

In 2009, a twin-engine Cessna Skymaster, a tiny plane only big enough to carry a pilot and five passengers, started flying long sweeping lines back and forth in a grid over the ancient city. This was the work of the National Center for Airborne Laser Mapping (NCALM), an academic group centered at the University of Houston. Over the course of five days they had lasers actively pulsing at the city from above for a total of 9.5 hours.[4] That is the same length of time as a one-way commercial flight from Washington, DC, to Moscow. The survey flights were low, much lower than commercial airlines fly, at an altitude of eight hundred meters.

FIGURE 9. Airborne lidar-derived images of the city of Caracol. A digital elevation model has been modified using the hillshade function to make it easier to see subtle features, like terraces. The authors note groups of (a) houses, (b) fields, and (c) roads, as well as (d) a reservoir and (e) a natural sinkhole. Source: Chase et al. (2014).

The result was a point cloud of 4.28 billion points and a breathtaking snapshot of Caracol, minus the jungle, that made headlines around the world (see figure 9).

In less than a week, lidar gave us ten times more of Caracol than had been covered on foot over the previous two decades. The distribution of structures and roads showed no signs of stopping at the edges of what had been flown and the Chases and NCALM wanted to document more and at a higher quality. In 2013, the plane was back over Belize. The original two hundred square kilometers was expanded by another one thousand square kilometers. They flew at a lower elevation, six hundred meters, and got twice as many ground returns, improving from 1.4 points per square meter to 2.8 per square meter.

The story of Caracol is being repeated every day. A new study from the heart of the Maya area reported 2,144 square kilometers covered by lidar, which allowed the team to map 61,480 individual structures (Canuto et al. 2018). Airborne lidar has been taken up around the world and every time it is applied we get locational data across a larger amount of land than could be walked by a survey team.

As cool as airborne lidar is, and it is, consider what we can do with lasers on the ground.

. . .

All digital technology becomes more and more portable over time. In the 1990s, an engineer in the San Francisco Bay Area named Ben Kacyra was hard at work trying to make a laser scanner that you could take anywhere. In 1997 his team's working prototype was by today's standards incredibly cumbersome and slow. To get it around it had to be mounted in a VW van and unlike modern machines that blast out one hundred thousand pulses per second, the prototype could only measure thirty points per second. It was nonetheless a technical success and a few years later Kacyra sold his company to Leica Geosystems, who still make a large portion of the world's "terrestrial laser scanners," the term we use for lidar when the machine is on the ground.

Ben Kacyra and his wife, Barbara Kacyra, are now the heads of a nonprofit aimed at documenting the world's cultural heritage. The venture, CyArk, has since 2003 used terrestrial laser scanning as a technical solution to counter the information lost with the destruction of archaeology due to disasters, both natural and human-caused. The first models they produced were stunning in

FIGURE 10. 3-D scanning of ancient architecture. The CyArk 500 project has made photorealistic 3-D models from around the world available online. This example from the cliff dwelling at Balcony House in Mesa Verde, Colorado shows a number of complex details that would be difficult to appreciate without a 3-D model. Source: cyark.org; artsandculture.google.com/project/cyark.

their level of architectural detail as well as looking futuristic, with their brightly colored red or yellow clouds of points on a black background. Over the years, scanning hardware and software have continued to improve. New scanners now come with high-definition cameras that allow the point cloud to come out with photorealistic quality.

In October 2013, CyArk launched an ambitious effort to digitally preserve five hundred locations in the next five years.[5] There are a number of lessons that we can learn from the CyArk 500 project, but to start let's have a look at the tools that have been helping make it happen (see figure 10).

Most terrestrial laser scanners work on the time-of-flight principle but with some important differences from airborne lidar. The laser scanner is typically placed on top of a tripod and programmed to scan the environment around it. The laser beam sweeps up and down as it slowly turns 360 degrees. The scanner combines the resulting splashes of points to make a single point cloud for the location where the machine is set up.

The cloud includes every surface the machine had within a clear line of sight. That means a high density of points all around with the exception of a tight circle directly below the scanner, and laser shadows. Laser shadows are cast by fully solid objects, which the lasers never reach past. To fill in these blank spots you move the scanner to a new position where it does have a line of sight, and repeat.

The goal of a terrestrial laser scan is to create one seamless model. This begins with reconnaissance of the place to be scanned, to work out exactly how large an area will be targeted and how this will be accomplished with the fewest number of stations (places where the machine is set up on the tripod and turned on). There is no perfect way to do this, but there are some common problems that surveyors know to watch out for, like areas that will have laser shadows and require closer stations to create more overlap. Many machines require control points (targets at fixed locations with known coordinates) that are scanned and used later to combine individual station scans into a single point cloud.

There are other things besides laser shadows that are important to look out for when doing a laser scan in the field. For example, every survey will produce noise, that is, points that will have to be cleaned or filtered out of the data. Noise is unavoidable, but can be minimized by doing things like keeping people from walking in front of the scanner when it is going.

With those caveats, laser scanning itself is easy and fast. If you are scanning something straightforward, like the outside of a building or a ruin, it may only take a single day. The interiors of buildings, and things like caves, require a lot more stations for a terrestrial laser scanner, which is why more archaeologists are turning to mobile laser scanning.

Mobile laser scanning works by taking all the parts that would normally be mounted on the bottom of an aircraft or placed on top of a tripod at a survey station and shrinking them down to fit within a handheld device and backpack. A mobile laser scanner can build a continuous point cloud as you walk around and sweep the device back and forth, based on technology called SLAM, for simultaneous location and modeling. As you move around the lidar is pulsing out lasers and building a 3-D model at such an incredible speed that it can follow your relative position within the model as it is being built. SLAM has been tested in driverless cars to build up a picture of what is around the vehicle in order to avoid accidents. Like driverless cars, mobile laser scanners have a lot of potential but are still rare today.

Lasers are not the only way that we build 3-D models. Many of the most detailed models are made by software that uses overlapping images, a process called photogrammetry. Photogrammetry uses photos taken from different locations to measure distance. Those distance measurements can be processed to create a point cloud. The technique has a long history but took off when smartphones had both good quality cameras and processors. It is a passive technique—that is, it passively takes in visible light bounced off surfaces—and so is subject to the limitations of the camera, the amount of overlap between photos, and the environment. And just like laser-made models, some are compiled from airborne images while others are from images taken close to the ground, and some models use real geolocation while others float in digital space.

Drones often use photogrammetry to create 3-D models of archaeology and to survey hard to reach places (Cowley et al. 2018).[6] The drones in use today are either miniature helicopters with multiple rotors keeping them aloft, or fixed-wing craft that look like tiny gliders. Each has its advantages and disadvantages in terms of flight time (a limiting factor for the amount of area covered), stability, and payload (which sensor, or sensors, can be put onboard).

Drone experts Pablo Norambuena and Juan Sainz have recently flown the entire island of Rapa Nui, better known as Easter Island (Norambuena and Sainz 2016). Rapa Nui is featured on the cover of archaeology textbooks about as often as Egypt because of the hundreds of *moai*, stone statues, that dot the island. The ancestors of the people of Rapa Nui left behind more than *moai*; there are stone foundations of homes, fields, and more, that can be seen on the ground surface today. The drone survey used a 1.5 meter-wide fixed-wing drone programmed to fly in straight lines about 25 to 28 kilometers long. Because the island is pretty tiny, about 164 square kilometers, it took only fifty-two flights to create a seamless single picture of the island out of 21,840 overlapping pictures.

From these fixed-wing drone data one can build not just a seamless single air photo but also a point cloud of the entire ground surface; however, to map archaeology in detail a much higher resolution is necessary. That is why another team has recently flown a small section of the island, about nineteen square kilometers, also a using fixed-wing drone, taking just about the same number of photographs as the island-wide survey, with the aim of achieving ten times the resolution (Dahlberg 2016).

If you want a really, really detailed photogrammetric model you have to get up close and personal. For example, a number of

FIGURE 11. A statue named Hoa Hakananaiʻa. This image of a Rapa Nui statue *(moai)* currently in the British Museum was created from overlapping images. The entire model is a small 3-D object file (.obj), only 23MB. Data source: uploaded to sketchfab.com by user light_heists, model captured on 30 March 2015; displayed in Meshlab (2016.12).

people have used overlapping photos to create a 3-D model of a *moai* that is in the British Museum (see figure 11). His name is Hoa Hakananaiʻa.[7] He is 2.42 meters tall, and he's got some astounding tattoos. But in order to capture the intricate carved images on his back, care needs to be taken with lighting and considering the perspective of the viewer.

You can also find 3-D models of *moai* in place on Rapa Nui that have been generated based on photos that people have taken when they have visited. The quality of these is much more variable since there is less control over the distance to the target, lighting, and so on. Nonetheless, some archaeologists in other regions are starting to use tourist photos to crowdsource the raw data for photogrammetric models.

No matter how you create a point cloud, the most time consuming and difficult part is the postprocessing. Point clouds need to be joined together in space and cleaned up to eliminate noise so you can start to make a visualization. Further steps, like creating a digital mesh and adding texture, are necessary before you can export real-istic static images or animate a fly-through.[8] And when you are done, you are still only going to be looking at the surface. Next, let's look at some different scanners, scanners that try to peak underground.

.   .   .

The original *Jurassic Park* opens with fictional paleontologist Dr. Alan Grant, played by Sam Neill, blasting a shotgun at the ground and imaging in perfect detail a fossilized dinosaur underground. This iconic scene is based on a real technique called geophysical diffraction tomography. One of its pioneers, the nonfictional geologist Alan Witten, used to use an eight-gauge seismic shotgun that he named Betsy. The idea is that you place sensors (called geophones) around the area, you point Betsy at the ground in the center of them, Betsy goes ka-boom and creates an energy wave, and then the sensors detect how the energy's path is deflected by things underground.

But I am afraid that you will not find a seismic shotgun in an archaeological toolkit. Science fiction rarely gets archaeological geophysics right. As in most things, it overreaches. For example, we cannot use scanners to get that kind of detail that you see in *Jurassic Park*. It is not possible to see artifacts underground. So, how does underground imaging work? What can you see?

The goal of an underground geophysical survey is that it shows us something out of the ordinary, and the term for that result is one you will find throughout science fiction: an anomaly. There are two basic ways to peak underground and detect anomalies without digging. One type, called passive, uses sensors to detect small changes in the properties of the ground. The most common passive tool for archaeology is a magnetometer.

A magnetometer is basically a really, really sensitive metal detector. We all know that a compass needle naturally aligns with the Earth's north-south magnetic field but that a much, much weaker magnet placed close to the compass can interrupt it. For these sensitive instruments the source of the disruption can be the presence of metal, or stone, or some other soil property that messes with electromagnetism over a short distance. Typically, two sensors are placed close to one another, maybe a meter apart, and then walked, dragged, or driven slowly over a survey area. There are a number of different types of sensors, but they work on the same principle.

On a magnetometer survey the person operating the machine has to remove any metal on them. This so that the surveyor who calibrates and operates the machine (or their footwear) is not the source of anomalies. As the array of sensors travels over an area it records even the smallest changes in electromagnetism. Like other scanning in archeology, the resolution depends on the rate the machine is taking in data and the speed it travels, and it is greatly influenced by ferrous objects (bits of metal or stones with high natural iron content). For example, a survey at a section of a UK cemetery for 2,861 "unclaimed patients" appears to show the locations of about two hundred graves (Gaffeny and Gaffeny 2011). In practice, these are not the locations of the graves themselves, but those of buried metal grave markers. That is an important distinction because the small markers tend to get moved around over time and not all graves had markers to begin with.

The other type of geophysical survey, the active type, introduces energy and sees how it behaves in the environment. For example, the passive magnetometer, one of the most popular methods with archaeologists, is often paired with electronic resistivity. Resistivity works as a survey method for the same reason you do not put a toaster in a bathtub: water is a great conductor of electricity. Even slight changes in moisture in soil are detectable by making a small electric field on the ground. You will see the results of surveys using this kind of instrument discussed in terms of resistivity or conductivity.

It works like this. Your resistivity machine has a positive and negative end placed on the ground. The power source lets you move electrons from one end to the other. For this method, the power does not need to knock your socks off, like Betsy-the-seismic-shotgun, in fact, some are run on just a single nine-volt battery.

The damper the ground, the faster the electrons make the trip; the dryer the ground, the more resistance to the electrons and the slower the trip. You walk, drag, or drive your resistivity machine over an area, and what shows up are the kinds of things that make crop marks, such as buried earthworks. This makes sense since the reason we can see crop marks is because archaeology has in some way changed the moisture in that area. Incidentally, in that same cemetery where the magnetometer showed lots of grave markers, resistivity showed no graves at all, just slightly darker patches along old pathways between sections of the cemetery.

These methods—magnetometry and resistivity/conductivity—can be used to work out how deep an anomaly may be but they tend to be better at showing the outline of things in two dimensions. Where you want to get an idea of how deeply something is buried, especially for smaller areas, archaeologists will often use ground penetrating radar.

We have already seen radar do a pretty neat trick: it was radar waves from space that NASA used to detected massive dry riverbeds under the sands of the Sahara. Ground penetrating radar is a type of scanner that is moved across a surface, sending out radar waves and receiving back signals from as deep as several meters below the ground depending upon the setup.[9] At that UK cemetery, ground penetrating radar scans showed anomalies at distinctly different depths at the same locations, suggesting multiple internments; people had been buried in the same plots at different times. This is why archaeological prospection has been called a "four-dimensional puzzle" (Gaffney and Gaffney 2011), with time being the fourth dimension.

.   .   .

Natural phenomena, like the Saharan radar rivers, accumulate over long, long time periods and leave the biggest, oldest, and therefore most obvious anomalies. Geology is usually the target for nonarchaeological geophysical surveys. For example, while seismic survey is rarely used by archaeologists, it was essential to private companies who mapped the bottom of the North Sea looking for oil and gas. A boat motored along creating a seismic energy source as it navigated its survey line, while behind the boat a string of sensors detected the energy waves that bounced off the bottom to create a seafloor model.

After prospecting for natural resources in the North Sea was completed the data were shared with a group of academic archaeologists, but they were not interested in looking for sunken ships. They were after a landmass that once connected Britain to the European mainland, a place called Doggerland.

Around ten thousand years ago, the Mesolithic people of what is now Britain and Ireland lived on a peninsula jutting out from

Europe into the North Atlantic. Over the next twenty-five hundred years, the intervening land was swallowed up by rising seas, separating the British Isles from one another and from mainland Europe—the original Brexit.

Armed with a digital elevation model of the seafloor and other data, archaeologists have now made an atlas of a twenty-three thousand square kilometer portion of these lands (Thompson, Fitch, and Gaffney 2007). They have traced almost seven hundred kilometers of former coastline, sixteen hundred kilometers of rivers and streams, and two dozen low-lying areas that at one time may have been lakes. They did not find the camps that people would have lived in, nor would we expect them to be able to do so with the data that they have, which covers a total area about the same size as Wales. But what they have done is shrink down the area where we should be looking for them; that is the name of the game in archaeological prospection.[10]

There have been improvements in geophysical sensors over the years, but the real change from the perspective of archaeology has been the evolution of fast, multisensor, high-resolution surveys over large areas. The Stonehenge Hidden Landscapes Project (2010–14), put these advances into action. Over 120 days of fieldwork, the team scanned a massive area mapping the locations of twelve hundred buried ritual monuments from the Neolithic and Bronze Ages. This survey also improved the interpretation of known features. For example, a low mound, originally thought to have been a barrow, was scanned by a combination of ground penetrating radar and magnetometer to reveal that it is in fact something quite different (Gaffney et al. 2012). To investigate further, another machine capable of measuring both the magnetic field and electronic conductivity was carried over the feature at settings that

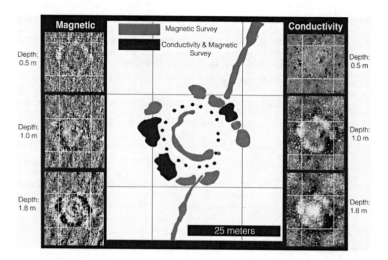

FIGURE 12. Imaging underground using geophysical survey. This example shows the kinds of data we use to image structures underground without excavation. Two soil properties—magnetism and conductivity—were measured at increasing depths below the ground surface to create a composite picture of a small monument near Stonehenge. Source: Bonsall et al. (2013).

were ideal for imaging three different depths below the surface (0.5, 1.0, and 1.8 meters) (Bonsall et al. 2013) (see figure 12). Together, these multiple scans allowed the team to reclassify the mound as a "mini-henge," known as a hengiform monument. This miniature version of Stonehenge, about eight hundred meters northwest of actual Stonehenge, has pits defining an enclosed area, instead of a continuous ring-ditch, and the interior likely has pits and burials. Remarkably, until the scans, it was hiding in plain sight.

How reliable are the results of archaeological prospection? Looking for agreement between different geophysical instruments, like the magnetic and conductivity results at the hengiform monument, is one way to measure confidence, but direct observation is best. Direct observation in this context means some kind of excavation. The United Kingdom and Ireland have the most data on this, with hundreds of geophysical surveys conducted for archaeology each year picking up features from a range of time periods. A look back over a decade's worth of survey data for roads in Ireland had the great advantage that most of the scanned areas were subsequently mechanically dug, stripping away the top soil, thus allowing us to check the results (Bonsall, Gaffney, and Armit 2014).[11] James Bonsall (of the Institute of Technology Sligo) and his colleagues determined that several factors are key to reliability: what you are looking for, how cooperative the underlying geology is for that search, how high a resolution your scanning is, and the interpretive skills of the archaeologists processing and reading the data from visualizations. For example, earthworks, like the one described above, have a really good chance of being found in almost any conditions, but small features, like postholes, were invisible in even the best conditions at the locations examined in Ireland.

When a geophysical survey suggests there will be buried features, but we fail to see anything in excavations, most of the time that is chalked up to signals giving a false positive. It happens all the time. But in some cases, and these are rare, a geophysical survey may be telling us about something that is invisible to the naked eye but remains detectable through soil properties, something called "ghost features" (Bonsall, Gaffney, and Armit 2014, 12). This is one of the many reasons that we need the power of human reasoning to weigh the evidence at hand and that we are unlikely to be replaced altogether by machines.

. . .

Scanners are a big deal for archaeology because they change what we can see. We can see through jungle without cutting it down. We can see archaeology in 3-D without visiting in person and we can revisit it again and again. We can to some degree see under the ground without digging. Seeing is important because it is the first step in the creation of new knowledge about the past and is necessary to preserve that which has survived the forces of entropy.

Some of the techniques we use, like geophysical survey, will probably remain the domain of specialists. But others, like creating 3-D models with photogrammetry, use technology that is already widely available. One estimate suggests that the total number of cameras in the world will exceed more than forty-five billion in the next few years. And the fusion of different technologies, like drone-based lidar, is poised to give us some unbelievable results. It is amazing to me that there are millions of people living in the world today who will never know a time without these amazing technologies. They are sometimes called the digital natives, as opposed to folks like me who are adult adopters, digital immigrants.[12] In the next chapter I want to tell a small part of the story of how data in archaeology went from being almost entirely created in an analog form to being "born digital."[13]

5   *Digital Worlds*

If I could give just one piece of advice to time travelers it would be this: you cannot rely on old maps to navigate the past. Here's why.

There are examples of extremely old art—carvings etched on bone and cave paintings from the last Ice Age—that could have been maps, but we cannot be certain. This is understandable given the circumstances. For example, the stick charts that navigators in the Pacific have used for centuries would be just as difficult to classify as art or maps had traditional navigation techniques and knowledge not survived to the modern day. So, right off the bat, that ambiguity puts most of human history out of reach. Thanks, equifinality.

Writing was first invented about five thousand years ago in the Middle East, and there are enough examples of clay tablets that have survived with images that look like maps to convince me that mapping, as we known it, was invented around the same time or soon after. Maps made over the next few thousand years expanded, in terms of the amount of the globe represented, but were still working on the assumption that the world was flat. In truth, there are extremely few historic maps that are more than five hundred years old. So, even if there were lots of great maps around way back when, they are gone now. Thanks, entropy.

Most of the surviving examples of old maps were made by Western explorers and surveyors in the centuries that followed Columbus making his way to the New World. There is something charming in their imperfections, with coastlines that almost look right, but not quite, and huge blank spots. There have been a number of efforts to transfer these to a digital format, among them the David Rumsey Historical Map Collection, which currently has hundreds of maps with real-world coordinates viewable on Google Earth. I particularly like the ones that look like one of those oversized antique globes that open at the equator to reveal a miniature bar.

Many of these old Western maps stand on their own as historical documents, and even as works of art, but they are deeply, deeply problematic for retelling history. The problem is not that the people who made the maps were necessarily sloppy or bad at making maps, it's that they were too good at mapping what they wanted to see. And what they often wanted to see was a land erased of its indigenous people and their histories.

It is one thing to say historic maps are not objective, it is another to see a familiar place mapped from a different perspective. That is the goal of an online project called the Decolonial Atlas. It is based on the premise that, "the orientation of a map, its projection, the presence of political borders, which features are included or excluded, and the language used to label a map are all subject to the map-maker's bias—whether deliberate or not" (decolonialatlas.wordpress.com/about). Some of my favorite maps currently hosted on the website show regions of North America without modern political boundaries, with their names given in the languages of Native American peoples. Take note, would-be time travelers: knowing what local people call landmarks, like rivers and mountains, is going to be more useful to you than knowing your position relative to boundaries that were not drawn until the recent past.

These two examples—the superimposition of historic maps onto the modern digital globe, and the creation of maps that force the viewer to confront the colonial biases in those historic maps— are relying on the same set of geospatial technologies to create contrasting versions of the world. Taking the long view of humanity, I wonder if these technologies will bring a return to the kind of creativity in mapping that our species probably enjoyed for a long, long time before the paper map came along. Just think about all the options that the map on your smartphone opens up. You can zoom in and out, you can search by text, you can switch between maps and satellite images—try that with a paper map. We even have the capability of creating new layers on top of the real world that we interact with through augmented reality. That's why when we make maps today what we are really doing is creating digital worlds.

In this chapter we explore the ways archaeologists make digital versions of the ancient world. The paper map served archaeology well and is still one of the tools in our toolbox, but we have been able to accomplish so much more using technology like geographic information systems (GIS), global positioning systems (GPS), and new super-high-resolution satellite imagery. As we will see, working with these geospatial technologies can be one of the hardest things that archaeologists do. It requires a lot of decisions based on little and incomplete information, as well as working within a computer framework that was not created with archaeology in mind. We will look at some of the clever technical solutions archaeologists have come up with for adapting these advances for our purposes, through things like enhancing tiny changes in topography to make archaeology visible and developing algorithms to teach machines to find archaeology.

Today the stakes for handling locational information correctly could not be higher in terms of protecting archaeology. For example, a few years ago, I had the privilege of mapping an incredible piece of architecture in the Hawaiian Islands. It is largely intact, and it is associated with a well-known event from history, but its location is not well known to the broader public. In a place like Hawaii, which sees millions of visitors every year, it makes sense to obscure the location to protect it from a swarm of unregulated visitation that, even if visitors were careful, would damage it. This specific location is in good hands; it is actively looked after by the local community and archaeologists. But we cannot expect that to work in all cases. For many communities, displaying the locations of archaeology is a necessary prerequisite to advocating for their protection. In the Middle East, for example, there is a real problem with looting for the antiquities trade. International efforts to show the locations of archaeology, and the impacts of looting, have been an effective avenue to raise awareness and discourage further damage. That is our constant conundrum: we must keep from drawing unwanted attention to locations with intact archaeology, but we also must show the public that, while archaeology is precious, it is not rare. It is everywhere and it needs our protection.

. . .

Coming to the subject cold, there are a few things about the use of GIS in archaeology that you should know about. The first is that it is best thought of as a highly specialized branch of computer

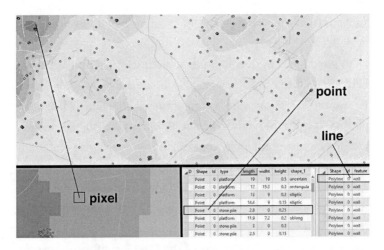

FIGURE 13. How the world is simplified in a geographic information system (GIS). A GIS represents things in the real world through data models: vector and raster. Vector data—points, lines, and polygons—have a string of information attached to each object in a corresponding spreadsheet. Raster data represent a single variable, on this map the density of points, in pixels. Data source: Swedish National Data Service, created by Olof Håkansson.

science (see figure 13). As such, the experts in the field want to see it used both well, as in for sound archaeological scholarship, and correctly, in a technical sense. The book you are reading is meant only as a brief introduction. For those looking to get into this in much more depth there are two books that have tackled the topic that I highly recommend: one is by David Wheatley of the University of Southampton and Mark Gillings of the University of Leicester (Wheatley and Gillings 2002), the other is by James Conolly of Trent University and Mark Lake of University College London (Conolly and Lake 2006). Neither is strictly speaking a handbook or technical manual. They are more like guides to best practices, and they have been a big help in navigating the hype that surrounds this technology and in learning how to use the tools available.[1]

A good place to start to understand the underlying principles behind GIS is to consider what goes into creating a GIS database. For example, GIS software is programmed to operate in data models that simplify the world in a few different ways. The archaeology visible on the ground today could be represented by a point, or by a polygon outlining the footprint of a building foundation or where a scatter of artifacts was observed. Points, lines, and polygons are together known as vector data, as opposed to the other basic data model: raster data. Raster data stores information in a grid of pixels, like a photograph. The size of the pixel is uniform across the data and defines the resolution of the dataset. The value ranges in a raster will depend on what is being represented. They could be binary (present, absent), an ordinal scale classification (1, 2, 3), or a continuous variable (1.2, 1.3, 1.4).

It is fitting that we call these vector and raster data models "GIS primitives" because they are simple, and they have been carried over from the earliest days of the technology. They can be displayed at the same time, but each layer of data must be a single type (i.e., a layer can have points or polygons, not points and polygons). They have other special qualities that make them distinct. Vector data will have a spreadsheet in which each object (each point, line, or polygon) has a corresponding row, and columns represent different quantitative and qualitative information, called attributes. GPS data recorders collect data in vector format whereas remote sensing data (e.g., satellite imagery) mainly comes in raster format.

The third dimension, elevation, is typically either the primary variable in a raster layer called a digital elevation model (DEM) or one of the variables in a vector data table. In that sense, GIS is said to be more than two-dimensional but not truly three-dimensional; it is sometimes described as two-and-a-half-dimensional. Computer-aided design (CAD) has had three-dimensional display sorted out for a long time, and there are a number of stand-alone programs that will let you view and manipulate point clouds in 3-D, but they do not operate in true geographic space or have the capacity for spatial statistics or storing rich databases. Over the years, archaeologists have come to work more and more with natively three-dimensional datasets, specifically point clouds, and fortunately for us, GIS programmers continue to make improvements on handling the third dimension. However, it generally remains a weak spot.

Frustratingly, there have been few improvements over the years in how time is integrated within GIS.[2] From the perspective of the software, data have time stamps that can represent when they were created or when they were updated. From the archaeological user's perspective neither is as important as the time when the observation was made (i.e., when something was found), or the time to which a building or deposit or artifact dates. Further, GIS is not well designed to compute or display things like duration, or change over time, or the probability error bars that come with lots of archaeology. There have been some creative work-arounds, like making short videos to show how the distributions of archaeological phenomena change over time.[3]

Time in an archaeological GIS database is innately problematic. To use GIS we force our data into layers. Digital layers at first glance can make it look like everything was created, used, abandoned, and discovered at the same time.[4] But buildings or deposits from one time period, and one time period only, are the exception rather than the rule. Most locations will have archaeological deposits from across time. Further, it is commonplace to know precisely where something was found but not know precisely when that material dates to.

The limitations that data models put on us have led some to hold an extremely dim view of GIS. They see it as a "technology without intellectual vigour, overly dependent on simple presuppositions about the importance of spatial patterns in a dehumanised artificial space" (Connelly and Lake 2006, 10). In other words, GIS is too boring, dumb, and fake to be useful for reconstructing the past.

Here's the problem with that view: the same could be said for just about anything we do with computers. Computers must start with simple presuppositions and abstract data models before they can scale to complex and real-world problems; they are built to discern pattern from noise. That's why they need a great deal of help from us. Just feeding them all the data and crossing our fingers that something useful will come out, violates the "garbage in, garbage out" law of computing. It is also unrealistic to think GIS is the right tool for every job. So, how exactly are archaeologists creating good locational data and information?

. . .

Let's start by looking at the online GIS databases that exist today that give us ways to share and display what we have found. It is hard to capture all the ways that archaeologists and other scholars do this. Nonetheless, I did a survey of the kinds of places where archaeologists might go looking for larger databases, and this is what I found (McCoy 2017).

Some of the biggest datasets of archaeology available today are in locational indices and digital atlases. Locational indices are similar to Google Maps. They are built for displaying information, searches, and answering simple spatial queries like: How many locations have already been recorded in this study area? Digital atlases are more like Google Earth. They are built for exploring a particular time and place. Both indices and atlases, generally speaking, are point layers, in which each point represents a place where archaeology has been reported.

Some atlases are the result of collaborative projects in the digital humanities. For example, Pleiades (pleiades.stoa.org) is a "community-built gazetteer and graph of ancient places" and includes thirty-six thousand points around the Mediterranean. This crowdsourced dataset includes archaeology and things like place-names that are important for mapping classical texts onto the real world.

Other atlases focus on a certain kind of archaeology from a particular time period. For example, the Electronic Atlas of Ancient Maya Sites, created by Walter R. T. Witschey of Longwood University and Clifford T. Brown of Florida Atlantic University, is a point database focused on just Maya settlements. It can be viewed in Google Earth or imported as a layer in a GIS of six thousand points that includes place-names, if known, and an ordinal classification of settlement size (e.g., rank 1 are the largest; rank 5 are the smallest).

Locational indices tend to catalog all locations where archaeology has been recorded, regardless of age or type. The Digital Index of North American Archaeology (DINAA), for example, includes more than three-quarters of a million records from all time periods and types of archaeology and so is a "uniquely comprehensive window into human settlement across North America" (ux.opencontext .org/archaeology-site-data/) (see figure 14). The project, which began in 2012, is led by David G. Anderson (University of Tennessee,

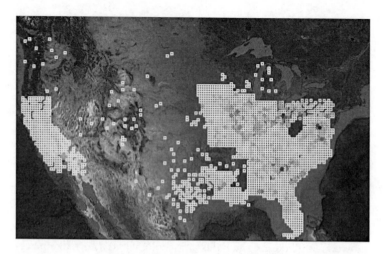

FIGURE 14. The Digital Index of North American Archaeology (DINAA). DINAA is an archaeological locational index of over three-quarters of a million records. Indexing is a critical first step in conducting scientific research and caring for archaeology. Accessed December 19, 2018.

Knoxville), Joshua Wells (Indiana University, South Bend), Stephen Yerka (University of Tennessee, Knoxville), Eric Kansa (Open Context), and Sarah Whitcher Kansa (Open Context), and has grown to include most of the US Southeast, some of the Midwest, and California.[5] There are a number of contributing institutions, and the largest number of records are from centralized state-level government agencies. As new data are added records are classified by what was found and the time period, or periods, to which it belongs, to allow the user to look at the distribution of archaeology in ways that have been impossible until now.

How many records will DINAA have when it finally covers all of North America? That is difficult to say, but the total will be in the millions.[6] One reason I think that will be the case is what I see in the distribution of radiocarbon dates over this same region. The

Canadian Archaeological Radiocarbon Database (CARD), started by Dick Morlan of the Canadian Museum of History and currently managed by Andrew Martindale of the University of British Columbia, is a clearinghouse of radiocarbon dating results from studies around the world, but mainly in North America. This is a crowdsourced effort among archaeologists, and while it is not a complete record of every single result, it nonetheless shows the volume of archaeological research.

GIS databases at a continental scale are necessary to try to tackle big problems, like estimating the impacts of climate change on coastal archaeology. The DINAA database was used to identify thousands of locations with archaeology in the US Southeast that are projected to be underwater in the near future (Anderson et al. 2017). And those are just the ones we know about. In Scotland, GIS is being used to mobilize the public to help protect, salvage, and record archaeology as it is exposed and swallowed up by the sea (scapetrust.org). GIS has also been used as a collaborative tool to help indigenous groups advocate for the protection of sites on their lands (O'Rourke 2018).

In parallel to the creation of locational indexes, we are seeing more archaeological GIS data being shared and archived online. Much of this is project-specific data, such as the Paleoindian Database of the Americas (PIDBA), which tracks early stone artifacts (Anderson et al. 2010). That database includes over thirty thousand artifacts from about six thousand locations.

There are also data repositories, such as the Archaeology Data Service (ADS) in the United Kingdom, and the Digital Archaeological Record (tDAR) in the United States. The ADS has been running for a long time, and like tDAR, it is a data omnivore, taking in all sorts of digital records.[7] These repositories will have a larger and larger role in archaeology as there is a shift toward recycling existing data-sets (which is not as common as you would think) and making our digital data accessible over the long term (see Marwick and Birch 2018).

There can be a great deal of secrecy around locations where archaeology has been found, especially in the United States.[8] Web-based GIS all have protocols in place to keep from disclosing loca-tional information that would invite looters. Some limit how closely a public user can zoom in. Others, like DINAA, lump records into polygons to obscure their precise location. Archaeological loca-tional data on federal land in the United States is inaccessible out-side of the government agencies that hold those data since the location of known archaeology falls under a rare exception to the Freedom of Information Act. That is a good thing, especially since the amount of funding to actively protect these places is being slashed and the amount of land protected is being cut. There have been a few high-profile cases where thousands of locations have been accidently disclosed online in federal reports, but this is the exception to the rule. Generally, archaeologists employed by state and federal governments do a good job of keeping locations protected.

The Endangered Archaeology in the Middle East and North Africa (EAMENA) project takes a different approach. Much of the design of their website centers on the notion that it is only by draw-ing attention to archaeology that we can educate people about the past and alert the public to the damage done not only by looting, but also by natural disasters and development. This design ele-ment is, in part, why the EAMENA website looks much more com-plete and gives details and maps of individual locations. The casual user glancing at EAMENA and then at DINAA might think that the

Middle East is full of sites and the middle of the United States has no archaeology. In reality, that is simply not the case.

The necessity of protecting the locations of some of the things we find means we cannot give the broader public complete access to the digital worlds we create. That is why I think it is important to talk about the advances we have made in creating and maintaining good GIS databases, even if the data remain behind the scenes. Next I want to give you an idea of what those advances have been and how they are changing the way that archaeologists do their jobs.

. . .

One geospatial technology that has fundamentally changed how we do field work is GPS. In the analog days, a field survey involved a lot of time and effort spent navigating around and plotting on a paper map the things that we found. GPS makes those aspects of what we do incredibly efficient, meaning we can record more, faster, and over larger areas. It also makes us better at working cumulatively, by making it easy to share data and easier to find where sites have already been reported. In many places, the larger and more complete datasets that come from these small changes in fieldwork are already allowing us to ask bigger questions in archaeology.

Now that it has become easy to figure out in real time the geolocation of the things that we find, we are moving toward fully digital field survey. GPS today can achieve centimeter accuracy using real-time kinematic (RTK) positioning (Limp and Barnes 2014). Kinematic refers to the kind of mathematics involved in figuring out positions using geometry. For decades, RTK GPS were extremely expensive and the domain of professional surveying. Today, the technology has come down considerably in price, and can be linked to other devices—like a tablet—or attached to a drone to allow it to fly a preprogrammed flight plan. In other words, as long as we can get a good satellite signal, we can know exactly where we found something.

High-precision GPS allows us to collapse the two typical scales of field recording—the survey area map and the site map—into a single GIS database. A GPS records location in vector formats and you can attach a near limitless amount of information to a specific point, line, or area. These can be used in downstream products, like raster images representing the density of finds or static maps for reports at different scales.

Changes in how we survey go beyond how we map what you can see on the surface when you are at the site. When you pour data from historic maps, air imagery, geophysical survey, and field survey together, you can talk about the history of the landscape in a way that we could only do by excavation before. In other words, our field is shifting its basic unit of observation from a few square meters, to hectares and square kilometers (Kvamme 2003).

Some archaeologists have advocated a kind of all-out "total archaeology" approach, using high-tech and traditional survey to amass large GIS databases (Campana 2011, 33; 2018). The idea is that the more methods are applied, and the more features discovered in an area, the less need for salvage archaeology ahead of development. That's the practical benefit in terms of preservation. The larger intellectual benefit is we are free to ask, and answer, questions about life outside the places that archaeologist often look. In Italy, for example, archaeologists have traditionally been keen to excavate urban centers—understandably so, as they were home to thousands of people in the past, most of whom are not represented in the written record. It would be easy to see the places between cities as empty because all too often they remained underexamined. Today, with the help of technology, that is changing and we are learning more and more about the lives of people who lived in rural areas (Campana 2018).

With more and more geospatial data, the boundaries between sites become eroded into a continuum of individual features and artifacts. This is because our GIS databases are "born digital" in their real location. This was the dream of siteless survey. For practical reasons, we still create inventories of sites to organize what we find for data management purposes, but, in future, we may talk about distributions of features and artifacts as much as we currently do about sites (see Howey and Brouwer Burg 2017).

If I have made this sound easy, the reality is that it is not. There are a number of technical hurdles to a modern survey. Actually, I mean a lot of hurdles.[9] Next I turn to how we are employing computers to help us leverage what we learn from fieldwork and remote sensing into better pictures of the distribution of archaeology.

.   .   .

In the 1990s, imagery and elevation data had long achieved near global coverage, but if you were looking in that data for archaeology, you could forget about it—there just was not high-enough resolution. And so, for a time, satellites remained a poor alternative to what had proven useful: air photographs.[10] Even in 2004, when Google Earth came along, satellite imagery was only just starting to become useful, with the development of, and this is literally the technical term, "very high-resolution" satellite imagery.

What counts as very-high resolution is a slippery metric, but generally we are talking about pixels representing spots that on the ground are about a meter or less in size.[11] The demand for this imagery is often filled by private companies like Maxar (formerly DigitalGlobe) whose WorldView, QuickBird, and GeoEye satellites offer twenty-five centimeter resolution images. These will not let you read a newspaper from space but they are much more useful to archaeology than Landsat.

At the same time that images were getting better, the global digital elevation model (DEM) improved in detail and coverage. The Shuttle Radar Topography Mission (SRTM) covered 80 percent of the planet's surface at ninety meters resolution. The next generation, the Advanced Spaceborne Thermal Emission and Reflection Radiometer (ASTER) model in 2009 improved that to 99 percent coverage at thirty meters resolution. Not as good as airborne lidar, but the coverage is incredible and higher resolution data are on their way. The German TerraSAR-X Next Generation (TXS-NG) satellite, for example, is capable of twenty-five centimeter spatial resolution elevation models.

As technology improves, Google Earth has added on details and features that make the virtual globe more realistic. For example, a few years after its initial release Google added bathymetry of the ocean floor.[12] But maybe the most impressive shift has been the addition of 3-D photorealistic models of the surface of the earth. For that the company has had to fly airplanes with multiple cameras over cities to create a photogrammetric model that is georeferenced within the virtual globe.

The virtual globe is bound to get more and more lifelike. The real challenge is how we leverage these richer remotely sensed data to make larger and more detailed archaeological locational datasets. For that, we have turned more and more to automation.

.   .   .

In field survey, we rely on our eyes to detect changes in the shape of landform as a clue to the presence of archaeology. To take a surface model of the ground, a DEM, and turn it into something that shows us where archaeology may be is a different task. And for that task we have created a number of digital tools to make archaeological features pop out from the natural contours of a study area (see figure 15).

The hillshade function is a popular choice for trying to make archaeology stand out from the natural topography. With a digital elevation model you can use elevation to calculate the direction of slope, otherwise known as aspect, everywhere in the model. So, if you put your digital sunshine in the northwest then the southeastern sides of hills will be darker, and will grade to lighter as you wrap around to the northwest sides that are facing the sun.

But because this is a digital world, there is no reason you have to have just one sun. You can add another source of light coming from somewhere else, and just as having two lights illuminates the subject of a photograph, the shadows in your DEM change. This is the multidirectional hillshade function, and it is behind some of the better-looking digital topographical maps because it catches landform at its best and can make archaeology pop out.

A team of experts in remote sensing based in Serbia at the Institute for Anthropological and Spatial Studies and headed by Žiga Kokalj created a useful piece of software that they call the

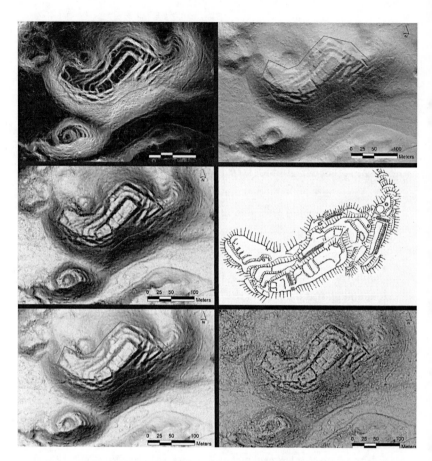

FIGURE 15. Topography of a hill fort. One of the challenges for archaeology is turning high-resolution lidar data into images that clearly show subtle changes in topography. The Relief Visualization Toolbox was created by Žiga Kokalj and his colleagues in order to take a digital elevation model and quickly create a number of different ways to look at the same place. Here a Maori hill fort (Puketona Pa) is shown as (from left to right): Top: slope; multi-hillshade; middle: openness-positive; not-to-scale hand-drawn map field map; bottom: anisotropic sky-view-factor; and sky-view-factor. Source: McCoy (2017).

Relief Visualization Toolbox (Kokalj, Zakšek, and Ošti 2011). As the name implies, you feed it your DEM and it throws a bunch of algorithms at it to highlight topographic relief, including hillshade and multi-hillshade functions. The idea is that we cannot be sure which of the manipulated digital images will allow for archaeological phenomena to pop out, so why not hit the data with all of them?

When it comes to manipulating DEM to create images, the multidirectional hillshade function is just one of many tools in our toolkit, and not even the strangest one. The names of the digital tools in the kit take a bit of explanation.

One of my favorites is sky view factor. Here's how it works. If you walk outside and take a 360-degree picture of the entire sky on clear day, it is unlikely you will actually see the entire sky. If you are out in the middle of a field a large portion of the picture, let's say 90 percent, will be blue sky, because there are trees or hills in the distance. But if you are standing immediately next to a building in that field, now maybe 45 percent of your picture is sky. Stand on top of the roof of that building and now you are back to 90 percent. When you use sky view factor, the building's outline shows up clearly, as low values. Many people use sky view factor and other topographic-enhancing techniques to trace over places in the data where they think they see archaeology.

Another way to build up a GIS database is to take observations where archaeology has been reported and use those locations to predict where you should find more (Kvamme 2006).[13] This approach, called site locational modeling or site predictive modeling, has gotten more and more sophisticated, and some of these programs use artificial intelligence (AI), specifically machine learning and automated feature recognition.

Machine learning is the process of teaching a computer to get better at something without having to be updated by humans. It mimics human learning in that it is hierarchical: it starts out learning how to make basic distinctions, then moves to finer ones. In archaeology, it has been most profitably applied to generating images showing hot spots of higher probability for the presence of individual archaeological features. With the right tools a human could achieve this; what would be virtually impossible for a human to achieve is the replicability and the scale of an automated approach.

Another distinct but related branch of AI, called automated feature recognition, is not that different from facial recognition in photographs, in that it is an algorithm that is programed to identify and classify things in images. This AI requires a training dataset—one showing specific places where you already know that archaeology is located—before you let it loose. For this to work you also need a validation dataset—one showing places not included in the training dataset but where again, you know where things are—to check how well it did.

Automated feature extraction methods such as these tend to do well within narrow parameters. For example, it helps if you are looking for things that fit a particular shape template that rarely occurs in nature. If your archaeology comes in a lot of different shapes, humans are still probably better at picking things out of images. The trend now is to improve manual extraction (Casana 2014; Quintus, Day, and Smith 2017) and push automated extraction protocols as far as is possible. Some have used different AI programs on the same study area to show that even if AI programs do not agree perfectly with one another they produce similar densities of features: hot spots where there are many things, and cold spots where there are few (Freeland et al. 2016). Others are looking at how we can use semiautomated methods based on the two data models used in a GIS (raster and vector) (Sevara et al. 2016).

Other fields have developed AI approaches that are being incorporated into archaeology. One popular software is MaxEnt, short for maximum entropy.[14] MaxEnt has been used by thousands of biologists who want to work out the spatial distribution of species (Phillips, Anderson, and Schapire 2006). It strikes an ideal balance between the type of field data available and the multiple continuous environmental factors that contribute to defining a habitat.

If you want to know, for example, the extent of the habitat of a rare bird so you can protect the species, points where the bird has been spotted only tell you where one of these birds was at one time. If you feed the point locational data into MaxEnt it will compare the observations relative to a dozen or so environmental factors in nongeographic statistical space and then chose which combination of weighted variables is the best fit. That alone would be useful for figuring out which variables are the best predictors of the geographic distribution of the birds. But the software does more than that. It also turns the model back into geographic information in the form of a raster distribution map showing the probability of encountering the bird. In coming chapters, we will see how archaeologists have used this software to predict the locations of archaeological features based on the distribution of known features.

There are a number of reasons that archaeologists have not, and likely will never, turn things completely over to machines. The method you chose, human or machine, depends a lot on the scale of your project, the level of detail you wish to get out of the dataset, and how you define success (Opitz and Herrmann 2018). The rates of success for human versus computer vary widely, making it almost impossible to say ahead of time which will produce a better product.

.   .   .

There is a website called Open Street Maps that is essentially a crowdsourced Google Maps. It has been useful in crisis mapping tasks by distributing the work of remotely mapping, say, refugee camps or the extent of natural disasters, over hundreds or thousands of volunteers. Some of the most high-profile cases of crowdsourcing in archaeology, like crisis mapping, capitalize on citizen scientists willing to do repetitive mapping tasks.

Nearly a decade ago, Albert Yu-Min Lin, then a University of California, San Diego-based engineer, began attracting thousands of citizen scientists to go online and classify high-resolution imagery of Mongolia in the search for the tomb of Genghis Khan. On the face of it, a search for the lost tomb of one of the historical figures featured in *Bill and Ted's Excellent Adventure* sounds a lot like treasure hunting. But the project was technically innovative and taught us a great deal about remote sensing and citizen science in archaeology.

The Valley of the Khans search area in Mongolia was big, covering an area twice the size of Yosemite National Park (Lin et al. 2014). Lin estimated that viewing the satellite images at their native resolution on screen (0.5-meter resolution, GeoEye) you would have to look at twenty thousand screens of nonoverlapping sections of Mongolia. Lin asked volunteers to classify what they saw. They could pin natural features, like rivers, and human-made things, like modern roads and buildings, as well as out-of-the-ordinary things that looked to be ruins of some kind.

To scale-up remote sensing like this required solving some basic problems. The volunteers doing the classification were untrained and thus created noisy data. They logged on inconsistently; most of the edits were done following major press coverage of the project, which one would expect, and Lin and colleagues actually documented this phenomenon. There was the worry that in the pool of volunteers were people who were working together. That sounds innocent but would invalidate the important idea that each observation was independent. And because it is the Internet, there was the worry that the effort would be sabotaged by trolls, or exploited by people who would use the data to find and then loot sites.

The team put in place some simple solutions to these problems and tested out different formats. To keep people doing the work of classifying, the interface had a gamification element in which volunteers leveled up as they worked. Some volunteers were given feedback based on peer coding while others were allowed to classify in isolation. There was a slight improvement in classification quality by those using the peer method, again not a surprising effect, but well documented. To work around collaboration, trolls, and other bad actors, imagery was cut into over eighty-four thousand semi-overlapping tiles that onscreen were not georeferenced and were presented in a random order. To address all the noise in the data, that is to say, lots of irrelevant or incorrect data, a kind of consensus map was created based on an interpolation (kernel density) of thousands of tags.

What did they find? Not a lot. Only fifty-five locations with archaeology surfaced over that vast area. The good news is the false positive rate was rather low if you focus on consensus hot spots. And because these were humans doing classification, lots of different types of archaeology from different time periods were found, something AI is not always great at. The bad news is the accuracy rate was awful and the labor-to-discovery return rate was a problem. By the end of the project, thirty thousand hours were logged by ten thousand users. If that work had been done by a single person, she or he would have been working for more than three years continuously and finding only one possible location with archaeology per month. That kind of ratio between effort and return is just abysmal.[15]

One solution to quality control when scaling up is to hire and train people in identifying archaeology in remotely sensed data. Jesse Casana, who is now at Dartmouth College, hired a small group of four part-time employees to search an area in the Middle East. Their study area was much larger area than the Valley of the Khans and at a lower resolution (Casana 2014). Imagery was cut up into about three thousand individual scenes. The classifications came with self-defined probability ranking. When a settlement, fortification, or some other type of archaeology was found, it was ranked as definitely something, probably something, or possibly something.

The Middle East is a more target-rich environment for archaeological remote sensing than Mongolia and over a few weeks the team identified fourteen thousand locations that looked like there had been archaeology there in the 1960s, an average of four to five places per image. The quality of the results needs to be assessed in detail but is consistent with the density found on previous surveys in the region. That is of course just assessing the presence or absence of archaeology. When it comes to actually mapping, results have been more mixed.

In southern Africa, for example, archaeologist Karim Sadr found that making detailed maps using remote sensing led to a somewhat confusing result (Sadr and Rodier 2012; Sadr 2015a, 2015b). Sadr was looking to map the stone wall corrals that herders made over an eight thousand square kilometer area during the Iron Age. Like the Middle East, southern Africa is a target-rich environment, and more than seven thousand of these wall corrals are visible on Google Earth. They are widely variable in terms of size and shape, factors that may indicate something about the history of herding in this part of the world.

Sadr repeated this study twice, once with students and once with a private company that does surveying by remote sensing. On a regional level, intercoder reliability was good. But the mapping of individual features was a mess. They were unacceptably variable when the results for individual corrals was compared. In other words, Sadr discovered that, at least in this case, people were good at consistently showing where in the region there is archaeology but no good at consistently mapping. This does not mean we must give up on using people power for remote sensing. What it does mean is that we have to take care to know the limitations of the massive amounts of geospatial data that we are creating today.

As archaeologists develop better workflows for remote sensing it is likely that we will see methods and results evaluated for how well they produce different kinds of locational data and information (see Cowley 2012). In many of the examples I have described, the techniques performed well in one aspect of creating locational data: detecting the presence of archaeology. They answer the question: Where is it? But, as we have seen, it is possible for people, or machines, to perform well in one task but perform poorly in others. Tasks such as mapping involve creating locational information; that is to say, they must answer the question, What is at that location? And, once the data are mapped, the natural next step is to interpret them: What were people doing here? All of that is necessary before we can make the leap to locational evidence, asking: What does it mean that we have found this here?

In this chapter we have looked at how archaeologists make maps, or really, how we create digital versions of the ancient world. The fact that we keep at least some locational information obscured from public view, together with the technical nature of our work, means we do not always get to share our results. So, what have we been doing with all this information? What is it we are doing better now thanks to advances in geospatial technologies? In the next few chapters I look at research on movement and mobility, on how our ancestors fed themselves, and on the kinds of societies they created. We have learned about these topics through attempts to understand long-term processes that unfolded over centuries, or millennia, ones that no one person in the past could have appreciated in a single lifetime. We have also learned about these same topics through attempts to imagine what it was like living in the past. Together, they show how we can use technology to expand our natural historical curiosity.

Part III

6 *Retracing Our Steps*

Migration, Mobility, and Travel

One of the most unusual things I have ever recorded on an archaeological field survey was a beat-up strip of asphalt, maybe a few hundred meters long, running parallel to the highway in New Mexico.
It was an abandoned piece of Route 66, a four thousand kilometer
road built in the 1920s to connect Chicago and Los Angeles.[1] Even
though it has been over twenty years since I did contract archaeology in the American Southwest, I still remember this short bit of
road because as I dutifully filled out the required paperwork I naturally began to wonder not only if it was worth the time or effort to
record, but also how we even begin to reconstruct something as
inherently temporary and transitory as travel.

Route 66 has been called America's Main Street. In the lean
years of the Great Depression it carried refugees escaping the Dust
Bowl to California. Then, in the economic prosperity of the 1950s
and 1960s, big shiny cars roared down Route 66; their image is
cemented in the collective nostalgia surrounding the great
American road trip though the route was replaced by the interstate
highways forty years ago.

That collective nostalgia is a whitewash.[2] To take one example,
Route 66 was a dangerous place for African American travelers,

who were subject to a patchwork of Jim Crow statutes in isolated small towns.[3] So much so, that by 1962 the Green Book—a travel guide to places willing to serve African Americans by Victor H. Green—had a circulation of two million.

The idea that the fabric of American society in the twentieth century—the good and the bad—can be described by focusing on travel along Route 66 is in line with a trend in the social sciences called the "mobility turn" (Szymanowski 2016). This turn to consider how people's mobility, both spatial and social, has changed over time is, to me, a natural progression from the closer attention that scholars have paid to how we inhabit the world around us through the study of space and place (Brunn and Dodge 2017). Archaeology should in principle be able to tell us about people on the move over the long arc of history. However, to get at this aspect of the past requires some creativity, and this is something that geospatial technology has helped unlock.

This chapter centers on innovative approaches to examining the distribution of archaeology to reconstruct ancient mobility, migrations, and travels, and what those journeys can tell us about human history. I begin with human evolution and our first steps upright, then move to how geospatial technologies are being used to map major migrations. Geospatial technologies have also been used in some imaginative ways to learn about transportation networks, like the Roman roads across the Old World. Today, when I think about that small piece of old Route 66, I do not think of it as unusual at all, but as an opportunity to tell a more dynamic, and in many ways more real, human story.

. • .

One of the fundamental questions that nags at our historical curiosity is "Where are we from?" To access deep time in our history, we are almost entirely reliant on fossils and artifacts found in deposits that date to the last Ice Age.[4] The places where fossils or chipped stone artifacts were recovered have been subjected to the agents of entropy for so long they are sometimes referred to not as sites but as "localities."

Paleoanthropologists, specialists in human evolution, have to cast a wide net when they go out prospecting for new fossil localities.[5] They begin by using previous data and experience to narrow the search to places where geological layers are exposed and likely to produce fossils. For example, research in Ethiopia beginning in the 1980s pointed to the Fejej area as having previously unexamined fossil-bearing deposits. Field-checking led to what was at the time one of the oldest-known hominin fossils, dating to about 3.7 million years ago (Fleagle et al. 1991). Further remote sensing-guided fieldwork in the southern Main Ethiopian Rift resulted in the discovery of stone artifacts in younger deposits associated with manufacturing and using Acheulean hand axes as well as of the remains of *Homo erectus* (Asfaw et al. 1992).

With advances in geospatial technologies have come more and better geological maps that have helped in the search. Large GIS databases of fossils have generally been slow to develop but there are nonetheless some standouts.[6] For example, the website fossilized.org, maintained by Henry Gilbert at California State University, East Bay, gives visitors a novel way to visualize data. The site advertises itself as "the largest collection of paleoanthropology localities in the world" and can be searched through either specimen identification number or species. While the underlying dataset has basic latitude/longitude coordinates for fossils, it is also able to visualize the density and age ranges of different finds organized by geographic region. What I find valuable about this kind of collection is that it shows how few useful specimens we have with which to reconstruct such a large piece of our history, and why a small number of new finds can sometimes change the story.

Satellite imagery, a detailed and complete global DEM, high-resolution geological maps, and computer simulations of past environments together should result in geospatial predictive models that narrow the search for fossils down considerably. But, as Robert L. Anemone, biological anthropologist at the University of North Carolina, Greensboro, has shown, it is not that easy.

Anemone and his colleagues have been looking for fossils in the hills of Wyoming and Utah, specifically for evidence of New World primates and other mammals that lived long before the first humans evolved. They were first guided by Landsat-5, then Landsat-7, and most recently Landsat-8 to find fossils based on known localities (Emerson et al. 2015). The team first had the problem of overprediction. Productive localities that are only five thousand to twenty thousand square meters remained anonymous in big splashes on the map with the same or similar values. Using higher-resolution data and a machine learning method (GEOBIA, or geographic object-based image analysis) gave much more specific search locations and most of the eighteen localities predicted to have fossils did, in fact, have fossils.

With geospatial models like the one developed by Anemone and his colleagues now giving fine-grained results, the question becomes not if an automation can find new localities, but how efficient is the process, and how complete of a picture of the past does it give us. Let's say, for example, we want to know about the mobility patterns of ancient humans. How will we know which of the many possible localities pointed out by a geospatial model will have the specific fossils useful for that endeavor? That's a tricky question to answer. Fortunately, we do not rely on fossils alone. The studies of our closest living relatives—chimpanzees—and of how modern people move around give us independent lines of evidence to work with.

. . .

One of the ripple effects of advances in geospatial technologies is that we have rich, high-precision data on the movements of just about every kind of creature on our planet. The new field of movement ecology is helping turn mountains of locational data from GPS tagging things that crawl, climb, fly, and swim into coherent pictures of not just where and when they move, but how and why (Kuhn, Raichlen, and Clark 2016; Nathan 2008).

New locational data and information on our closest living relatives confirms they are capable of thinking in complex ways about the costs and benefits of moving around. Karline Janmaat, a Dutch primatologist based at the Max Planck Institute in Leipzig, has chased chimpanzees around Tanzania and Ivory Coast (Janmaat, Ban, and Boesch 2013; Janmaat et al. 2016) to collect geospatial data on where they nest at night and where they gather food during the day. She has done this over long periods, usually for months at a time and sometimes for nearly two years.

For paleoanthropologists, Janmaat's work is critical in that it quantifies the geographic ranges of chimps in different environments and relative to specific resources, like fruit trees, and how these change from season to season and year to year. This is better than just tagging individuals, although that is good too, because we get behavioral data tied to geolocation that let us work out why chimps choose to roam around the way that they do.[7]

As if chasing groups of chimps around was not challenging enough, Janmaat has run into some geospatial data-collection problems. Her typical routine involved using hiking-grade GPS to track her own movements all day as she tracked the chimpanzees. Ideally speaking, that would yield data on all the places the chimps went, from the tree they woke up in to the one they nested in at night, as well as the timing and speed of their movement between locations.

But Janmaat found that GPS location would drift during the day, making it look like the chimps were moving at impossible speeds; they sometimes appeared to be clocking in at over one hundred kilometers per hour. At other times the GPS data made it look like the chimps were on the move when in fact the researcher, and the GPS, were stationary. The solution was lots of data cleaning, working out when the signals were bad and eliminating those errors.[8] A similar thing, known as the noisy telemetry data problem, happens with GPS-tagged animals; it is generally overcome with probability estimates for where and when creatures stop and start.

Technical issues aside, the GIS data show strong evidence that chimps are incredible spatial-temporal thinkers. Not only will they remember the fruiting patterns of specific trees from season to season, but female adult chimps choose nighttime nesting trees specifically to minimize their travel time to breakfast the next morning. Katharine Milton, an expert in primate diets at the University of California, Berkeley, proposed that primate cognition more broadly may have evolved in the context of solving spatial-temporal puzzles presented by foraging for seasonal fruit (Milton 1988). From that perspective, the reason you and I can imagine the movements of our ancestors in the distant past may ultimately be tied back to some of our ancestors being better at imagining the places and times they could eat figs.

Paleoanthropologists have been interested in mobility for a long time and especially want to know about how we came to walk around on two legs. This is not just because it is one of the fundamental physical differences between ancestral humans and other apes. Our inherited capacity for hiking for long distances also gives us a huge advantage as hunters and gatherers. We are able to access broad territories when looking for food, and when we come across something that is bigger or faster than us in the short run, we have the ability to slowly stalk it to death. Taking a long walk in the woods may sound like the most harmless activity imaginable, but because other animals are not as good as us at sustained hiking, it is one of our more deadly adaptations.[9]

Recently, geospatial technology has been used to investigate the evolution of walking upright at Laetoli in Tanzania, where fossilized footprints dating to three million years ago were found in 1976. The creatures that left footprints in wet volcanic ash all those years ago were clearly walking on two feet. They left behind three tracks, one that was made by a single individual walking (a track called G1) and two trackways interspersed along the same path (G2 and G3). At first this made it difficult to work out the sizes and gaits of the individuals. Matthew R. Bennett of Bournemouth University and his team revisited Site G, where the trackways were found, and used a tripod-mounted laser scanner (Konica-Minolta Vi-900) to create incredibly detailed contour maps of each footfall, disentangling the tracks (Bennett et al 2016).

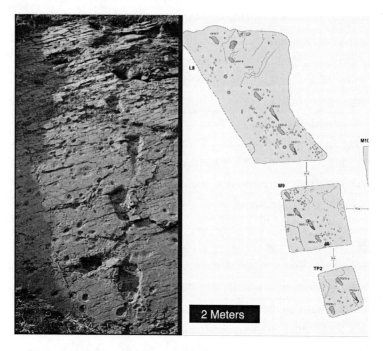

2 Meters

FIGURE 16. Three-million-year-old footprints. These footprints were made when an archaic human walked over wet volcanic ash in Laetoli, Tanzania. They were first uncovered a few years ago not far from where similar prints were found in 1976. The 3-D model, created by photogrammetry (structure-from-motion), shows two-millimeter contour lines (left). Overview photo (middle) and map (right) show the footprint in the context where it was found. Source: Masao et al. (2016)

Soon after, in 2016, Fidelis T. Masao of the University of Dar es Salaam and his team announced that more footprints had been found at Laetoli, at Site S, apparently from a much larger-bodied, taller individual with an estimated height not seen in the fossil record for another million years (see figure 16).[10] The team nicknamed this surprisingly large creature Chewbacca. When the other footprints at Laetoli were reported in the 1970s they were shown in photographs printed in newspapers and textbooks. In contrast, Chewie's footprints, one of which graces the cover of this book, were captured in 3-D through photogrammetry, and have been shared with the world through a digital repository for scans of biological specimens (morphosource.org). This gives other scientists a chance to examine their claims—and gives the rest of us a chance to see and interact with something that hasn't seen the light of day in over three million years.

. . .

Today we have an incredible amount of movement data on humans, generated by fitness trackers and GPS in our phone, far more than the entire contents of the largest GIS databases that track animal movements. But, to generalize all that data that into locational information we can use to understand the distant past requires some out-of-the-box thinking.

To get an idea of how our hunter-gatherer ancestors traveled, biological anthropologist David A. Raichlen of the University of Arizona turned to the Hadza, a group of people who live in northern Tanzania. His team recruited about forty adults who were willing to wear Garmin Forerunner 205 GPS watches from dawn to dusk (Raichlen et al. 2014). This was not the first time that modern hunter-gather mobility was the subject of anthropological study. Previous research gave us a pretty good idea of how mobile people are under different environmental conditions—hot or cold, wet or dry—which is of course linked to how much potential food will be encountered when one is out and about (Kelly 1983).

The news coverage of the Hadza mobility study tended to focus on the fact that the volunteers—people who have to hunt and gather for their food—are far more active than other people living today, covering on average six kilometers every day (men averaging about ten kilometers, women about four kilometers). That might be enough to shame people into keeping their New Year's exercise resolutions, but it is hardly surprising. What is more interesting is the *way* they moved around the landscape as they searched.

I was at the Monterey Bay Aquarium with my family recently and we caught a show about sharks that was full of maps of their movements around the Pacific Ocean. Free-range predators, like sharks, will shift their search patterns depending upon how dense and reliable the prey are (Humphries et al. 2010). If prey are abundant and easy to find, they will change their direction, and the duration of their search in that direction, more or less randomly. That pattern is referred to as Brownian motion, the same pattern seen when molecules randomly bounce off one another, constantly changing their direction and duration of travel.

If prey are hard to find or sparse, a Brownian search is not optimal. Instead what you see is what we call Lévy flight foraging. The Lévy pattern also involves a lot of random changes in direction and duration of search, but there are far more short moves interspersed with long moves in one direction. It turns out the Hadza follow a Lévy search pattern, which makes sense in the sparse landscape of northern Tanzania. But before we jump to the conclusion that this is something unique to hunting, it should be said that people walking around Disneyland also follow a Lévy pattern. To me the lesson here is this: if we reduce our movements to a mathematical model it reveals that we have much more in common with other complex animals than we might think.

Most archaeological data are too coarse-grained to be able to show direct physical evidence for the different search patterns we see in modern people. But advances in our ability to match stone artifacts to their natural source and in lithic technology analysis (the study of how stone tools were made) have given us a leg up in working out the mobility of ancient hunter-gatherers in different contexts.[11] For example, in the Middle Stone Age in southern Africa (Nash et al. 2016) and in the Upper Paleolithic in Europe (Tomasso and Porraz 2016), we start to see regular discards of chipped stone whose original source was more than one hundred kilometers away. These longer-distance trips suggest an evolutionary shift about forty thousand to fifty thousand years ago in our ability to use landmarks for wayfinding.

Wayfinding was the center of a GIS study in northern Spain focused on topography that could have been used as landmarks by early modern humans. Locations that have been more or less stable for thousands of years and scored highly in a legibility index—meaning that people could recognize them at a distance—were more likely to have early archaeology within about two kilometers (Guiducci and Burke 2016). It makes sense. But it took the right combination of GIS tools and creative thinking to put the pieces back together and work out when and how people learned to navigate in unfamiliar landscapes.

.   .   .

We live during a pause in the long, long history of peopling.[12] The last major movement to permanently occupy a substantial landmass previously unoccupied by people, not counting Antarctica, was no more than forty human generations ago, with the initial colonization of the islands of New Zealand in the far South Pacific. The living descendants of the wayfinders who accomplished that feat, the Māori, recall in their genealogies the names of the canoes that brought their ancestors to a place they named Aotearoa, the land of the long white cloud.

I wonder if, when we put human settlements on the Moon and Mars, the ships that bring the founding populations will occupy the same place in future genealogies. Maybe it is because those next big moves are untold generations away, or because we glorify colonizers in Western popular culture as adventurous and independent, but one thing is clear: a great deal of effort is expended by archaeologists to work out when and how we came to be the dominate life-form on Earth.

The number of books and articles on the timing, rate, and route of the dispersal of our species is staggering. These studies are, at the end of the day, about good geospatial data and information. But the real advances that geospatial technologies have offered have been in terms of formalizing models. We have, for example, a number of much more specific simulations of how some early humans left Africa and spread across the Old World. These models are necessary because retracing our steps is not simply a matter of connecting the dots.

One complication is that the Earth today is not the Earth as it was during the last Ice Age. And so if you want to study how and when early *Homo sapiens* spread across the African continent you have to modify your GIS to mimic that previous landscape. That's just what a recent study did. They used a modified global DEM and paleoenvironmental data from 125,000 years ago to suggest that people may have dispersed through the Sahara along one of three major river corridors; rivers that disappeared many years ago, not to be seen again until they appeared as radar rivers (Osborne et al. 2008).

Virtually all of the Earth's coastlines were different during the Pleistocene. With so much water trapped in glaciers there was a lot more seaside real estate. This is especially frustrating since it is along these paleo-coasts—which like the drowned coasts of Doggerland, are gone today—that people may have found their way from Africa to what is now Australia.

Australia, or more correctly, the former uber-continent of Sahul, which combined mainland Australia, Tasmania, and New Guinea, is important to the dispersal of our species. For geospatial models, it is the canary in the coal mine that tells us that some of our ancestors left Africa. The problem with deposits of this age in Europe and Asia is that other members of our genus, *Homo,* were already wondering around there, and this muddles the signal of the spread of modern humans. But because Sahul remained separated from Southeast Asia, it was never occupied by archaic humans, and it offers our first unequivocal evidence for both the use of water-craft and our spread out of Africa.[13]

The crossing to Sahul is not the only reason to think that our spread out of Africa had a distinctly coastal element. Julie S. Field of Ohio State University is an archaeologist known best for her work on Pacific Island archeology, but she also has the distinction of having made the first geospatial model of our southern dispersal out of Africa to Australia (Field, Petraglia, and Mirazón Lahr 2007). Starting in East Africa, a simulated group of digital wanderers were sent out in a GIS with no knowledge of what was over the horizon, but with simple instructions: to follow the path of least resistance. The results were then compared with the real-world distribution of archaeology from this time period.

The method Field used is a version of something called the "least cost path" function. There are a number of ways to calculate it, but in its simplest form, you tell the GIS you want to travel between two points, and it will find the best route between them. In a perfectly flat plain that would be a straight line, but in reality, it will mean hugging the contours of hills, rather than marching over them, and following gentle slopes where they occur in nature. The digital wanderers in this model, who were not given a target, eventually found their way to locations outside Africa where early archaeology had been reported, and when you look at their various paths together, you see that they often did so by following paleo-coastlines.

A recent discussion of these findings takes the importance of coasts and coastal environments even further (Erlandson and Braje 2015). Jon M. Erlandson of the University of Oregon and Todd J. Braje of San Diego State University argue that major river mouths, which were troublesome to cross for the digital wanderers in the southern dispersal geospatial model, were in reality rich mangrove forests that early bands of people would have been attracted to. I have hiked through my share of mangrove forests. There is plenty of life, certainly attractive for hunting and fishing, but they are also not easy to traverse.[14]

There is a growing consensus that paleo-coasts were the route taken by the first people to colonize the Americas from Asia (Gustas and Supernant 2019; Pedersen et al. 2016). We have not thrown out the scenario that you probably learned in school, that people came over from Asia via a land bridge that is now drowned. Several lines of evidence now point to the earliest of these moves having hugged the paleo-coast of the Pacific, including the confirmation, nearly twenty years ago now, that one of the locations where we have definitive evidence for early Americans is located all the way down in Chile.[15]

Archaeologists have had some time now to come up with plausible scenarios to explain the apparent rapid spread of people from northwest Asia all the way down to South America. One of the first teams to take this on was David G. Anderson of the University of Tennessee, Knoxville and J. Christopher Gillam of the University of South Carolina, who proposed a new way to think about how the first generations of people who lived in the Americas might have occupied these vast continents.

Anderson and Gillam (2000) noticed that when you look at all the reported finds of stone points made in the earliest styles on a single map, their distribution is patchy. They drew their initial artifact maps based on the Paleoindian Database of the Americas (PIDBA), which today is one of the largest GIS databases of a single artifact type. There are good reasons to think that some of the concentrations of artifacts are due to biases in how the database was created, but Anderson and Gillam argue that perhaps what the distribution is telling us is that people did not spread evenly. The idea is that over the years when populations grew and a new group broke away to live elsewhere, they would not go immediately down the road, but "leap frog" to the next good patch of land.[16] Like the results of the study on early wayfinding, this conclusion makes sense, but it took the right combination of data, GIS tools, and creative thinking to create this formalized model of peopling.

Let's return to the last phase of peopling of the planet: Aotearoa and the other islands of the Pacific. Over the years a few Westerners, including Thor Heyerdahl, have voiced skepticism about the ability of Polynesians and other Pacific Islanders to search, discover, and colonize islands on purpose. Heyerdahl is famous for sailing a balsa log raft he called the *Kon Tiki* from Peru to French Polynesia in 1947. He held the opinion that the Pacific was settled by "white

Indians" drifting over from South America (see Holton 2010 for a recent review). Even if we put aside the landslide of evidence that tells us the ancestors of Pacific Islanders came from the Asian side of the Pacific *and* the racist overtones, we can thank computer models for soundly refuting Heyerdahl's watery publicity stunt.

Computer models of long-distance voyaging across the Pacific have disproved the idea that these were accidental trips.[17] In the 1970s, one of the first geospatial simulations in archaeology sent digital canoes out at the mercy of the seas and showed that the probability of drift voyaging ending in landfall is exceedingly remote (Levison, Ward, and Webb 1973). In the late 1980s, computing power had increased, as had the data on winds and currents, and new models showed that searching for new lands required increasingly better technology and navigational knowledge over generations (Irwin 1992). Digital canoes found New Zealand, the largest potential target in the remote islands of the Pacific, during the last pulse of simulated exploration because doing so required abandoning a safe method of searching directly upwind of a home island and adopting a risky method of tacking back and forth across the wind in the cold southern seas.

The notion that over generations people were learning to be better at wayfinding helps explain why in the radiocarbon dating of the earliest archeological evidence across the Pacific there are pauses, when no new islands were settled, and pulses, when many new islands were settled rapidly. We have nonetheless not stopped looking for alternative explanations, and geospatial technologies have again helped in that. Just as today we have more and better environmental data that we can use to look at peopling across the land, we also have better monitoring of storms, currents, and wind patterns that gives us a more complete picture of how the Pacific

Ocean operates in practice. More-detailed climate records give us a better notion of periods of more or less frequent El Niño/Southern Oscillation (ENSO). Together these have been used to shift the debates around voyaging to consider the probability of different hypothetical scenarios (Montenegro, Callaghan, and Fitzpatrick 2016), like how closely natural patterns in ENSO match the pauses and pulses in the discovery of the remote islands of the Pacific (Anderson et al. 2006).

There is a big difference between the sorties of sailing canoes that brought the ancestors of Pacific Islanders to their new remote island homes and the groups of people who made their way from Africa to Europe and Asia, and then over to Australia and the Americas. Ice Age-era people were foragers and hunters. They traveled with the clothes on their backs and the things they could carry. The double-hulled sailing canoes of the Pacific were filled with farmers. They brought with them the domesticated plants and animals they needed to start over on the next island and settle down there. And so they were simultaneously the most recent case of peopling and part of the movement that Gordon Childe brought to the world's attention: the Neolithic Revolution.

·　●　·

The detritus left over from the spread of farming has been recognizable since Childe's day. And so a number of different hypotheses have been proposed for the origins and spread of domestic plants and animals. The origin of rice, for example, has been retraced based on the plant's genetics, maps of the words for rice in different languages, and archaeological evidence. Unfortunately, because domestication was likely a long process and involved backcrossing with rice's wild relatives, the modern genetics of rice varieties are tricky to work out. The archaeological evidence for cultivation—such as preserved early fields—is extremely rare, as is direct evidence for domesticated rice.

Fabio Silva and his colleagues at University College London have created the Rice Archaeological Database, a GIS database that covers an area of about eighteen million square kilometers and includes four hundred radiocarbon-dated sample locations (Silva et al. 2015). But limiting the database to the locations of the earliest examples of rice in different regions severely cuts the sample size. At that density, the number of available samples becomes analogous to having only one hundred samples for an area equal to the entire European Union. And so they had to find a clever way to search for the likely location rice was first domesticated that would be the best fit to the data, as thin on the ground as they may be.

The model created to search for the original homeland of domestic rice began with a few simple assumptions. First, some places were taken out of contention for being too cold (like the Russian Far East and high in the Himalayan Mountains), too dry (major deserts, like the Gobi), or too far offshore (more than forty kilometers). Second, they made two assumptions about the spread of rice: that it would follow the path of least resistance and that the rate of its spread would increase as it moved away from the core. This is known as the "fast marching" version of the least cost path function. Next, a few hundred arbitrarily chosen locations were laid out in a massive grid and subject to over six hundred million simulations to determine which distribution map best fit the current locational data for the spread of rice.

The winner was a location on the Lower Yangzi River, a location that archeologists had suspected as the center of domestication.

But Silva and his team did not stop there. They ran the test again using six locations that had been proposed in the archaeological literature. They found that if you combine the results of two of these—an origin on the Lower Yangzi and another upriver in the Middle Yangzi—the combination is a better fit than the single origin result in the unconstrained test. It is remains unclear what exactly having two origins points along the same river means for prehistory. This is nonetheless an important result because archaeologists are naturally hesitant to take sparse spatiotemporal data and then advocate a complex solution—but history sometimes does not follow Occam's razor.[18]

Another good example of archaeological data pointing to a more complex historical process than we once thought possible is in the spread of farming and herding to southern Africa, a momentous shift that came only in the last two thousand years. Until then, places like the Kalahari Desert had been exclusively home to hunter-gatherers for the entirety of human history. For a long time archaeologists had speculated that domesticated animals had been adopted or taken down to the western half of the region during the Late Stone Age, many generations before a well-documented expansion of Bantu-language speakers to the east.

Separating out the actual data for these processes from the voluminous speculation about it has been difficult, to say the least. At the time of writing, there are more than 1,450 publications that cover six million square kilometers over fifteen hundred years (550 BC to AD 1050). I know this because Faye Lander and Thembi Russell, archaeologists at the University of the Witwatersrand in Johannesburg, complied a geospatial database of all the types of archaeological evidence used to identify the spread of pastoralism and farming into southern Africa (pottery, livestock, metal, metalworking, cultivation, structures, stables/byres) as well as a second GIS database sorting out all that has been written about it (Lander and Russell 2018).

I have to hand it to them. It was not easy, and the results are a bit disheartening because while this topic has attracted a lot of attention, it is not the kind that produces lots of good locational data. For example, there are just over two hundred sample locations; that's an even lower density than the ratio of sample locations for early rice in Asia. There are a lot of radiocarbon dates, but only forty direct dates on domesticated animal remains and pottery, and new ancient DNA results have shown that many of the animal bones once identified by their shape as a sheep, dog, or cow, were in fact from Africa's many wild animals (Horsburgh, Orton, and Klein 2016).

There is good news. By considering these various metrics for herding, farming, and making iron separately in eight time-slice maps, Lander and Russell (2018) were better able to visualize something that in the past had been only represented in rather confusing maps. Even with the caveat that there are serious spatiotemporal gaps, the current evidence shows two unexpected trends. First, cattle and sheep spread south before farming, giving herders a foothold in southern Africa perhaps as many as thirty-five generations before farmers eventually migrated down. Second, those farmers brought with them Bantu languages, plants, and iron, but strangely, not livestock, which based on the current evidence, they seem to have adopted from resident pastoralists.

When it comes to early wayfinding and peopling, or the spread of farming, geospatial technology has proved useful in helping reject incorrect models, build new models, and in some cases show that the past was more complex than we would presume based on the principle that all things being equal, the simplest explanation is the best. This does not mean that archaeologists are done arguing about the timing and direction of migrations. We are constantly quarreling over arrows on maps. What it does mean is we are in a much better position to narrow down why people packed up and started new lives far from the places they had known.

. . .

Roads are so ever present in modern life it is hard to imagine that they are an invention, and a quite recent one in fact. There are enough examples of paths and trails in different times and places to say they are probably a universal feature of human life.[19] Roads are different. Roads are built by hierarchical societies—chiefdoms, states, empires—to "facilitate and formalize movement" along routes with major infrastructural improvements (Earle 2009, 257).[20] And so, though the exact dates depend upon where in the world we are looking, humanity did not start road construction in earnest until sometime around the Bronze Age.

For archaeologists, a network of roads is more than the byproduct of travel or commerce. We read it as a big, sustained construction project underwritten by an elite class. The network of Roman roads, for example, while mostly unpaved, covered four hundred thousand kilometers; that's more than the distance between the Earth and the Moon (see figure 17). Roads were also investments in urban centers. The Mendez Causeway at the Maya city of Tikal for example is estimated to have taken ninety-three thousand person-days to build (Keller 2009). We also see roads as vital to over-the-top displays in much the same way as monuments. After all, if you want to have a parade, you need a road.

Another important piece of the story of ancient transport is travel along and over water. Archaeologists have repeatedly

FIGURE 17. The roads of the Roman Empire. This GIS layer contains lines representing all known roads built and maintained by the Romans. Their total length is about the same as the distance between the Earth and the Moon. Source: McCormick et al. (2013)

pointed out that while there tends to be an implicit bias that categorizes water as a barrier—something that requires a bridge to get over—shorelines, rivers, canals, lakes, bays, and the ocean are the real highways of the ancient world. This gets tricky for scholars, and not just because watercraft are preserved only under extraordinary circumstances. Waterways are dynamic, they change constantly, and in many cases it does not require much modification to make them suitable for launching, landing, or anchoring crafts. Nonetheless, like roads, large maritime infrastructure—systems of canals, breakwaters, and piers—is associated with hierarchical societies. The technology of the day also influenced where people went and how they moved things around. Foot traffic has been joined over the centuries by pack animals—

like donkeys or llamas—and riding animals—like horses, camels, and elephants.[21]

With those basics in mind, there are three ways that geospatial technologies are helping better understand ancient travel and transport. The first is how these technologies are being applied to systems of roads that are already well known to us.

.   .   .

For many years archaeologists noticed segments of long, straight tracks crisscrossing northern Mesopotamia that were obvious on air photos but nearly impossible to see close up because they were only subtle changes in topography. In 2003, Jason Ur, an archaeologist at Harvard University, began using declassified Corona satellite imagery to create a complete map of tells—villages and some of the world's oldest cities—in northeastern Syria (Ur 2003). He would eventually also map six thousand kilometers of roads (Ur 2010): about one-and-a-half times the length of Route 66, all within a study area about the size of New Hampshire.

There were roads going everywhere. Roads within and around settlements, roads that connected settlements to one another (village-to-village), and other roads that radiated out from a settlement and seemed to fade to nowhere. But these were not mysterious roads to nowhere. They were what here in Texas we call farm-to-market roads, created by people and animals moving between the hinterland and the city. Mapping these old farm-to-market roads from satellite imagery helped identify regions that were farmed during the Early Bronze Age (2600–2000 BC).[22]

Remote sensing is giving us more rigorous ways to investigate roads across the US Southwest that are associated with the Chaco

Phenomenon. The ancestors of Pueblo people, who traditionally had rarely consolidated into large single settlements, built monumental scaled architecture, or subscribed to a uniform set of art, architecture, and artifact styles over a large region, relatively suddenly did all those things at once.[23] At the center of this activity was Chaco Canyon in New Mexico, with its massive great houses containing hundreds of tiny apartments, and great kivas, round buildings built partially underground and intensely painted inside with murals.

A network of tracks across one hundred thousand square kilometers of the San Juan Basin region—also referred to as Four Corners because it is where Utah, Colorado, Arizona, and New Mexico meet—have been called the Chaco Roads. They are associated with Chaco-styled architecture that is dotted across the region, and some lead straight to Chaco Canyon, running more than fifty kilometers in a straight line.

John Kantner, an archaeologist at the University of North Florida, helped demonstrate the utility of GIS to archaeology by showing that documented segments of Chaco Roads do not follow the least cost path given the landform, but rather follow natural features with ideological significance (Kantner 1997).[24] New research using airborne lidar has started documenting road segments in and around the canyon itself over a study area of forty-two hundred square kilometers. Like the northern Mesopotamian tracks, some of these would be invisible on the ground because they are marked by such subtle depressions.

The most studied, and largest, network of roads and ports in the ancient world belonged to the Roman Empire. The richness of the historical records and the enormous size of the transportation networks built and maintained by the Roman Empire, has attracted innovative, if at times somewhat bizarre, approaches.

Time travelers thinking about a holiday to the Roman Empire will be pleased to know there is a website to help them plan the trip. It is called ORBIS and it was built by Walter Scheidel, a professor of classics at Stanford University, and digital humanities specialist Elijah Meeks, who now works at Netflix as a senior data visualization engineer. The ORBIS model covers an incredible ten million square kilometers. The team focused on 632 well-known settlements, about half of which are on the coast and serve as the bases for estimating sea routes. The land routes cover more than eighty-four thousand kilometers, and that is still only about a fifth of the total length of the old Roman roads. In addition to the roads, the web map includes 28,000 kilometers of navigable rivers and canals, and around 119,000 kilometers of sea routes (the duration of sea travel varies based upon the season of travel).[25]

The goal of ORBIS is to show the specific costs of connectivity—travel and communication—that ordinarily would be thought of as determined only by distance, but were in fact also influenced by the season, mode of transport, and other details. So if, for example, one wanted to go from Londinium (London) to Roma (Rome) in summer, ORBIS calculates that the trip would take only thirty days by sail. But if you went primarily by donkey, in winter, the website estimates it would have taken eighty-two days. It even calculates the travel cost in silver coins *(denarii)*; not surprisingly the faster trip was more expensive. The value of translating things into variables like logistical time and money means we are in a better position to understand how news, ideas, and customs were spread from one place to another across the Roman world.

There is good reason to believe that the old Roman road network had impacts long after Rome fell.[26] Archaeologist Stuart Brookes at University College London and mathematician Huynh

Hoai Nguyen of Imperial College London wanted to identify which towns were particularly well placed in the late Roman period, and how they fared later on in medieval Britain. To work out which of the many towns situated at crossroads had an advantage in the network they used PageRank, an algorithm developed by Google. PageRank works out the rank order of the most important websites for the topics you search.[27] The data in this case was not websites but position in the road network. They showed that good placement within the network was a predictor of future success.

The hands-down winner for the most bonkers approach to studying the Roman roads involved petri dishes of slime mold. At some point you have noticed how spatial patterns in nature—like the veins and arteries pumping blood through our bodies—can look like tiny road systems. Andy Adamatzky, director of the Unconventional Computing Centre at the University of West England in Bristol, noticed this too. He collaborated with some archaeologists interested in the Roman roads across the Balkans and made a scale model of the distributions of seventeen towns and cities from the middle and late Roman periods (Evangelidis et al 2015). The model was on a good-sized petri dish (twenty-two centimeters by twenty-two centimeters) with oat flakes representing towns. After he had made eighteen copies of the model, some of those oat flakes were then coated with slime mold *(Physarum polycephalum)*, and over the course of a few days, the mold spread, creating a natural network.

Did it work? Sort of. As it spreads out and searches for nutrients the mold leaves behind thicker protoplasmic tubes between the oats along natural least cost paths. Many of the experimental mold-maps mirrored corridors that we know were important in the region and the results are surprisingly close to what a computer model of the same process shows. But, while I love fun science experiments, they are much less efficient as visualization tools then making digital people build digital roads.

. . .

In addition to helping us understand well-known ancient road systems, geospatial technologies are also helping us work out where artifacts circulated before they ended up where we find them.

There are some fundamental facts that make the whole enterprise of sourcing artifacts—that is, working out where people got the raw materials to make things—difficult and in fact can doom the search before it starts. Natural sources for raw material are seldom nice and geographically discrete. A good source for obsidian can be cut through by a river, making it impossible to say if people quarried that kind of stone directly from the source or picked it up a great distance downstream. Ceramics are even more problematic because they are constructed from a recipe of clays and other things added together. And, if that were not bad enough, there is received wisdom among many archaeologists that working out the spatial pattern of artifacts relative to where the raw material occurs does not tell us anything interesting.[28]

Not everyone is as pessimistic about the value of sourcing. My own experience looking at how the ancestors of Native Hawaiians (also known as *Kānaka Maoli*) quarried stone convinces me that this is an area of research where we will see a lot more innovative geospatial archaeology.

The volcanic islands of the Hawaiian archipelago give you two basic choices for tool-stone: hard gray basalt, which is great for making adzes, chisels, and a variety of other tools, and volcanic glass. Volcanic glass is in the obsidian family. It can be chipped into flakes with razor sharp edges, and naturally occurs in hundreds of locations across the islands. Most research has looked at basalt adzes to try to work out interisland exchange, identify examples of craft specialization, and consider the controls that the elite may have had over both.

My colleagues and I were interested in volcanic glass precisely because it was not intrinsically valuable, and therefore was a good metric of how people interacted with each other on a day-to-day basis (McCoy et al. 2011). One particularly important source is located on a small hill called Puʻuwaʻawaʻa.[29] About half of the three thousand artifacts we examined were matched to that source. Unsurprisingly, travel time turned out to be a good predictor of the proportion of this source used at any one location, but that was hardly the point of the study. Next, we looked at the artifacts themselves and tried to get an idea how the stone was being quarried and exchanged relative to known boundaries between communities and districts.

There is no technology, no method, which will tell you all the places a stone artifact has been from the day it was carried away from its source as a raw cobble. But when we look at a large number of artifacts at once, interesting patterns can emerge. At places that are within one day's walk of the Puʻuwaʻawaʻa source—meaning you could wake up, go to the source, and be home before sunset—we found bits of weathered surfaces on some chips of volcanic glass. This is a telltale sign that someone worked down a stone that still looked a lot like it did when it was in its natural form. The collections of artifacts from further away had no weathered surfaces and were mainly pieces that were smaller and perhaps had already been used a bit before being passed down between neighbors. By the end of the line all you see are bits of Puʻuwaʻawaʻa volcanic glass almost too small to use. To us that suggested a degree of permeability of travel across community boundaries (in Hawaiian, called *ahupuaʻa*) that had not been documented before.

If we can source small stones, what about big stones? Detailed geochemical studies of the stones of Stonehenge and the Egyptian pyramids give us a pretty good idea of where people must have quarried them. But geospatial technologies are not often a major piece of these studies. There are some exceptions to this rule that, to me, demonstrate a lot of untapped potential.

Take for example the world's best known megalithic statues: the *moai* of Rapa Nui (Easter Island). The people of Rapa Nui carved about seven hundred *moai* from a single quarry located on the eastern side of their tiny island. There are no natural rivers to help move these statues. Very-high-resolution satellite imagery has shown thirty-two kilometers of tracks, most leading out from the quarry to some of the many places that *moai* have been found (Lipo and Hunt 2005).

There has been a lot of speculation about how these statues might have been transported. Carl P. Lipo (State University of New York at Binghamton), Terry L. Hunt (University of Arizona), and Sergio Rapu Haoa (Instituto de Estudios Oceanicos, Hangaroa, Rapa Nui/Isla de Pascua, Chile) used a 3-D scan of an intact *moai* to replicate it in concrete (Lipo, Hunt, and Rapu Haoa 2013). This was essentially a really, really big 3-D printing job so they could try out different ways of moving a *moai*. When it was finished a small coordinated team made the concrete *moai* statue "walk" by wobbling it back and forth down a path. The experiment, along with some assessment of what was going on with the center of gravity as the statues were walked, was used as evidence to argue that they could have been made and placed by small independent groups using the tracks mapped by satellite imagery rather than an intensely hierarchical society capable of large coordinated labor projects.

Polynesia is home to rich oral histories and there are detailed early written records of life on these islands, but it is unrealistic to expect these records to reflect every aspect of what happened in the past. No historic record is capable of that. Through the application of geospatial technologies on stone artifacts, big and small, the innumerable trips people made to quarries come into focus. With this new knowledge we can flesh out our picture of the past by testing our underlying assumptions about what life was like.

. . .

The final way that geospatial technologies are helping us better understand ancient travel and transport is through visualizing the evolution of big patterns in boundaries and movement. Research taking on these types of problems tends to be technically challenging in terms of geospatial analysis, but it highlights the kinds of things that can be achieved with the right approach.

Studies of long-term and large-scale movement will often circle back to looking at political boundaries between ancient states. Recent studies from the Andes (Mantha 2009), the Basin of Mexico (Carballo and Pluckhahn 2007), and Crete (Bevan 2011) have found ways to measure interaction in cases where we do not have detailed maps showing the growth and decline of states. One interesting study looked at travel across the Alps to examine an aspect of state power we rarely talk about (Whitley 2017). It turned the least cost path function upside down and asked: Where should we find things left behind by people who were actively avoiding settlements and the paths between them? In other words, people going out of their way to not interact with others, like smugglers, bandits, or thieves looking to avoid authorities.

Other studies have tried to visualize what travel in different landscapes looked like given our tendency to use multiple informal pathways between locations and to travel over or along water. Meghan C.L. Howey, archaeologist at the University of New Hampshire used a program called Circuitscape. Circuitscape "borrows algorithms from electronic circuit theory to predict patterns of movement, gene flow, and genetic differentiation among plant and animal populations in heterogeneous landscapes" (circuitscape.org). Her study of Michigan in the centuries before European contact shows what travel could have been like outside the confines of estimating the least cost route between two points (Howey 2011).

Robert Gustas and Kisha Supernant from the University of Alberta used nontraditional variables to calculate the costs of movement around different locations in the Pacific Northwest (Gustas and Supernant 2017). Like Howey, their goal was to show not one path but general trends, in this case along a coastline with many offshore islands. Among the findings were two predictive models showing hot spots where archaeology should be found— one for if overland travel was allowed by the people living there, another for if it was prohibited.

Many of these studies speak to how people travel in the absence of roads, or when avoiding roads. For much of our history, it was on informal routes along paths and trails that our ancestors made their way in the world. This is one of the challenges to realizing the full potential of ancient mobility as a window into past societies, but it's one that we can make progress toward resolving with the right combination of data, tools, and creativity.

. . .

There is something poetic about using objects that have stayed in one place for thousands of years to reconstruct movement. And geospatial technology is helping us do that by allowing archaeologists to scale up from looking at a handful of locations and a small number of artifacts, or from retracing a few cases of ancient exploration or exchange, to constructing larger and more complete pictures of people on the move. In some cases, we have used sparse locational information as evidence to support some complex stories about the past. There are gaps and topics that have attracted much more attention than others. Geospatial technologies can make it a lot easier to see where our efforts need to go (see Gupta 2013), as we strive for a more complete accounting of where we came from, how we traveled around, and why.

Next, we are going to look at how geospatial technologies are helping archaeologists identify and understand the strategies people used to put food on the table. There is a great deal more to the story of our relationship with the natural world and our place in it beyond food. But we have to eat. And an impressive amount of the archaeological record reflects what people did to solve the ever-present problem of having enough food to live and thrive.

7   *Food and Farms*

How Our Ancestors Fed Themselves

Time travel stories, like any fiction genre, operate on a set of unspoken conventions. There are some things about the past that must be correct, or as correct as we can hope to be, or our suspension of disbelief is broken and the whole thing becomes silly. There are other details that we, the audience, are happy to gloss over. The method of time traveling, for example, can be short on explanation. We will accept just about anything. Characters have traveled through time as the result of a bump on the head, or magic. Time machines can take any form—a car, a telephone booth, a hot tub—it doesn't matter.[1]

One convention that I had not noticed until recently is that time travelers never seem to worry about feeding themselves in the past. Or to worry about how the additional mouths to feed on their visit to the past might influence the future. Why? The simple answer is that even though one out of nine people in today's world are undernourished, most other people do not think about going hungry.[2] The slightly more complex answer is deeply rooted in the time travel genre. In his book *Time Travel: The Popular Philosophy of Narrative,* David Wittenberg (2013) has made the argument that the cultural and literary soup that gave rise to the time travel novel was the late utopian romance genre. With that as base stock, it is not surprising that hunger is not a factor. There is no hunger in a utopia, so no need to pack lunch.[3]

Thinking that the past was a kind of utopia, or Garden of Eden, inhibits our historical curiosity about how people in the past put food on the table. And I don't mean what was on the menu, although that is interesting too. Many of the big questions about how human societies evolved are in some way rooted back to agriculture. This makes intuitive sense. In a world before capital, before money, food was the currency and a prerequisite for getting larger and larger groups of people to live in the same place. We can draw a straight line from so many things in history back to food.

In this chapter we look at a series of different kinds of spatial puzzles that center on how people managed to not just survive, but thrive, in the past. This requires us to be, in different ways, sensitive to what the natural environment in the past looked like. In that sense we have to think like historical ecologists. For example, figure 18 shows two caves, marked with circles. In the upper map we see them relative to the known distribution of a particular type of tree in the modern day; the map's darker shading indicates where there are relatively dense stands of these trees and gives us a picture of the local ecosystem. Then in the lower map we see what the environment around the caves looked like more than twenty thousand years ago. It was colder, and not only are the stands of these trees thinner, but also the coast is further away. In this simple example, knowing that resources that are abundant and close today were much further away during the last Ice Age is important context for interpreting what kinds of foods show in deposits at those cave.

In addition to thinking carefully about the ancient environment, there is the distinctly archaeological problem of working out

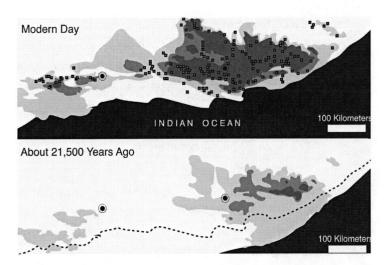

FIGURE 18. Reconstructing the ancient environment. To be able to work out what the distributions of settlements tell us about land use, it is helpful to have a model of what the environment looked like in the past. In this example from southern Africa, MaxEnt software was asked to reconstruct the Ice Age environment around two caves (circles) based on the modern distribution of a particular type of tree (squares). The results show the coastline was further away, because sea levels were lower, and the colder temperatures meant stands of these trees were thinner. Source: Franklin et al. (2015).

how people dealt with the constraints that nature put on their activities, and how they took advantage of different opportunities. We will begin with some fairly straightforward models that look at where people lived. These take advantage of the fact that when humans don't like the cards that they are dealt, or see something over the horizon that looks good, they often will vote with their feet. Next, we get into some more subtle strategies, like storing food and making friends, that humans use to get through shortfalls. The final examples center on complex scenarios in which rewards and risks become entangled and extreme. In these cases, computer simulation and modeling have proved useful to helping sort out the plausible from the probable, and may give us a clue as to the kinds of challenges we will face in the future as we try to feed more and more people.

．　•　．

The most obvious strategies in dealing with different environmental challenges and opportunities involve choosing where to live. And so a good place to start is to look at where people lived over long time periods, and over broad areas.

Archaeologist Peter Veth of the University of Western Australia noticed archaeology clumping at certain time periods in Australia, in places he called "islands of the interior." New research using a database of hundreds of radiocarbon dates representing time-slices between twenty-five thousand and twelve thousand years ago identified six to nine specific locations where people consistently lived (Williams et al. 2013). These were defined by taking the distribution of all dates from a two-thousand-year range and then using a cluster analysis (k-means) to pinpoint "islands." Some of the environmental factors that drew people in, unsurprisingly, involved access to fresh water, such as significant mountain snow-melt in summer that would have contributed to big healthy river systems.[4] The value of studies like this one is that out of all of the plausible environmental factors that might be drawing people to an area we can narrow things down to what was happening in a specific time and place.

Some of the most ambitious research in archaeology today takes on the problem of mapping out the distribution of people over time.[5] Michelle A. Chaput of the University of Ottawa and her colleagues transformed the contents of the Canadian Archaeological Radiocarbon Database—that's thirty-five thousand radiocarbon dates from nine thousand locations across North America—into time-slice snapshots of where people were living over the past thirteen thousand years (Chaput et al. 2015).

After some basic data cleaning, they had to figure out how to get around serious spatiotemporal biases that would skew population estimates. What do you do when there are more radiocarbon dates reported in one place than another, not because there were more people living there, but because more archaeology has been published from there? Or when multiple samples from the same location are from the same time period—should they count the same as a location with a single date? They also had to make some decisions about scale. How large an area can a radiocarbon date represent in a model that is built on a continental geographic scale? And how much time should be represented in each snapshot map?

The geospatial math behind this was in large part dictated by the scale of the project and of the radiocarbon data itself. To smooth out uneven sampling, a single location could only be counted once, provided that there was at least one sample from that time period. If multiple samples from the same location fell into the same periods, the location was still only counted once. They used a spatial interpolation (kernel density) to estimate the relative density of settlement across North America. It was determined that a six-hundred-kilometer bandwidth was ideal to smooth out patchiness in the data and represent each area fairly despite uneven reporting.

The result was a dozen "radiocarbon frequency population estimate" heat-maps, each representing all dated deposits from within five-hundred-year intervals. You can view them side by side, or as a video that opens by showing a few hotspots for foragers, followed by in-filling of those spots, and the heating up to red hot of the eastern half of the continent as farming becomes the dominant way of life over the past two thousand years. The final map, where the movie ends, is North America as it was when Columbus came along.[6] Before this study archaeologists already had a general idea that some of these patterns were emerging; what this model does is formalize those observations and tie them down more tightly to a specific time and place.

When we zoom in to look at how these changes in population play out in different environments we start to see how people's preferences changed and how they coped with big climatic swings.

In northern China there appears to have been a shift in where people preferred to live that accompanied the move from hunting and foraging to millet farming (Wang, Yang, and Jia 2016). Lin Wang of HuaQiao University and colleagues looked at the terrain around what are considered typical settlements from before, during, and after the transition to farming. To do this they broke the land around each settlement into concentric rings based on hiking times. The smallest rings represent the areas one could reach in just ten minutes and the largest show the land that could be reached in a two-hour walk. They found that hunters preferred foothills and mountains; transitional hunting/farming people preferred foothills of river valleys so they might experiment with cultivation while still having access to good hunting grounds; and dedicated farmers preferred broad valleys where farms could expand as the population grew.

In China we also find some clear signs of changes in land use during a major climatic shift, specifically, in the Bronze Age during the Holocene Optimum, a wet and warm period about six thousand years ago.[7] At that time China had become home to millions of farmers thanks to large swaths of land being used for millet farming, including the West Liao River Basin (Jia et al. 2016). When the Holocene Optimum ended, there was a "divergence of human subsistence strategies as well as the dispersal of settlements," due to a weakening of monsoons that drove millet farmers south and an influx of people from the west who practiced a mix of herding and hunting (Jia et al. 2016, 787). In tracking both this shift and the earlier changes in settlement, the geospatial model allows us to take general assessments of what might have been happening and tie them down to specific times and places.

New research in the American Southwest shows how in some cases people's strategies to deal with food shortages from drought influenced the types of social networks they built. To be clear, these ancient social networks are not like modern digital ones where we have lots and lots of individual-to-individual links that we can trace. What we have are pottery styles shared between neighbors that, at best, let us drill down to the level of a household, but are most revealing when we look at what happens on a regional level.

One study looked at if, in the long run, it was better for groups to be extroverts or introverts. Lewis Borck of Leiden University and his colleagues took twenty-two study areas in Arizona and western New Mexico, reconstructed their social networks based on pottery, and then counted up the number of ties to external groups as well as ties within each group (Borck et al. 2015). A group of extreme extroverts, who somehow avoided ties within their own group, would have a ratio of 1; a group with only ties within that group would have a ratio of -1. These extremes are pretty rare. The general trend over time was from slightly introverted (-0.2) to extroverted

(+0.5). What is particularly interesting is how and where the ratio changed over time and space.

During a well-documented extreme drought, lots of places were abandoned regardless of the orientation of their social networks. Nonetheless, external orientation turned out to be a good predictor of survival. There is an exception: some people made it through the drought yet maintained more internally oriented social networks. The authors suggest that this could be due to relatively higher population density, flexible settlement patterns within the group, and access to good agricultural lands. What sets this study apart from other examinations of the relationship between climate and society is how it used this fine-grained dataset to show quantifiable divergences in how people tried to solve a problem through relying on each other or by asserting their independence from others.

· · ·

Where I work, out on the islands of the Pacific, it is impossible to overestimate the importance of the ocean in how people fed themselves. The coast is where most people lived and if you look carefully you will find centuries of discarded remains of all manner of fish, shellfish, and other sea creatures that were on the dinner table. The same can be said for coasts around the world.

The Pacific coast of the American Northwest—places like Oregon, Washington, British Columbia, and Alaska—is a place where you will find archaeological deposits containing thousands of years of salmon dinners. Of course people caught and ate more than salmon. They commonly ate herring and more than a dozen other types of fishes; in fact, more than one hundred unique taxa have been recovered, including fish like sculpins, flatfishes, rock-fishes, greenlings, and dogfish.

We expect that, like us in the modern world, people in the past had cultural preferences for certain fish. We also expect that climatic shifts would change how much of different kinds of fish were caught. So, how can we work out if the type of fish that were being eaten at any one time is due to what was naturally available or to what people from that group preferred to eat? The Pacific Northwest is densely packed with dozens of distinct cultural groups, as well as diverse coastal microenvironments, both of which make answering this seemingly simple question rather difficult.[8]

Two archaeologists in Oregon created an incredible map of all the fish caught along the coast of the Pacific Northwest over about ten thousand years. Iain McKechnie, currently at the University of Victoria, and Madonna L. Moss, University of Oregon professor and curator of zooarchaeology at the Oregon Museum of Natural and Cultural History, pulled together a list of 222 locations where fish bones had been recovered. The painstaking task of identifying the thousands of fish bones was the result of forty years of work at more than a dozen different archaeological labs and the number of identified specimens totaled over half a million (that's 513,506 fish bones).

The results provide a kind of species-specific heat-map (inverse distance weighted) in nearshore waters that in some places shows a dramatic shift in the proportion of certain fish over short distances. For example, if you were fishing the southern shores of Vancouver Island it would not be unusual that you came home mostly with herring. Less than one hundred kilometers away, where the city of Seattle is today, herring were comparatively rare, making up less than 15 percent of the catch. McKechnie and Moss

(2016) knew that interpolating all the data from these many differ-ent locations from different time periods does not necessarily show what people preferred to eat or tell us about natural cycles in fisher-ies. Instead what they have done is to create a baseline to tell us about the general trend, something that is critical if we are to detect when something different is going on.

The meta-analysis of fish bones in the Pacific Northwest is, to me, a good example of how geospatial technologies can take some-thing for which we have lots of good locational data—in this case, where people were catching different sorts of fish—and start to, as best as we can, get an idea of what kinds of strategies they were using to feed themselves. Another place where we are seeing this is in the middle of North America, around the Great Lakes.

Archaeologists love it when people stash things in pits. Storage of food and other goods in pits is an extremely old practice but it is not universal; some times and places have lots of pits, others few or none. Logic dictates that if a pit was used as designed (meaning that whoever dug the pit came back and collected whatever was in there), we should not expect to find the contents. That's fine, because the thing that archaeologists are after is not necessarily the goodies that people stored away; what we want to know is why people thought stashing things was a good idea.

To learn why people gathered things in pits, it helps to know exactly where they are. Meghan C. L. Howey and colleagues worked with airborne lidar data to try to create a map of the places where people cached things, including preserved foods (Howey et al. 2016). On a field survey, the places where people stored things are visible today as tight clusters of shallow depressions that, when excavated, are clearly examples of storage pits. The problem is that surveying large areas for small targets is time consuming, but remote sensing is almost always going to result in a lot of false positives where there are also natural and modern human-made depressions.

For this study, the team used a custom automated routine to identify more than 2.5 million possible pits in a portion of Michigan. That was clearly way too many. Next they were able to winnow it down to a more reasonable number of locations based on the known sizes of the features. Not surprisingly, many pits were found around lakes, but the study also showed clusters far from lakes where archaeologists were not actively looking for them. The lesson here is that remote sensing can give us survey-like results, but only with careful application and a good working knowledge of the targets.

In these unrelated studies we see how geospatial technology can be applied to generate a snapshot of some fundamental decisions that people made in order to put dinner on the table.

.   .   .

When I was kid, maybe eleven or twelve, I was obsessed with a time travel book series called *Grail Quest* by J. H. Brennan.[9] These choose-your-own-adventure books were set in King Arthur's court and each one began with Merlin casting a spell to call the reader's mind back to that time. One of the things that made it stand out from other choose-your-own-adventure series is that it had a *Dungeons and Dragons* element. For some critical decisions you had to roll dice to determine if you moved on or if you died. To make it through one of these books you had to die and restart a lot.

The world's first generations of farmers faced real-life choices that involved variables that people who got their food from hunting, gathering, and fishing did not have to think about. What to grow, where to plant, when to plant, how many animals to keep, what kinds, and how to feed them: these would become the central concerns of many of the world's people. Spatial analysis and remote sensing give us a good idea of the kinds of strategies that people took up, but it has been through simulation—a high-tech version of a choose-your-own-adventure book—that we are getting insights into the fundamentals of the lives of early farmers.

Arizona State University's C. Michael Barton has created and killed thousands, and possibly millions, of digital farmers in computer simulations for the Mediterranean Landscape Dynamics project (MedLanD for short). But, to be clear, the goal was "*not* substituting a computer simulation of the human past for narrative prose," or trying to come up with the perfect recreation of the past (Barton, Ullah, and Mitasova 2010, 366; emphasis in original). The goal of simulation was to expose what underlying factors narrowed down the number of winning solutions.

The MedLanD team had several things working in their favor in their search to uncover what about the dynamics between human land use and the natural environment had shaped the course of history. They began with high-quality geospatial data, specifically, the distribution of environmental variables that influence susceptibility to soil erosion (like the slope of land), as well as the locations of different-sized settlements in two study areas on either side of the Mediterranean, in Jordan (Wadi Hasa) and in Spain (Penàguila).

The locational information from archaeology and the local environment were the independent variables in this experiment. As in any laboratory experiment, the MedLanD team knew that they must be able to make adjustments to the dependent variables—like how to farm and what to farm—to see what the long-term impacts would be under different conditions. To do this they wrote modules that run in an open-source GIS (QGIS) and also have taken advantage of MaxEnt.

Unlike the speculations of early armchair scholars, the results of the MedLanD project spell out the fundamental choices that farmers likely made, and their specific consequences.[10] For example, in Wadi Hasa there were basically three moves that kept farming communities from having to abandon the region. One was to maintain small groups, thereby keeping intensive farming and herding from tipping the environment toward a one-way downward spiral of soil degradation. Another was to let groups grow larger but to shift toward putting more and more land in grazing, again to keep the increasing demands on the environment from going down that spiral. The third option was to invest in infrastructure that could offset the impacts of intensive land use, things like terraces and irrigation.

The Mediterranean was the stage of important shifts in the big story of humanity and so it is important to develop a realistic picture of when people there adopted different strategies. The modeling tells us that the scale at which the environment would be impacted by these choices was detectable over a single person's lifetime. That suggests that while there are only a few ways to survive this choose-your-own-adventure, they were actual choices, not just history being batted around by natural forces.

Having said all that, there is also good evidence that even some of their neighbors were, over the long term, somewhat at the mercy of the ability of the land to sustain them. J. Brett Hill of Hendrix College tracked generation-scale movements of villages around his study area in Jordan and found that in the north, people built new villages not far from the ones occupied immediately beforehand (Hill 2004). In contrast, in the south, there were times and places were people would just abandon areas and completely reorganize, a state of affairs that environmental conditions largely dictated.

. . .

The isolation of the Hawaiian Islands in the middle of the North Pacific kept people from finding them and making them their home until about AD 1000. For eight hundred years, the descendants of the first Polynesian settlers saw their numbers grow, perhaps up to close to half a million. To feed the growing population, and to appease the demands of society's ruling class for surplus, land was farmed more and more intensively over time. By the time of first contact with Westerners in 1778, valleys had been transformed into irrigated pondfields to grow taro (you may know it from the dish poi), and vast swaths of the islands were planted in crops like sweet potato that were watered only by rainfall.

The ancestors of today's Native Hawaiians, *Kānaka Maoli*, invented—or from the perspective of world history, reinvented—kings and queens. And changes in how people fed themselves went hand-in-hand with this seismic shift in society. One way we can see the connection between food and society is through the ways different natural constraints and opportunities shaped the political histories of individual islands.

Archaeologist Thegn N. Ladefoged of the University of Auckland, along with an interdisciplinary team investigating the same kinds of human-environment dynamic relationships that were being modeled in the Mediterranean, wanted to know exactly where farmers could have planted (Ladefoged et al. 2009). While

FIGURE 19. Farmland in the Hawaiian Islands. This predictive model shows every location in the Hawaiian Islands where environmental conditions would have allowed farmers using traditional crops and techniques to grow food intensively. Source: Ladefoged et al. (2009).

this was not a simple task, it was made a great deal easier by data on which soils had the nutrients necessary for intensive farming and other environmental variables.

The predictive model of where people could have intensively farmed turned out to be a great match for large integrated field systems and prime planting areas known through coarse-grained information such as limited archaeological field surveys, air photos, and historic records (see figure 19). Further detailed environmental data have helped refine this model, but it is remarkably complete and gives a clear snapshot of how different the potential for intensive farming was on the extreme ends of the island chain. On Kaua'i, an island not known for launching campaigns to fight neighboring kingdoms, people relied almost entirely upon irrigated valleys. On Hawai'i Island, an island well known for internal fights to consolidate power and for many off-island campaigns, the opposite is true: most food comes from massive field systems on the dry sides of the island.

The geospatial model is a good fit for something Patrick V. Kirch of the University of Hawai'i, Mānoa pointed out in his book *The Wet and the Dry:* that the expected relationship between environmental risk and political action is flipped on many Pacific Islands (Kirch 1994). You would think that the chiefs or kings with fields that produced more food would be out competing with their neighbors. But it was those who inherited lands with few or no opportunities for irrigated fields, and thus prone to heavy losses when droughts would come along, who were most likely to take up arms to try to place themselves in the ruling seat and control the better lands of their neighbors.

Not long after the predictive model told us where people *could* have farmed, a lidar survey told us where and how they did farm. The first airborne lidar survey for archaeology in the islands of the Pacific was flown over a place called Kohala. The target: abandoned agricultural fields. At the controls of the plane tacking back and forth over the northern tip of Hawai'i Island was Gregory P. Asner, director of the Carnegie Airborne Observatory. Asner, a remote sensing expert who has used lidar to look at global-scale problems with human land use, ecology, and climate change, had flown for ecological surveys many times before, but not for archaeology.

I first met Asner in 2008 at a lu'au in Hilo.[11] Over forkfuls of *kalua* pork, Thegn Ladefoged and I made the case to him that airborne lidar was going to be the next big thing for archaeology. The next time I saw Asner it was in his computer lab at Stanford. He had completed the flights, but with the severe winds across that part of the island pushing the plane around, he had nearly crashed in the process. Now the ball was in our court to tease out archaeology from the hard-won data. Thanks to some creative efforts at extracting individual features from the lidar data, we worked out precisely where people built their farms—and how they built them. The map of agricultural infrastructure covered nearly 240 square kilometers, about the same size as the first lidar survey of the Maya city of Caracol (Ladefoged et al. 2011; McCoy et al. 2011).

On the windward side of the island, the half that faces the trade winds and receives the most rainfall, we could plainly see a couple of dozen irrigated fields built within the confines of narrow valleys—they were visible because of a halo effect that terraces, with their artificially flat middles and artificially steep edges, make in the data (McCoy, Asner, and Graves 2011). The extreme detail of lidar also allowed us to map large areas next to these fields where it was possible, through the use of long irrigation ditches to expand how much land was farmed.

On the leeward side, in the rain shadow of the Kohala Mountains, farmers built hundreds of kilometers of low windbreak walls to keep crops from being destroyed by the trade winds as they rushed down the mountains to the sea. Airborne lidar allowed us to see the density of these features, a metric for the state of fields when they were abandoned. When brought together with environmental records of droughts and new radiocarbon dates on fields and houses, it became clear that as the need for food ramped up, people began taking more and more risks.

If a society and economy ramping up and taking more risks sounds familiar, as by now it should, let us return to the Maya.

. . .

Simulations in archaeology are most useful when they help explain the spatiotemporal patterns we see in locational data.

MayaSim is an agent-based model for the rise and fall of Classic Maya society. In it the agents are settlements and there are a number of things that vary as they grow and interact with their environment and their neighbors. The model has two broad categories that can be adjusted, the biophysical and the anthropogenic. The biophysical are things like climate, hydrology, and soil. The anthropogenic factors are population size, agriculture, and trade. Time in this digital world is marked out in steps and something interesting happens at around three hundred to four hundred steps. People begin farming in riskier areas, forests are cleared away, and soils become degraded. Soon after, the map goes from what looks like a healthy, thriving civilization to the collapse that the Maya have become famous for.

This simulation certainly looks like the Maya collapse as viewed from space, or as it might look in a version of the computer game *Sid Meier's Civilization*.[12] But that is not the only outcome. When population growth and soil management are adjusted, the collapse becomes a smaller reorganization, an endorsement of the idea that those are the key variables. Computer models, like MayaSim, are being used more and more to make links between data and evidence. And with results from airborne lidar being transformed into survey-scaled digital maps, we are beginning to see the kinds of data that are necessary to make regular use of computer models in archaeology.[13]

Simulations based on large and detailed geospatial data—on both the environment and archaeology—are showing us ways to be more certain about our interpretations. It is nonetheless hard to shake the uncertainty that is built into the fragmentary nature of our evidence and the nearly boundless alternatives we have to choose from when creating historical narratives.

. . .

There are innumerable ways that we can learn about how people in the past put food on the table through geospatial technology. We can look at the places where they chose to live and when they chose to leave; the times and places that they chose to stash food away; when they reached out to neighbors and when they took a more self-reliant path; and how farmers tried to balance the need for food, and surplus, against the pressures that farming places on the ecosystem. As our datasets grow, we can move beyond general observations with regard to how people dealt with the natural environmental constraints on their actions, and consider how they took advantage of the opportunities before them in specific times and places.

Just as ecologists have turned to computer simulation to try to understand the interconnected ways that ecosystems work, archaeologists today turn more and more to modeling to tell us which explanation, out of the many plausible ones, is the one that our datasets are most likely telling us about. The knowledge that we gain is invaluable to understanding the course of history and some believe it gives us the only real preview we are likely to get of the future. After all, the same things that farmers faced on a small scale a millennium ago in terms of the rewards and risks of pushing production up to, and past, its limits, are being repeated today on an industrial and global scale.

In the next chapter, we look at another essential element of the past: ancient society. It is an exciting time in archaeology. We are learning more and more about the premodern roots of the kind of society we live in today, and exploring further what it might have been like to live long ago.

8 *Living in the Past*

Reverse Engineering Ancient Societies

We know that life in the past was different than in the present. It is hard to miss changes within our own society, large ones and small ones, for good and for bad, as one generation passes and a new one comes along. We can read about life centuries ago when social norms and ideals were so different that it has been compared to a foreign country.[1] But what about the far distant past? Can we hope to catch a glimpse of what it would have been like to live in societies that came and went thousands of years ago?

One of the pioneers in trying to reverse engineer what ancient societies were like is our old friend Gordon Childe. Childe noticed that long after the Neolithic Revolution, starting about six thousand years ago, we start to see the coincidence of a number of new things: the world's first cities; the first signs of distinct professional classes like artisans, soldiers, and priests; truly impressive monumental architecture; complex long-distance trade networks; writing; the collection of surplus food as tax or tribute; and authority over people by a divine monarch, a king or queen, as opposed to authority being solely organized by kinship. He collectively called these changes the Urban Revolution (Childe 1936).

Michael E. Smith, an archaeologist at Arizona State University, has pointed out that the Urban Revolution has often been misunderstood and that those misunderstandings have had knock-on effects. Maybe the biggest is that the Urban Revolution is not about cities: it is about an "interconnected series of changes" that resulted in the first state societies (Smith 2009, 7). In other words, the creation of cities were just one of the things that let us reverse engineer that society had changed to become more hierarchical, and more like the world we live in today.

We are living through what Andrew Bevan of University College London has called a "data deluge," where we face "floods of new evidence about the human past that are largely digital, frequently spatial, increasingly open and often remotely sensed" (Bevan 2015, 1473). Much of these data come from increased geospatial data on ancient cities and their hinterlands—from decades of field survey, excavations, and remote sensing. The first half of this chapter centers on what these new maps tell us. We have far more information on cities than Childe did when he defined the Urban Revolution, but it is also important to recognize that having more and richer locational data does not instantly yield knowledge.[2]

Abandoned ancient cities are beautiful. It is completely understandable that the focus is too often on the city, rather than the society that built it. The problem is that "fanciful speculation about the past on merely common-sense grounds" and "uncritical extrapolation from the present" have flourished at the expense of "an empirically sound account of what people actually did, and how they organized their affairs, in the distant past" (Smith et al. 2012, 7620).[3] Some of that speculation has come from an uncritical reading of the spatial layout of cities and of monuments. When archaeologists have produced maps of orderly streets, they have often assumed that that order must reflect the power of the monarch. Large monuments, again, are assumed to reflect a powerful autocrat with thousands of obedient people. Some of these interpretations may hold water when tested, but the larger problem is that if we think too narrowly we create a cartoonish picture of the past.[4]

In the second half of this chapter we will consider how archaeologists have tried to work out what it would have been like to experience a range of different places, everything from monuments, to fortifications, to farms, to the interior of a room. If by the end of this chapter you are skeptical about some of the interpretations we have come up with, you are in good company. Archaeologists are constantly at odds with each other over how to turn our ideas into metrics and tie our metrics back to how people experienced the world. Geospatial technology is useful in that it gives us tools that we could not have dreamed of in the days of analog maps but it also gives us a platform whose limits we have yet to find.

There are so many reasons why we try to reverse engineer ancient society, or figure out how people experienced the past, instead of focusing our energy solely on topics that seem more straightforward to investigate. For example, as a social science, our inferences about the past hold authority because we have a more complete picture of what happened than other scholars. With that comes a responsibility to retell as much as we can, and when we fail to do that, we lose that authority and unwittingly create blank spots in history. That is bad science, to put it mildly, and it is why we should listen when the humanities perspective in archaeology warns us of the dangers of dehumanizing the past. The forces of entropy and equifinality guarantee incompleteness and ambiguity in interpretation and it can be all too easy for the people we are writing about to lose their humanity. The best reverse engineering, in my view, populates the past with real people.

. . .

A big part of recognizing changes in human societies turns on the ability to recognize inequality. Inequality is at the heart of the shift to a state society. So how do we know that there was inequality in ancient societies in the first place? Surely it cannot have been exactly the same everywhere. And if it was different, then how can we compare societies thousands of years apart, in different parts of the world?

One measure of economic inequality across a group is the Gini coefficient. Named for its inventor, Corrado Gini, it yields graphic and numerical indices to represent the relative distribution of wealth in the modern world. Inequality in the Gini coefficient calculation is a measure of how far any one group is from perfectly even wealth distribution. If for example you had a group in which everyone had equal wealth and you compared their incomes, those incomes would be proportional to the total income of the group (e.g., in a group of ten thousand people, everyone would earn one ten-thousandth, or 0.01 percent, of the total income).

A collection of archaeologists led by Tim Kohler of Arizona State University and Michael E. Smith, have generated Gini coefficients for the ancient world. The method does not require any special geospatial technology—all that is needed are measurements of the footprints of houses (Kohler et al. 2017). The summed area of all houses is treated like the total income, giving archaeologist a way to measure inequality at a number of spatial and temporal scales. A great deal of the world—South America, Africa, South

Asia, and Oceania—has not yet been well studied using this measure but results suggest a significant divergence in the trajectories of the Old and New Worlds, with the former trending toward levels of greater inequality rarely seen in the latter.[5]

There is good reason to believe that more, larger, and more detailed databases of architecture of ancient urban landscapes will tell us not just about the distribution of wealth, but possibly also about the underlying source of that wealth. Archaeologists at Purdue University working in Mesoamerica, Richard E. Blanton and Lane F. Fargher, have used multiple lines of evidence to argue that two contrasting pathways to power are imprinted on the layouts of ancient cities (Blanton and Fargher 2008).

One route to power is authoritarian. In this scenario, the state is headed by a powerful monarch, whose wealth is drawn from monopolizing resources and trade; therefore decisions regarding how the city is laid out and operates need not reflect the needs of the people. In central Mexico, the city of Tenochtitlan is a prime example. Its ceremonial precinct and palaces are centrally located, making them obstacles to travel since all major roads route through the center of town.

The alternative also has a powerful leader, but one who is reliant on taxes and therefore must put their more despotic impulses somewhat in check. These are not exactly democracies, nor are they socialist collectives, but states where leadership comes from reading and responding to the will of the people. Also in central Mexico, the city of Tlaxcallan could not be more different from its authoritarian neighbor. In Tlaxcallan, public spaces are dotted around the city and the palace is situated unobtrusively on the edge of town.

There are a number of good reasons to preserve archaeology, but a reason that these contrasting examples of state power highlight is the need to create an archive of the many different ways that people have organized themselves in the past. The worry is that if we are too narrow in what we choose to preserve today, we could inadvertently lock in a particular version of what the past was like for future generations. Ideally, by thinking more broadly about what we preserve, archaeology is in "a unique position . . . to prefigure future understandings of political organizations that do not enforce or grow social inequality" (Borck 2018, 235). In other words, because we know that people in the future will also be curious about politics in the distant past, we can choose to preserve archaeology that show how remarkably creative our ancestors were when it came to engineering societies, not just monuments to kings and queens.

.   .   .

As the datasets that will help create a more realistic picture of what life was like in the past come online, we are starting to appreciate how ancient cities operated. Some of the best examples come from airborne lidar used to create large continuous GIS datasets of the urban and rural landscapes in the Maya region.

Archaeologists Marcello A. Canuto of Tulane University, Francisco Estrada-Belli of Boston University, and Thomas G. Garrison of Ithaca College, along with their colleagues, have created the largest single map of the Maya lowlands to date (Canuto et al. 2018). It covers just over 2 percent of the region (2,144 out of 95,000 square kilometers), but allowed the team to map 61,480 structures: everything from temples and roads, to defensive features, house sites, and agricultural field systems.

The survey was flown in a dozen discrete blocks, some with large cities like Tikal, others with almost no evidence of people at all. This is actually a huge advantage. This kind of data can be used to extrapolate a number of trends, since they are more likely to reflect a representative sample of the entire area, the same way a modern census interviews only a small number of households, but selects at random those households from a cross-section of geographic regions, economic classes, and ethnic groups.

Using these data the team classified land on a sliding scale, from urban core (more than 300 structures found per square kilometer); to urban (150–300 per square kilometer); to suburbs, or to use their term, "periurban" (60–150 per square kilometer); to rural areas (fewer than 60 per square kilometer); and finally to places that were vacant with almost no sign of settlement or any other activity (fewer than 10 per square kilometer). They took these data and broke them down to generate a ratio of farmland to residents. As you might expect, the downtown areas do not have enough fields to produce the food necessary to feed residents. But the urban and periurban areas immediately around the urban centers have the capacity to produce way more than they could eat themselves. That is a strong confirmation that farmers within a day's walk from city centers would have had to have been producing the food surpluses necessary to keep cities going.

There is good reason to think that these cities relied on an even larger but poorly understood integrated system for maintaining food supplies over an extremely large suburban and urban area. The four most urbanized survey blocks, even with all possible food surpluses being moved to where they were needed, were still overpopulated by 50 to 125 percent beyond the capacity of the farmland within each block. In the eastern sampled areas, where most cities were located, even those survey blocks that were not as urbanized were calculated to be at full capacity. In contrast, the western survey blocks had vast areas that were capable of producing three times local needs, or even six times local needs.

Food security is of course just one element of a successful city, but it is remarkable that even the ancient urban sprawl of the Maya did not completely negate the inherent problem of feeding massive numbers of people. Given the fact that archaeologists have access to thousands of years of successful and not-so-successful cities, some have argued that we have a lot to contribute to urban planning and that ancient cities should be at the center of research on sustainability. Indeed, depending upon your perspective, cities are either the least sustainable or most sustainable things we humans have created. Some were abandoned, while others far outlived the states that built them.[6]

. . .

One stunning example of an ancient city that was abandoned is Angkor Wat in Cambodia.[7] Angkor Wat was the capital of the Khmer Empire at the height of its power until its collapse sometime in the fifteenth century AD. Around the thirteenth century, the city sprawled over one thousand square kilometers set between mountains to the northeast and a lake to the southwest. The natural rivers and streams that cross the area were diverted into canals that irrigated fields and fed the massive rectangular reservoirs at the city's center. The managed water system was also an integrated part of the temple complexes, as can be seen in the layout of the Angkor Wat temple complex, located just south of the central temple (see figure 20).

Every remote sensing technique possible has been thrown at Angkor Wat and its surroundings. It makes sense. The study area is

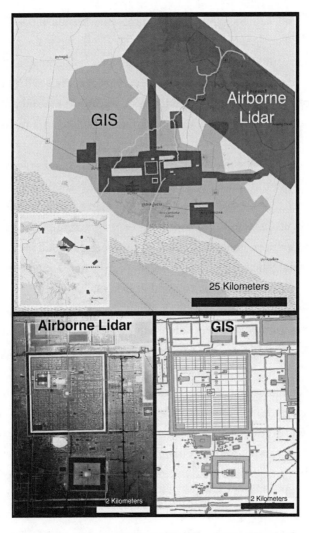

FIGURE 20. The city of Angkor Wat. Here airborne lidar (middle) has been used to create a GIS map (right) of artificial water features (canals and pools), streets, temples, and other buildings. The reservoirs cover an area one thousand times larger than that of Washington DC's reflective pool at the Lincoln Memorial. Source: Evans (2016).

large, and Cambodia has a serious problem with unexploded land-mines. The Greater Angkor Project has been responsible for the most recent remote sensing efforts using airborne lidar. In 2012, 370 square kilometers were flown, and today there are data from 2,230 square kilometers, including a large section of the mountains outside the city and smaller settlements around this region of Cambodia.

The results of the Greater Angkor Project, like other large airborne lidar projects, are still unfolding. Nonetheless, three advances are already evident. First, the map of city is better now than it has ever been. The footprints of architecture, roads, canals, water features, temples, and so on have been captured in remarkable detail; this technical achievement can be hard to appreciate as the results are spread over a number of studies.[8]

Second, excavations within temple complexes give us clear metrics for the density of settlement, which can in turn be linked to the larger GIS map (Carter et al. 2018). New research suggests that "temple enclosures were high-density residential zones" rather than the "empty" sacred landscapes they appear to be today (Carter et al. 2018, 503). A single temple complex could have housed several thousand people with a density of anywhere from 900 to 3,500 people per square kilometer. That sounds crowded, but for context you should picture a density like sprawling modern Houston (1,300 people per square kilometer), not Paris (20,000 people per square kilometer).

Finally, the mapping of Angkor's hydraulic engineering has presented a possible reason for the abandonment of the city (Penny et al. 2018). A computer model of how the water system worked, at peak construction, shows a vulnerable upper elevation portion where it drew water out of rivers and streams. The authors note that

the downstream end of the system—those beautiful canals border-
ing temples and the massive reservoirs—may have been to blame,
since so much of the system was engineered around aesthetics.

As Monica L. Smith (2014), an archaeologist at the University of
California, Los Angeles, has pointed out, the creation of the world's
first cities six thousand years ago marks changes in ancient societies that we are now appreciating in ways that Gordon Childe simply could not have. We can look at the variability within and around
cities, rather than thinking about them as dots on the map. Next,
let's have a closer look at how archaeologists have used geospatial
technology to approximate what it would be like to visit the past.

.　•　.

When it comes to reconstructing the past, archaeologists want to
achieve something that is authentic, a faithful representation. We
want it to be real. And creating an authentic past is important for
more than scientific reasons: it is an explicit rejection of a dehumanized past.

One of the best examples of how archaeologists have grappled
with authenticity was kicked off by a tool widely available in GIS
software packages: viewshed. To use the function all you need is a
DEM raster layer representing the ground surface, and a location
represented by a point. If you ask the GIS to calculate the viewshed
what it will return is a map showing all the places, under ideal conditions, that could be seen from that point.[9] The tool is fine if you
are using it for what it was designed for, like working out where to
build a house so that you get the best views. But there are a bunch
of commonsense problems with viewshed that archaeologists have
struggled with.[10]

If you press the viewshed button in a GIS you are making a number of assumptions. I am not the first to point them out; archaeologists are well aware of them. Here is a short list: you assume you know the height of the viewer, leaving out everyone not that exact height and anyone sitting down; you assume everyone has the same capacity for sight, leaving out many people who do not see well at certain distances or do not see at all; you assume that topography is the main thing that will block views, leaving out nontopographic things such as trees or buildings or fog; you assume that sight is binary (seen or hidden), and fail to distinguish between something close up and something far; and you assume your viewer is stationary, failing to account for the fact that as we move around our views change on a moment to moment basis.

Christopher Tilley, who you will remember from Stonehenge, goes so far as to reject digital reconstructions of what people experienced in the past, like push-button viewshed studies, as doomed from the start. He prefers the more hands-on approach of visiting places. That way he has got not just his sight but all his senses with him to evaluate each place.

Mark Gillings, archaeologist at the University of Leicester, takes Tilley's objections seriously but instead suggests a number of possible solutions, including shifting away from a narrow application of viewshed to a broader study of perceiving the world around us. Drawing on work by psychologist James J. Gibson, he argues that there are properties of the environment around us that shape the way that we, and other animals, see and travel around a given location.

Gillings did an intense study of the landscape around five small stone features in Cornwall. Archaeologists had suggested that these mini-megaliths, if you will, were built specifically in places that were naturally hidden from view (Gillings 2015). To capture how places were more, or less, naturally visible, Gillings ran over 150,000 viewshed calculations, taking more than one thousand hours of computer processing time. As it turns out the features "are neither visually prominent or show any evidence of being concealed, hidden, or deliberately tucked out of view" (13). Gillings (2017) has also highlighted topographic features common to the area, like the shoulders along natural drainages, and how they have special properties for how we perceive the world. His work illustrates the real technical barriers to doing these sorts of analyses in terms of the size of the area studied and the number of different iterations one can reasonably do.

Steve Wernke and his colleagues at Vanderbilt University have used advances in field recording and spatial analyses to examine how people experienced a town created by forced relocations in the Andes during the 1570s (Wernke, Kohut, and Traslaviña 2017) (see figure 21). The Spanish colonial government was clear about their goals when they created new towns for more than a million indigenous people. We have a great deal less information about what life was like in these towns and how they related to previous settlements in the same locations.

The colonial-era town of Mawchu Llacta, located high in the Andes, was fairly modest, about eleven hectares, with a population of about one thousand people in the early 1600s. It was abandoned in the 1840s, and today this ghost town is perfect for aerial survey since the outlines of buildings and streets are clearly visible. Wernke and his team tried out a number of different methods—including drones and a weather balloon—and after some trial and

FIGURE 21. Simulated life in a small colonial town. In this GIS study of movement, two hundred thousand simulated walks between buildings were used to replicate what it would have been like to travel around a small town in Peru in the 1600s. Thicker lines show heavier pedestrian traffic. Source: Wernke, Kohut, and Traslaviña (2017).

error were able to create a photorealistic 3-D model at high resolution, each pixel representing four centimeters on the ground.

The subsequent archaeological map is equally high resolution, with the footprints of 479 buildings, including a main church and fourteen chapels, plazas, and streets. Field checking of the results confirmed details like where doorways were placed and the likely height of buildings based on what remains of their walls. The production of this detailed a map was a feat, but it was not the goal: it was the first step.

The first time I saw what Wernke and his team had done with their super-detailed map I was reminded of Henry David Thoreau's *Walden*. Thoreau flips the travel novel around in *Walden* and gives the reader a deep read on the place where he lives, exemplified by the line, "I have traveled a good deal in Concord." Using the town's layout, the team modeled 196,806 different routes between the doorways of buildings and other destinations. From that they were able to create a kind of foot-traffic report; its hot spots are places where people were more likely to be as they traveled around the town. Next, they made a map of what buildings and spaces travelers could see from those densely traveled places. Within the city, perhaps not surprisingly given the history of the town, what people saw were areas that had religious architecture.

Something that makes this study different from other studies of motion or vision alone is that instead of using landform and location to assert what kinds of experiences people could or could not have had, this study worked more like a computer simulation, aiming to expose the underlying social engineering that went into town planning.

Another favorite target for viewshed studies are fortifications. They are perfect in that they are fixed on the landscape and we assume that the ability to perceive threats will have been a big part of the process of deciding where to build them. But, not all forts are the same. And so, when archaeologists find abandoned forts we have to stop and ask ourselves what strategies are evident and what factors may account for why fortifications were built in that place and in that form.

Andrew Martindale and Kisha Supernant devised a way to assess how naturally defensible locations would have been (Martindale and Supernant 2009). They looked at things like how much of the area immediately around a fortification could be viewed and what directions would have been viable approaches for an attacking force. Their results are encouraging but they also ran into the same problems as other viewshed and site location studies: you can have different defensibility scores depending upon where you are within a single location.

Moving away from fortifications, Elaine Sullivan, an archaeologist at the University of California, Santa Cruz, has shown how sensitivity to the intentions of architects can produce remarkable results. Her study of Karnak, a monument complex near the Egyptian city of Memphis, used 3-D reconstructions of structures to investigate aspects of visibility like shape and perspective (Sullivan 2017, 1228). It took a lot of effort, moving data between different software platforms, but in the end she created an immersive reconstruction of what Karnak looked like when viewed from the city of Memphis. As it turns out, architects in the later periods built pyramids close to the city at locations that would block the view of older pyramids, despite these older ones being a great deal larger.

Eleftheria Paliou, professor of archaeoinformatics at the University of Cologne, and her colleagues have taken viewshed calculation and applied it inside buildings from the Late Bronze Age (Paliou, Wheatley, Earl 2011). Like the better-known site of Pompeii, Akrotiri, on the Greek island of Santorini, was buried by a volcanic eruption, making it possible to recover the interior layout of buildings and some of the murals painted in them. For one room, Paliou and her colleagues created a density map of one wall mural that corresponded to how many times it could be seen from different places in the room.[11] Parts that were often obscured by the room's layout would have only have been visible in a handful of places, whereas others were visible from nearly everywhere. They also projected this assessment in reverse, showing which places in the room were best to see the entire composition of the mural.

Efforts to make a more authentic assessment of how people may have experienced different places have led to efforts to assess other senses, including sound, taste, and smell. Sound is the most developed of these, and its study has picked up the moniker "archaeoacoustics," which to me sounds like it would make a great band name for a folk trio.

Sound is something you can model in geographic space, given a certain set of assumptions and a 3-D model of the area of interest. For example, Kristy Primeau of State University of New York, Albany and David E. Witt of State University of New York, Buffalo took a tool developed for modeling the potential impacts of human noise on wildlife—something that is important if you are trying to work out where a noisy factory may be the least disruptive—and used it to make a kind of sound map of Chaco Canyon (Primeau and Witt 2018). They knew that the great houses were the center of ceremonies that included playing a shell trumpet, something that a nearby hearing person could not avoid perceiving, but what remained unclear was how much of the surrounding area could also perceive it above the ambient sounds of the world around them. As it turns out, if you blow a shell trumpet, people all over Chaco Canyon will hear it.

Sight or sound is one thing, but taste, how are we to get back to that? One group has made an effort to reconstruct taste by creating maps of what they call flavorscapes (Livarda and Orengo 2015). They started with a great deal of data from excavations around

London dating back to the early and late Roman periods, when the city was called Londinium. Over this time we start to see evidence for more than fifty new plant foods from outside the British Isles, mostly fruits, but also herbs and veggies. Places that naturally sit at central locations around the city, perhaps unsurprisingly, show a greater diversity of these exotic plants, which would have been rare in their time. The study then interprets changes in this flavorscape over time as they relate to the broader Roman economy.

But what about smell? Can we really smell the past? And if we could, would we really want to? The augmented reality and maker worlds say, "Challenge accepted." Stuart Eve of University College London began by building an app that would allow you to see a site reconstruction overlaid on the view from a tablet's camera, but then moved on to try to do the same for how places might have smelled in the past. The prototype smelly box emits a preprogrammed odor based on where you are on a site. Where do these odors come from you might ask? It turns out there is a company called Aroma Prime (formerly Dale Air) that will sell you any of three hundred aromas, named things like Barbeque, Dirty Linen, or Farmyard. Do you want to smell Bronze Age sheep? I expect some of you will say, "Why not," and others, "No, thank you." Regardless of your answer, we have the technology.

. . .

What started as small glimpses of ancient societies, hard won from years of survey, excavation, and analyses, has today grown into rich biographies of different times and places, in part thanks to geospatial technologies. Ancient cities have revealed themselves as settings for creativity in political organization and, to a degree, as natural experiments in environmental sustainability. Archaeologists have accumulated lessons about how to create a more and more authentic version of how people experienced the past by working with GIS tools like viewshed, and by expanding that work to include all of our senses. As I said at the start of the chapter, if you are skeptical about some of these interpretations, you are in good company. But, it would be a mistake to dismiss these types of studies out of hand as inherently beyond the limits of archaeology. Down that road lies a dehumanized past.

In the final chapter of this book I want to return to where we started: historical curiosity. By now you have a good idea of what geospatial technologies can do, and of the ways we have used them to retrace how people moved, how they fed themselves, and what it might have been like to live at their times and in their societies. But, the benefits of this technology have not been felt evenly, and there remain times and places that are featured more than others. The next natural question is: How can we use these technologies to expand our historic curiosity?

Conclusion

9 *Archaeology as Time Machine*

For more than a century, fictional time travel stories have teased us with the possibility of going back to the distant past. Research in physics, partially inspired by those stories, tells us it is theoretically possible. Stephen Hawking famously tried to determine if we would ever invent a working time machine by throwing a party for time travelers. As an experiment he withheld the invitation with the date and location until after the event. No future time travelers showed up to his party. Not a great result for anyone holding out hope for the invention of time travel.

Archaeology is as close as we are going to get to visiting the past. It may not literally transport us there, but it is an excellent way to guide our natural inclination to be curious, even to speculate, about an authentic picture of the ancient world. But, sadly, we are underusing our time machine. When I was doing research for this book I found thousands of great examples of archaeologists applying geospatial technologies around the world. Indeed, one of my primary motivations for writing this book was to try and get across how we were creating and interpreting all these new data. However, as I read more and more, it became painfully clear that just a few time periods and places have received most of that attention. This was not particularly problematic twenty years ago when geospatial technology occupied a small, high-tech niche in archaeology. But after the geospatial revolution, attention is important for a number of reasons, specifically because these technologies are fundamental to archaeology, and because the data they produce do not speak for themselves.

Why has our attention been so uneven? Some regions and time periods have had a head start in the sense that they attracted research by early adopters of geospatial technologies. But to me, this is an open question, and is likely answered differently for different places. What we can be more definitive about is what the knock-on effect is: historical silences. Anthropologist Michel-Rolph Trouillot (1995) defined "historical silences" as times, places, and events that are omitted, ignored, and denied because they do not fit orthodox historical narratives. In other words, gaps in the story. Archaeologists have the duel responsibility of creating the digital archive of life before the time of writing and of interpreting it. That makes it easy for us to create unintentional gaps in our narratives, and when we do, who would even notice them with the current flood of data produced?

I believe it is possible to leverage this technology to create a better retelling of the past, not just for a few places, but for everywhere. At this point I have talked a lot about what technology can do and how it has benefited archaeology. In this chapter, I want to talk about three facts that I want everyone know. Three facts that put us in a much better position to take advantage of archaeology as a time machine.

. . .

Before I get to those three important facts I want to spend just a little time talking about what it means to archaeologists when we say that we do not know something. The philosopher of science Alison Wylie of the University of British Columbia wrote a great essay on how archaeologists deal, or do not deal, with ignorance. In it she points out that ignorance is a "matter of uncertainty and incompleteness" (Wylie 2008, 183). Entropy guarantees incompleteness, and, if we presume that the human story is complex, then with complexity comes uncertainty. Given that both incompleteness and uncertainty are baked-in features of archaeology, what does that mean in terms of the application of geospatial technologies?

Having an incomplete body of evidence is not unique to archaeology, but can be taken in slightly different ways depending on if we are emphasizing the science or the humanities side of archaeology.[1] Incomplete geospatial data, for example, could mean there are known locational data that are not included (i.e., missing data) or it could refer to a reconstruction that is somehow narrowly conceived (i.e., missing perspectives). I expect if you polled archaeologists you would find more agreement than not on what is meant by incomplete, in part because so much of what we do is based on good locational data and information. We all want to know where something was found, how old it is, and how it might have gotten to where it was found. So, to put it in as simple terms as possible, incompleteness generally means blank spots on the map.

Uncertainty is not unique to archaeology and, again, it can mean slightly different things (Brouwer Burg 2017). For example, uncertainty in a GIS database could mean that locational data are fuzzy (i.e., locations not known with strong precision or accuracy) or it could refer to some other ambiguity, like not knowing exactly how variables were defined. Here again, so much of what we do is based on good locational data and information, that I expect there is more agreement than not among archaeologists over what is meant by uncertainty. To put that more simply, uncertainty, for our purposes, means not knowing the quality of the map.

There is one more additional factor that contributes to ignorance. It is incredibly rare that a map reflects everything we have learned that is relevant to archaeology in that particular place. That might sound like a trivial problem. After all, my smartphone app updates its map automatically. But there are barriers to creating an archaeological map that is up to date, such as the need to keep locations hidden from those who would mistreat, intentionally or unintentionally, what is found there. The most up-to-date information can also be missing from our maps due to a need for more technical expertise, or a need to include local knowledge held by the community who lives there. The problem of up-to-dateness is not quite a problem of incompleteness, because the skills and knowledge are out there, and not quite a problem of uncertainty: it is a wicked problem. It is not wicked like the Wicked Witch of the West, but it is so inherently difficult, persistent, and complex that it is intractable.

To be clear, these are not unsolvable difficulties, but they are universal, which means we are going to have to tackle them if we want to see the benefits of the geospatial revolution expand and fill in the gaps created when we focus our attention on just a few times and places.

. . .

Fact #1. *Archaeology is precious but it is not rare.* Archaeology is precious because it has survived entropy and it is our link to the past. But in the United States alone, there are millions and millions of places where archaeology has been recorded and more locations with intact artifacts, deposits, and features are being recorded every day. The reason they are so common is not hard to understand. People in the past did not live their lives glued to one spot the size of an archaeological excavation. They moved around the landscape, modifying it for their purposes, and so it makes sense that we find things everywhere.[2]

There are no empty places. Geospatial technology is helping us demonstrate this by defeating the things that make archaeology appear much rarer than it really is. The Maya, for example, were like other early urban societies in that they had to solve the logistical problem of feeding a dense population.[3] But for a long time we have lacked basic information on the location and layout of farms abandoned long ago because today they are under a thick tree canopy. The latest airborne lidar survey of the Maya region yielded over sixty-one thousand features, of which many, if not most, are evidence of agriculture (Canuto et al. 2018). In mere days, we had the raw data necessary to create field-survey quality maps over a total area equal to New York City. That would have taken decades, if not lifetimes, on foot.[4]

Geospatial technology is also helping get across the astounding scale of the debris left behind from previous eras. Out in a rural part of Syria called the Upper Khabur Basin, satellite imagery has been used to map settlements, like the tell of Hamoukar (Menze and Ur 2012) (see figure 7 in chapter 3). Over an area the size of New Hampshire are fourteen thousand villages, towns, and cities, some of which go back to the Bronze Age. In order to really appreciate how much archaeology that represents, the team who mapped these settlements also estimated the cumulative volume of "collapsed architecture and other settlement debris." The final measurement: seven hundred million cubic meters. That is almost three hundred times more than the volume of the largest Egyptian pyramid, and likely a greater volume than all of Egypt's pyramids put together.

Detecting, mapping, cataloging: these are tasks that play to the strength of the sciences. We are not, however, purely analytical creatures. We want to connect to the past and technology allows us to access and experience the physical record of it like never before. We have the capacity to create realistic 3-D models, through terrestrial laser scanning and photogrammetry, not only of individual buildings but also of major ancient cities. Hiking through ruins is no longer a pastime limited to nineteenth-century antiquarians or wealthy tourists. With a few clicks anyone with a strong Internet connection can be in the middle of the Maya city of Copan.[5]

The sheer number of 3-D models online today is perhaps the ultimate demonstration that archaeology is not rare. CyArk and others have made realistic images of so many different places it would take a long, long time to visit them all through a web browser or explore them via virtual reality. There are, however, a few dangers that are worth mentioning. One is that a scan is just that, a scan. It is not the same thing as the site itself. I say that because having scanned something does not mean we have saved the site itself; we have just made a copy of what we can see. There is always more below, and just beyond, the edges of the 3-D model. Other issues that have been raised include the question of how we should store and display all these virtual copies. And who owns them?[6] As we scale up to millions of these models it will become more and more important to keep these issues in mind.

Though it is difficult to predict exactly where the virtual and augmented reality worlds will take us, one promising direction is digital storytelling (Earley-Spadoni 2017). Virtual Rosewood, for example, is a project centered on retelling the story of a small town in Florida that was abandoned in 1923 following a racist massacre by a white mob (González-Tennant 2018).[7] Edward Gonzalez-Tennant of the University of Central Florida collected stories from survivors and other historical information and created an immersive virtual version of the town as it was in the 1920s. Virtual Rosewood is notable for a number of technical achievements, including the application of GIS to integrate qualitative information, and is a good model of what it looks like when we scale up geospatial technologies to look at places and times that have otherwise been overlooked.

Building a time machine is not free. All the time and effort spent—and technology used—in reconstructing the past costs money. Some efforts rely on philanthropy, but philanthropy alone is not how we are going to take full advantage of our time machine. That is going to take public funding. I know this because the public paid for much of the research that I have described in this book. In the United States, blue-sky research in archaeology is supported through institutions like the National Science Foundation and the National Endowment for the Humanities. On top of that, government archaeologists, in one way or another, do most of the day-to-day care for archaeology in the United States. They enforce regulations and professional standards and protect and interpret sites on government lands. When our governments fail to keep these kinds of institutions fully funded and open for business, we all lose. Sites do not take care of themselves, and there are lots and lots to take care of.

. . .

Fact #2. *Learning about the past requires teamwork.* This one seems obvious. But I worry that the image of archaeologist-as-treasure-hunter has created the additional problem of giving the impression that archaeology is somehow accomplished by single individuals. Nothing could be further from the truth. We need to work in teams that include not only other archaeologists but also experts in other disciplines, technologies, and forms of local knowledge, if we want to create an authentic picture of the ancient world.

One practical reason for this is the diversity of scholarship that is involved in deciphering archaeology. To return to an example from my own work, in a previous chapter I talked about how my colleagues and I matched volcanic glass artifacts back to their natural source, a single, small hill in the Hawaiian Islands (McCoy et al. 2011). That finding required geology and geochemistry. Next, we estimated about how long it would have taken to hike between where the artifacts were found and the source. That told us that people working volcanic glass within a single day's walk of the hill appear to have been able to access it directly. They likely passed some of that glass to their neighbors further away. In addition to archaeology, that deduction required geography and geographic information science. As best as we can tell, the fact that glass was being shared this way is evidence for the existence of resource rights and social networks that cut across known community boundaries, something which, to that point, had not been well documented. Now we were delving into politics, sociology, and economics. In the context of Hawaiian society, as it was known at the time of contact with Europeans, these networks may have been important in times of food shortfalls and for the sustainable management of the land. That suggestion required knowing the local ecology and ethnohistory.[8] This is what it takes to tell just one evidence-based story about the past.

The incorporation of expertise in geospatial technology in our teams can be tricky. One of the things that is great about GIS is that it can be useful even if you only use it casually. But there is a worry that it is so powerful that in the hands of the casual user it can produce results that mask uncertainty, error, and bias (Brouwer Burg 2017). Not everyone has the time or inclination to become an expert, and there are currently a relatively small number of people with the requisite background to be called experts in geospatial archaeology. So what can we do?

One option is to train more experts, or "power users," who can "straddle archaeology and GIS science, critically engaging in the theoretical and methodological aspects of GIS," and do "research on best applications in archaeology" (Brouwer Burg 2017, 119). Or to put that another way, the barriers to learning how to best use technology could be broken down faster if we had more people directly working on the problem of breaking down those barriers. Another option that is often raised is the potential for experts to engage with the public in mapping tasks that are exciting and can be made accessible (Duckers 2013). There is no one perfect solution, and it will probably take a combination of both and more.

Expertise in local knowledge relevant for interpreting archaeology is slowly becoming a more regular part of our teams.[9] Archaeology in general has gotten better at collaborating with the communities where we work over the past twenty years. It also helps that if archaeologists took a class picture every year, you would see us, in the most recent pictures, looking less and less like a club exclusively for white guys with beards. Over this same time, indigenous scholars have taken up GIS as a technology that meets a number of pressing needs. But as Kisha Supernant has pointed out, these parallel trends have not naturally produced spatial analyses that "account for the knowledge systems in the places where we work" (2017, 71). In other words, when archaeology and local knowledge fail to connect, the results are missed opportunities to expand what we know about the past.[10] Supernant's work on the history of the Métis is illustrative.

The Métis are a group that formed in the nineteenth century following the intermarriage of Native Americans and European settlers in Canada and the northern United States. What made them Métis, their identity, was wrapped up in how they "connected to the landscape, built complex webs of kinship, and had a lifeway that was both mobile and anchored to places on the landscape" (Supernant 2017, 65). When you try to recreate the historically recorded trails used by Métis with the least cost path function, the predicated paths almost never match up to the trails. To understand why requires thinking about seasonality, where people would have overwintered with kin, the relative importance of different places, the types of transport people used, and more—all elements that are not captured in a basic GIS spatial analysis.

Teams with different experiences and expertise are better suited to weighing independent lines of evidence and keeping each other honest. Thus, teamwork helps ensure a more authentic picture of the past because it is through teamwork that we decide between competing versions of what happened and win the fight with equifinality. Again, this seems obvious. But there are always some who will try to reconstruct the entirety of human history from single line of evidence, like genetics. That is no way to build a time machine.

. . .

Fact #3. *We hide from the public much of what we have discovered.* I wish this were not true, but it is. We are hiding things from the public. The ubiquity of GPS and accessible satellite imagery has made the job of archaeologist so much easier. But these technologies are a double-edged sword. They also make it easier than ever before for looters and vandals, and make it harder to manage site visitation. That means archaeologists have to use discretion about locations where we have found things. This genuinely makes it hard for us to advocate for the protection of archaeology.

To be clear, there are many places where we do not keep site locations hidden because they are already public knowledge. That is bad news for sites like Palmyra in Syria, which was captured by Islamic State (ISIS) fighters and severely damaged. Some groups make the location, and condition, of sites even better known as a part of a strategy to protect archaeology. The Endangered Archaeology in the Middle East and North Africa (EAMENA) project is a great example. EAMENA, as its website states, "uses satellite imagery to rapidly record and make available information about archaeological sites and landscapes which are under threat." It covers a massive region with more than 150,000 places where archaeology has been reported. Their website gives detailed case studies on how modern agriculture can damage archaeology, how modern construction can isolate archeological ruins in urban settings, and how large infrastructure projects, like dams and pipelines, can impact the integrity of entire landscapes.

In contrast, there are places in the United States and elsewhere where most site locations are not well known. In those cases it is sensible to keep locations secret to prevent criminal behavior, like looting or vandalism, and bad behavior, like tourists oblivious to how their visit might be damaging archaeology. We keep all this sensitive information in a guarded map vault the size of a football field at an undisclosed location high in the Rocky Mountains. I am kidding. That would be an improvement. In reality, all archaeologists and institutions that have locational data are left to deal with it in their own ways.[11] The lack of centralization, with the exception of recent digital repositories (e.g., tDAR) and site indices (e.g., DINAA), means we have an untold amount of locational data and information stored on researchers' hard drives. That secrecy makes it impossible to say what impacts development has had on archaeology. Take for example the Dakota Access Pipeline.[12]

The 1,886-kilometer Dakota Access Pipeline was built to take oil from North Dakota to processing plants in Illinois. Its construction brought intense protests in the tribal territory of the Standing Rock Sioux because of the pipeline's effects on water quality and impact on sacred cultural sites. Maps were part of the protest, an effort called counter-mapping, with some showing the route of the pipeline with Lakota/Dakota place names. But none of these maps showed the locations of archaeological sites along the pipeline, either at Standing Rock or elsewhere along the route (see Colwell 2016). Was that because no sites were found within, or near, the pipeline's corridor? That seems unlikely given it is almost half the length of Route 66. The real reason no sites were shown has to do with a rather complicated set of circumstances that are not at all unique to this pipeline.

Even today, years after the Standing Rock protests, it is not clear to the public which or how many sites were impacted along the pipeline. There are at least three groups of people who do know but, for different reasons, are not saying or cannot say: the pipeline's developers, contract archaeologists they hired, and government archaeologists with responsibility for regulatory oversight in their portion of the corridor. The pipeline's developers were obliged to pay for contract archaeology along the route. The contractors reported what they found to their client and the relevant state and federal agencies. The developers are not obliged to make site locational information public and the archaeologists they hired are bound by the terms of the contract they have with their client. Government agencies collected that information in their regulatory oversight role, and over the long term, are responsible for using it to help make sensible decisions about how to preserve cultural heritage in their area. They will not share it publicly, for legal reasons and out of an abundance of caution. This is why it is nearly impossible to know what exactly happened on any cultural resource management project unless you were in some way involved.[13]

The shroud of secrecy that archaeologists working in cultural resource management must deal with on a daily basis is one of the many reasons that digital repositories and indices, all of which have protocols in place to protect site location, are critically important. Without them, there will continue to be sites that are recorded for the first time on a contract archaeology project, then destroyed in the course of development, with the only records that they ever existed locked away where few will ever see them. To be honest, this is something that archaeologists will likely have to work out among ourselves. But there is something simple that anyone can do to help.

Archaeology is hard to avoid. In a way, the entire planet is one big site.[14] That means the chances are good that you will at some point find yourself at an archaeological site, come in contact with artifacts, or at the least, see someone's pictures online of their visit to a site or of artifacts they have come across. Most people behave respectfully and responsibly and would never dream of purposefully damaging archaeology. They resist the urge to take artifacts home as souvenirs and would find a way to alert authorities if they saw criminal behavior. That good behavior is necessary for the long-term care of our shared cultural heritage. A small additional thing that would help us save a lot more sites is to call out bad behavior. I recognize that "bad" is a subjective term, but think about this way: if you think the people who left behind those objects, and lived and died in those places, would object to what you are seeing, then find a way to call it out on their behalf.

. . .

I believe that a better retelling of the past is possible, and not just for a few places but for everywhere. We have a lot of work ahead. It pays to remember that the first decades of radiocarbon dating only gave us the broadest framing for retelling world history. It took many more years of research to get to where we are today. Just as radiocarbon is not appropriate for all time periods and places, not all the technologies described here will be universally useful. But everything is somewhere. That means there is lots of room to experiment, to build, to create, and to grow.

Now is the perfect time to rewire how people think about archaeology. To achieve that, I think we first need to abandon the adventure genre as the way archaeology is framed in our imagination. The time travel genre is a much better fit. It is about being curious about history. It is exploration tied to narrative, rather than to treasure. And it forces us to think about the relationship between the past and the present. It is time to say, "Goodbye, Dr. Jones. Hello, Doctor Who."

Glossary

ARTIFACT Any object that was created or modified by people in the past.

AUGMENTED REALITY "An enhanced version of reality created by the use of technology to overlay digital information on an image of something being viewed through a device (such as a smartphone camera)" (merriam-webster.com).

CROP MARK An unusual growth pattern in plants indicating the presence of buried archaeology.

DEM (DIGITAL ELEVATION MODEL) A GIS database representing elevation; typically a raster.

DRONE / UNPILOTED AERIAL VEHICLE (UAV) An aircraft with no onboard pilot that is directed by signals from a ground-based controller.

ELECTRONIC RESISTIVITY / ELECTRONIC CONDUCTIVITY Geophysical survey technique used to measure how resistive, or conductive, sediment is to electricity.

ENTROPY In archaeology, "a process of degradation . . . or a trend to disorder" (merriam-webster.com).

EQUIFINALITY "Having the same effect or result from different events" (merriam-webster.com).

FEATURE Discrete, often repeated, patterns of artifacts and/or deposits that suggest a particular set of activities. Features are not easily removed from where they are located; common examples include abandoned hearths, storage pits, and architectural elements (e.g., walls, terraces, etc.).

GEOSPATIAL REVOLUTION "Advances in the remote geospatial imaging of cultural landscapes, including ancient communities and their anthropogenic hinterlands" that are responsible for a "paradigm shift" (Kuhn 1962) in archaeology (Chase et al. 2012, 12916). The phrase was first used by Chase et al. (2012) in the context of lidar in Mesoamerica.

GEOSPATIAL TECHNOLOGY A "set of technological approaches, such as GIS, photogrammetry, and remote sensing, for acquiring and manipulating geographic data" (esri.com).

GIS (GEOGRAPHIC INFORMATION SYSTEMS) A type of software for viewing, querying, storing, and analyzing layers of geospatial data.

GNSS (GLOBAL NAVIGATION SATELLITE SYSTEM) The technical term for using satellites to determine geolocation. Satellite constellations currently in operation include the United States' GPS (Global Positioning System), the Russian GLONASS (Globalnaya Navigazionnaya Sputnikovaya Sistema), the European Space Agency's Galileo, China's BDS (Běidǒu Wèixīng Dǎoháng Xìtǒng), and India's Regional Navigation Satellite System (IRNSS).

GPR (GROUND PENETRATING RADAR) Geophysical survey technique that uses radar pulses to image under the ground.

GPS (GLOBAL POSITIONING SYSTEM) The vernacular term used to refer to satellite navigation. It originated with the United States' Global Positioning System satellite constellation, which began in 1978 and currently has 31 satellites in orbit. GPS require the user to be in the line of sight of a number of satellites so that position can be triangulated. The GPS receiver itself can be embedded within a device, such as a smartphone or a survey-grade GPS unit, or can stand alone and connect to another device, such as a tablet, that acts as data logger and display. External antennas are sometimes used to achieve better line-of-sight.

ICE AGE The planet has gone through a number of ice ages; the last one was the Pleistocene, a geological epoch from 2.59 million years ago to 12,000 years ago.

INTERPOLATION A method for deriving estimated values across an area based on sample data. GIS are capable of using a number of different interpolation techniques, like inverse distance weighting (IDW) and kernel density. The interpolation method used to create distribution surfaces is typically reported because without knowing what method was used it would be impossible to evaluate, or replicate, the study.

LEAST COST PATH The path of least resistance from one point to another as determined in a GIS. At the minimum, the user must enter a start location and end location, and provide a raster, typically a DEM, that will be used to rank the relative cost of movements. Other costs can be added and there are ways to customize the operation for different types of movement.

LIDAR A remote sensing technique in which laser measurements are used to create a three-dimensional point cloud representing the target. Lidar can operate in ground station surveys (terrestrial lidar), on aircraft (airborne lidar, or aerial laser scanning), as a vehicle-mounted or handheld device, or in laboratory settings. The term lidar is short for light detection and ranging.

MAGNETOMETRY Geophysical survey technique based on the measurement of magnetic fields.

MAXENT (MAXIMUM ENTROPY SOFTWARE) An open-sourced species distribution modeling program created by Steven J. Phillips, Miroslav Dudík, and Robert E. Schapire in a partnership between the American Museum of Natural History and AT&T Research.

NEOLITHIC REVOLUTION Term coined by V. Gordon Childe to describe the shift to agriculture following the domestication of plants and animals; it marks the beginning of the Neolithic Period, or New Stone Age. Its earliest signs appeared in the Middle East about twelve thousand years ago.

PHOTOGRAMMETRY A technique that dates back to the late 1800s, when it was defined as a method "of making reliable measurements by the use of photographs and especially aerial photographs (as in surveying)" (merriam-webster.com). Today, it is used to create a 3-D model out of 2-D images or video, based on reflected light; also known by the term "structure from motion."

POINT CLOUD A special category of point data, typically generated by lidar or photogrammetry, that can include millions or billions of locations (x, y, z) and can be displayed in 3-D.

RADAR RIVERS The nickname given to defunct Pleistocene river systems detected in the Sahara though the use of satellite-based radar imagery.

RADIOCARBON DATING A radiometric method of determining the date of death of an organism based on the known decay rate of carbon-14 and established methods of calibration relative to the carbon cycle.

RASTER A GIS data format that stores values in rows and columns of pixels at a fixed resolution.

SETTLEMENT PATTERN The spatial distribution of where people lived in the past; used to reconstruct ancient social networks, mobility, and other aspects of life.

SITE Any location where physical evidence of past activities, such as artifacts and/or features, has been recorded.

STONE AGE, BRONZE AGE, IRON AGE Also known as the "three age system," this concept divides the chronology of the Old World using advances in metallurgy.

VECTOR A GIS data format that stores data in a table tied to points, lines, or polygons.

VIRTUAL REALITY "An artificial environment which is experienced through sensory stimuli (such as sights and sounds) provided by a computer and in which one's actions partially determine what happens in the environment" (merriam-webster.com).

URBAN REVOLUTION Term coined by V. Gordon Childe to describe the shift to a premodern state society. It draws its name from the fact that in many cases, early states co-occur with the creation of a region's first cities. Its earliest signs appear in the Middle East in the Bronze Age, about six thousand years ago.

Notes

Chapter 1: Historical Curiosity

1. A note on dates: The dates given in this book for key changes in the history of humanity in the era before writing are approximations. New things are found all the time and archaeologists argue over dates a lot. For example, a recent study suggests the origins of art are much earlier than fifty thousand years ago (Henshilwood 2018). For a more comprehensive look at what happened in our history around the world, I recommend Robert L. Kelly's (2016) *The Fifth Beginning,* and Kent Flannery and Joyce Marcus's (2012) *The Creation of Inequality.*

2. Another note on dates: This is better known as the "three age system." We evolved during the last Ice Age, also known as the Pleistocene—a geological time period that started more than two million years ago and lasted until about twelve thousand years ago. During that time, archaic and then modern humans used stone for tools, and thus, it is called the Stone Age (in a few pages, we are going to divide up the Stone Age into three periods). In the Old World, the Stone Age continued until roughly five thousand years ago, when it gave way to the Bronze Age, followed by the Iron Age, which started two to three thousand years ago. The New World's timeline also goes back to the Pleistocene but is not tied to metallurgy.

3. Anthropology is the study of people. Archaeology is a subfield of anthropology devoted to the study of the human past through any physical material that can provide evidence of past activities.

4. The works of fiction mentioned in this book reflect my personal tastes. For an insightful and encyclopedic review of the time travel genre, I highly recommend James Gleick's (2016) *Time Travel: A History*.

5. For obvious reasons, my focus here is on time travel to the past, rather than to the future. For more on dystopian futures, nostalgia, and archaeology, see Bodil Petersson's (2016) discussion of *Waterworld* and a broad-ranging review by Dawid Kobialka (2016) that covers everything from *The Matrix* (1999) to the DC Comics character Hawkman.

6. I have singled out *Doctor Who*, but the same can be said for many popular time travel television and film franchises, such as *Star Trek, Back to the Future,* and *Terminator,* to name a few.

7. Some of you will remember Harrison Ford's Professor Jones recommending Childe to a student in *Kingdom of the Crystal Skull* or scrawling the word "Neolithic" across the chalkboard in *Raiders of the Lost Ark*.

8. Last note on dates: The Stone Age can be broken up into three periods: the Old Stone Age (Paleolithic), the Middle Stone Age (Mesolithic), and the New Stone Age (Neolithic), which begins at the end of the last Ice Age about twelve thousand years ago. So, to recap, if you are in the Old World, the chronology goes Paleolithic, Mesolithic, Neolithic, Bronze Age, then Iron Age.

9. Today, many archaeologists, myself included, try to limit our use of the terms "prehistory" and "prehistoric" for a couple of reasons. These terms can be applied to time periods long before humans evolved, which are irrelevant for archaeology. They also can carry the unintentional connotation of primitiveness when talking about people who had the same cognitive capacity as we do today.

10. Censorship is another problem. China's State Administration for Radio, Film and Television banned time travel on television in 2011, saying it didn't pay the proper respect to history.

11. Time travel on television does not have a great record on diversity. For example, there are few women. However, there are more women in lead roles than there used to be, the most high-profile of whom is Jodie Whittaker as the thirteen incarnation of The Doctor. Other recent time travel shows with great female leads include *Ashes to Ashes, Continuum, El Ministerio del Tiempo (The Ministry of Time), Future Man, Making History, Outlander, Timeless, Travelers,* and *Warehouse 13*.

Fans of *Doctor Who* would want me to note that over the years the series has had scores of recurring female characters, including, perhaps most relevant for this book, the time-traveling archaeologist River Song, wonderfully played by Alexandra Kingston. River Song, while an excellent character, disappointingly follows in the archaeologist-as-treasure-hunter mold. On the plus side, she did prompt The Doctor, then played by David Tennant, to say, "I'm a time traveler. I point and laugh at archaeologists."

12. Octavia Butler's (1979) novel *Kindred* is another good example of a story centered on a time traveler who must confront the antebellum period. For a comic take, I recommend the sketch on *Chappelle's Show* (Season 2, Episode 23) called "The Time Haters."

13. The term "site" has been used to refer to a location where archaeology has been recorded for as long as archaeology has existed. But it is problematic for a number of reasons that I will discuss in the next chapter. Nonetheless, it has been codified in law designed to protect archaeology, and so the term endures despite its well-known deficiencies as a scientific unit of observation.

14. There is a time travel romantic comedy called *Chronesthesia* (2016) by writer/director Hayden J. Weal. Weal plays the lead character, a barista who gets messages from the future. His previous credits include playing the body double for Bilbo in Peter Jackson's *Hobbit* trilogy.

Chapter 2: Finding Things Out

1. The dictionary definition of ethnography is "the study and systematic recording of human cultures" (merriam-webster.com). More plainly, it is when an anthropologist goes out and talks to people with the goal of better defining a culture.

2. To be clear, I did not invent the two-boxes explanation of entropy.

3. To make sense of how location relates to time, archaeologists have devised a schematic timeline called a Harris matrix (Harris 1979). Whenever I see a Harris matrix I am reminded of the great time travel novel by Kurt Vonnegut (1969), *Slaughterhouse-Five,* in which the author describes using his daughter's crayons to draw a timeline of the story's intersecting character arcs.

4. It can be impossible to reconcile previous field observations especially if all that is given is a general description of the location, as opposed to exact coordinates. For example, there could be five references to a stone monument in a certain place because there are five separate monuments, or because the same one was observed on five different visits, or something in between those

scenarios (Cooper and Green 2015). This is why in databases, ideally speaking, we assign a unique identification number to all observations, excavations, and artifacts from a given location.

5. It has been pointed out to me that this is not unlike how in biology a great deal of excellent research gets done despite a complete lack of agreement about what a species is.

6. I can still remember being drawn in by the artist's reconstruction of King Tut's gilded tomb when I was a kid. Seeing his final resting place, the Western obsession with all things ancient Egyptian seemed completely natural, even if it is weird and macabre.

7. At last count there are about eighty-one thousand archaeological site records housed at the Texas Archaeological Research Laboratory (TARL) and more are being reported every day.

8. GPS gives us geolocation, a location on the Earth, whereas a total station works on an arbitrary grid system (x, y, z), although some total stations now connect to GPS.

9. Michael F. Goodchild, an emeritus professor of geography from the University of California, Santa Barbara, has pointed out that you will often see decimal degrees reported to a ridiculous level of precision. So, for example, if you see a location reported down to eight decimal places, that final decimal place is giving you location to the millimeter. Unless that data was produced by super high-end survey equipment, that kind of precision is not justifiable.

10. There is also a mash-up field that combines computer science and geography, called geographic information science (GIS Science, or GIScience, or GISc).

11. Google Maps has a distinctly different function than Google Earth. Google Maps is a web-based GIS; it is all about organizing information geographically. Google Earth is a virtual globe; it is all about exploring a lifelike model of our planet.

12. There are some notable exceptions. The compelling, but at times confusing, movie *Primer* has the traveler move slowly backwards through time by means of a stationary box. In *Time Trap*, students get trapped inside a cave while searching for their lost archaeology professor and all the while time whizzes by outside. Austin Powers and others have been frozen and thawed out in the modern day, or brought back to life. And let's not forget that J. K. Rowling's

Harry Potter series features magical Time Turner necklaces that move the wearer through time but not space.

13. One additional possibility that was raised at the time was that the coin could have been a kind of hitchhiker. The scenario goes like this: The coin was carried to Roman Britain long ago and ended up in the River Thames. Then in the 1800s it got scooped up with gravels from the Thames that were used for ballast to balance a ship that was docked in London. When that ship dumped out its ballast upon arrival in New Zealand, the coin was redeposited.

14. Rachel Opitz of the University of Glasgow and W. Fred Limp of the University of Arkansas have called attention to how the ways that archaeologists think about things like form, shape, space, and place are changing due to the adoption of technologies which allow for high-density survey and measurement (HDSM). HDSM includes geospatial technologies as well as applications in nongeographic space, such as laser scanning artifacts to create 3-D models. They further make the case that these technologies "provide multiple bridges between scientific and humanistic ways of understanding the past" (Opitz and Limp 2015, 358).

15. The Maya rarely feature in time travel television. A notable exception is an episode of *El Ministerio del Tiempo (The Ministry of Time)* called "*Tiempo de Conquista*" (Time of Conquest) where the team goes back to Yucatán in 1516.

16. This is a bit of an unfair comparison since the theme park is only a fairly small part of Disney World's property, much of which remains undeveloped. By contrast, Stonehenge's surroundings, as we will see, are covered by archaeology.

Chapter 3: Views from Above

1. Today, we put the people who lived in Viru Valley in an exclusive club of societies that are so much like our own that we call them "archaic states," meaning they were ruled by a monarch who controlled a substantial territory. Most early states were founded as a result of copying their neighbors or being invaded. What makes Viru special is that it represents an independent invention of a state society, something that may have occurred as few as seven times.

2. It should be said that while crop marks often make beautiful patterns, they were not originally built to be seen from above; they are simply clues to

where we will find buried archaeology. Also, crop marks are not the same as so-called crop circles, the designs that modern people make in fields and erroneously attribute to aliens.

3. The summer of 2018 was an especially dry one and crop marks not usually visible started popping up all over the United Kingdom, only to disappear again not long after.

4. In the original study these are called moated sites.

5. Years ago, I requested an air photo finding aid for Honolulu and was surprised when the archivist came back with a composite of old black-and-white photos taped together with the words TOP SECRET stamped all over them. It turned out these pictures were taken in 1941 just prior to the bombing of Pearl Harbor. You could clearly make out the US fleet in dock, including the famous USS *Arizona*, completely intact. This was the first time I had requested these photos but they seemed strangely familiar to me, and then I remembered where I had seen them: the time travel movie *The Final Countdown* (1980). It's not one of the genre's most sophisticated stories but gets originality points for sending an entire aircraft carrier back in time.

6. Today, archaeologists use more than air photos in Flanders. Recent work includes some impressive remote sensing by airborne lidar of Spanish fortifications that are so realistic one can imagine the sixteenth-century character Alonso de Entrerríos on the TV show *El Ministerio del Tiempo*, played by Nacho Fresneda, shouting from the defenses, *"Por Santiago y por España!"*

7. For an interesting review of the history of mapping in Britain, see Wickstead (2019).

8. Hasselblad is a Swedish company best known for their high-quality medium format cameras. Mike Myers's time traveling character Austin Powers uses a Hasselblad on a fashion shoot in *Austin Powers: The Spy Who Shagged Me*. Elvis Costello fans will know it as the camera from the cover of the album *The Year's Model* (1978).

9. These film drops were usually somewhere over the Pacific Ocean so that if the midair retrieval failed the film would be fished out of the Pacific by the US Navy. If for some reason that failed, the cardboard box was designed to degrade over time and sink before being intercepted by the enemy.

10. They don't call it the "Great" Wall for nothing. At nearly nine thousand kilometers long, if it were stretched out it would be greater than the distance

between London and Beijing. On the ground, over a quarter of it is not actually wall but trenches and natural barriers.

11. If you want to go on your own hunt through declassified satellite images, you can get them all from the United States Geological Survey (USGS). The USGS maintains a catalog of satellite images, and lots of the other kinds datasets, online at EarthExplorer.

12. If you have every tried on a pair of night-vision goggles, you have come in contact with sensors that use infrared reflected energy in the absence of visible light. The next generation of night-vision sensors will combine infrared with other spectra.

13. Working with remote sensing data requires knowing what spectral resolution is represented; thus you see terms like panchromatic (meaning all visible light is represented), multispectral (meaning energy from across the electromagnetic spectrum), and hyperspectral (meaning energy from across the electromagnetic spectrum, but cut into many more, finer bands).

14. NASA can send data faster than anyone. Back in the 1970s Landsat satellites were initially sending data back to Earth at 15 megabits per second (Mbps)—that is, in the range of current broadband Internet. By the 1980s and early 1990s they were ticking along at a blazing 85 Mbps and the current satellite sends data at 384 Mbps, many times faster than current home Internet in the US.

15. To put that resolution in terms that are easier to visualize: at first, something the size of a grocery store would have been represented by two pixels in images; that was improved to four pixels. Better but not great.

Chapter 4: Scans of the Planet

1. Laser is an acronym for "light amplification by stimulated emission of radiation."

2. Nearly twenty years ago, the Caracol Time Travel Project (Hughes et al. 2001), anticipated the idea of 3-D immersive experiences as virtual time travel in their "virtual drama."

3. It is one of the sites in Bove's map of the Maya collapse; its last inscription was in AD 849.

4. The team could not just take off and start shooting. It takes time to maneuver into position. In fact, to get the plane in position took about twice as much time as it took to fly the grid lines.

5. When viewing these 3-D models, keep in mind there is always more archaeology beyond the edges of what you can see in a scan, as well as more below the ground.

6. Drone technology and its application in archaeology is evolving rapidly, too rapidly for me to fully capture it here, so I am giving only a broad outline of what they can do and what we are using them for today. I should also note that many prefer the terms unmanned aerial vehicles, or unmanned aircraft systems. I prefer drone because I think it is time to discontinue using the term "unmanned." NASA agrees and has adopted the term unpiloted aerial vehicles.

7. The statue was removed from the island by the crew of a British Royal Navy ship in 1868. A year later, it was placed at the front entrance of the British Museum. The people of Rapa Nui continue to petition for the return of their statue.

8. A digital mesh, or a triangulated irregular network (TIN), is made when you take a point cloud and connect the dots to create a single surface made up of many small flat surfaces.

9. Ground penetrating radar (GPR) is less frequently used but nonetheless has been tried out many times in many different environments. For example, a recent review of the use of GPR was based on information from six hundred different projects (Conyers 2013).

10. It should be noted that dredging of the North Sea has produced artifacts from the sea floor.

11. Want to see what one of these large excavations looks like in progress? Go to N 53°36′20.7″, W 6°38′48.9″ (or in decimal degrees: 53.605741, -6.646925) on Google Earth. You will be taken to what is today the middle of the M3 motorway. Next, set the imagery back to November 11, 2005. The road will disappear and you'll see a medieval settlement, the Dowdstown 2 site, in process of being exposed over an area of about 250 meters by 80 meters.

12. I like these terms in that they highlight a generational distinction in thinking about how we choose to use different types of technology, but it is important to recognize that there is a divide in the world between those who have access to all the latest-and-greatest, like me, and the millions of people who live on the other side of the digital divide, regardless of their age.

13. "Born digital" in this context means data that is first recorded in a digital format. There are archaeologists who work directly in a field variably called

digital archaeology (e.g., Huggett 2015) or cyber-archaeology (e.g., Levy and Jones 2018).

Chapter 5: Digital Worlds

1. A good place to start is to ask if GIS is the best tool for the problem at hand (see Lock and Pouncett 2017).

2. Michael F. Goodchild has thought a lot about time and GIS over the years and has come to the conclusion that a "space-time geographic information system is unlikely to emerge in the near future" (Goodchild 2013, 1072).

3. The technical term for what I am talking about here is geographic visualization or geovisualization. See Gupta and Devillers (2017) for an excellent review of the topic in archaeology.

4. Archaeological maps, both analog and digital, often give the illusion of contemporaneity. See Lucas (2005) for a good discussion of this.

5. Open Context is a publishing and data curation service maintained by the Alexandria Archive Institute, a 501(c)3 nonprofit organization. It hosts DINAA.

6. The United States has 93,530 locations listed on the National Register of Historic Places; some of these are archaeological, but most are historic-era buildings or monuments. While it was not created to do so, even a cursory glance at the list shows that the history of White colonial culture is overrepresented on the national register.

7. We may one day find that, in addition to digital records of physical archaeology, our archives will be filled with purely digital worlds left behind by abandoned video games. Andrew Reinhard (2018) and others working in the field of "archaeogaming" consider the digital footprints left behind by players in a fictional digital world, like the procedurally generated planets in the game *No Man's Sky,* as no different than an archaeological site.

8. In the United States, private land owners are, with a few exceptions, not obliged to disclose the presence of archaeology.

9. I have focused here on survey, in part because that is where my expertise lies and in part because the application of different geospatial technologies in excavations is a topic that is rapidly evolving.

10. Another factor that stalled the process of making imagery useful to archaeology was the Reagan-era privatization of the Landsat program, which

drove the prices of data thousands of times higher and impacted quality. Air photos by comparison were a lot less expensive; many of the images on earlier versions of Google Earth were air photos, not satellite imagery.

11. There are now a number of good volumes with examples of the use of very-high-resolution imagery in archaeology (e.g., Lasaponara and Masini 2012).

12. I get random emails from people who say they have "found Atlantis" at the bottom of the ocean on Google Earth. The things they point out are clearly accidental byproducts of how the elevational model of the ocean floor was made. These minor errors have a technical term in computer science, digital artifacts, that should not be confused with when we make digital copies of archaeological artifacts.

13. The topic of site locational modeling can bring out strong feelings among archaeologists for a few reasons. There is sometimes confusion over what is being modeled: Is it purely the likelihood of encountering archaeology, or does the model reflect decisions people made in the past (i.e., the reasons we find things there)? There is concern that predictive models only point us toward the kinds of sites we already know about and lead us to miss rare sites or patterns that are unique to a particular time or culture. There is often disagreement about if we should be using models in decisions about how to protect archaeology. For example, there is the danger that it will discourage gathering the kinds of primary data that are necessary to be good caretakers because computer modeling is faster and cheaper.

14. While entropy is the enemy of archaeology, it can be a useful tool in computer models. In this case, MaxEnt creates a bunch of hypothetical geographic distributions of a species, then discards ones that rely too much on single variables, until it has generated a model that retains the most entropy across the variables inputted.

15. The GlobalXplorer platform follows a similar layout as the Valley of the Khans project but the volunteer is asked to indicate the presence or absence of looting in a small tile of satellite imagery. Some have raised questions about how useful these data will be to people who are tasked with protecting known archaeology, since the most visible cases of looting could be many, many years old, and thus are already well known and certainly come too late after the looters have left the scene (Yates 2018).

Chapter 6: Retracing Our Steps

1. Laws designed to protect archaeology have created a one billion dollar a year private industry centered on cultural resource management, or CRM. CRM is also informally referred to as contract archaeology, or salvage archaeology, to distinguish it from the kinds of cultural resource management that is done by government archaeologists. In the United States, laws will vary from place to place, but are often based on a moving window, rather than a specific year, to define what might be considered an artifact or historic property. That is how something like Route 66 could be considered as eligible for protection.

2. Or in the words of The Doctor, "History is a whitewash" (series 10, episode 3).

3. For more, I recommend Candacy Taylor's (2016) article in *The Atlantic*, "The Roots of Route 66."

4. It should be noted that the first credible scientific attempts to pin down where our species evolved got the answer wrong. A century ago we thought we originated in Asia. It was a logical conclusion given that the oldest fossils that looked like archaic versions of humanity had been found in the islands of Indonesia and outside Beijing. The thing that overturned the Asian-origins hypothesis was a whole lot of new fossils found in Africa, later supported by genetic studies showing that our deepest divergences in modern humans can be traced back to Africa.

5. On *Doctor Who* there is an advanced reptilian species called the Silurians who evolved on Earth, predating human evolution by millions of years. A new paper in the *International Journal of Astrobiology*, "The Silurian Hypothesis: Would It Be Possible to Detect an Industrial Civilization in the Geological Record?" asks, if Silurians were real, would we even know it (Schmidt and Frank 2019)? It is a collaboration between NASA scientist Gavin A. Schmidt and astrophysicist Adam Frank, neither of whom are convinced that intelligent life evolved on our planet long, long ago. Their real point is to force scientists to try and extrapolate from the evidence of humans in the geological record now to formulate some criteria for recognizing something similar in the geological record of another planet.

6. One standout is the Stage 3 Project at the Institute for Quaternary Research at Cambridge University. Over the years, an interdisciplinary team of more than two dozen scholars has collected chronometric data on deposits

dated from sixty thousand to twenty thousand years ago, a period known among earth scientists as Oxygen Isotope Stage 3 (OIS-3), but referred to by archaeologists as Europe's Middle and Upper Paleolithic. These data are key to looking at things like the demise of the Neanderthals.

7. We know from previous studies that the geographic range of chimpanzees increases during dry times due to the scarcity of food. GPS and GIS give us the ability to look at more fine-grained behaviors. For example, chimpanzees also make and use tools and recently there was a GIS study of stone tool use among modern chimps (Benito-Calvo et al. 2015).

8. Everyone who relies on GPS for fieldwork has, through experience, worked out what works best for them. Right now, I have two kinds of GPS for fieldwork. One can resolve my location to within a few centimeters given the right conditions. It is expensive, cumbersome, and needs a daily recharge, but it produces useful GIS data for archaeological surveys. These kind of GPS are beginning to be replaced by GPS and tablet combos. I also have a smaller, cheaper GPS. It runs on two AA batteries and it has never let me down, but I use it mainly for hiking and geological survey because the quality is lower and data handling on the backend is not well suited for producing archaeological survey datasets. I also have a DLSR camera with a built-in GPS, but it takes a while to reacquire location after being turned off. That means it will sometimes geotag my photos in the last place I was, rather than where I took the picture.

9. See Kelly (2016) for a recent review of what archaeologists think about this theory.

10. Fossilized footprints have their own term—ichnites—and they caused a bit of a stir recently when it was announced that some had been found on the European coast of the Mediterranean dated to six million years ago. They were claimed to be evidence for bipedal locomotion (walking upright) much earlier than the three-million-year-old footprints at Laetoli. For a number of reasons this interpretation is unlikely, see Meldrum and Sarmiento (2018).

11. See Andrefsky (2008) for a recent review of lithic technology and sourcing.

12. Archaeology has turned "people" into a verb—peopling—to describe the process of humans spreading into areas where no people had been before (see Rockman and Steel 2003).

13. There has been, and will probably continue to be, a debate between early versus later dispersal of modern humans out of Africa, one which is beyond the scope of this book.

14. Erlandson and Braje (2015) further make the case that there was some leap forward in watercraft technology that spurred this along, which is certainly possible, but remains to be tested.

15. See Dillehay et al. (2015) for a recent discussion of the chronology for the site of Monte Verde in Chile.

16. Anderson, Bissett, and Yerka (2013, 197) have more recently identified about a dozen "hypothetical staging areas/locations of early settlement in North America."

17. I hate to dignify this kind of racist nonsense with a prolonged explanation of how much more likely it is that the Pacific was colonized by purposeful voyages of exploration followed by purposeful voyages of colonization. So I will just say one word: *Hōkūleʻa*. (Look it up.)

18. Occam's razor is the principle that among competing explanations, the simplest one is more likely to be true.

19. The scholarly literature can be a bit fast and loose with classifying physical remnants of foot and animal travel, but generally we can break them up into paths, trails, and roads (Earle 2009). The differences between them center on frequency of use, property rights, and the amount of labor put into infrastructure. Paths are the most basic; they require the least amount of effort and are intended for daily use. Then there are trails. These involve longer-distance travel, still only require a small amount of effort, perhaps minimal paving, short footbridges, or markers, and are not used as frequently as paths. They may be used only in certain seasons and knowledge of them does not need to be firsthand. For example, in Arizona, the O'odham have detailed geographic knowledge of a network of trails embedded in traditional songs (Darling 2009).

20. The chronology of roads is important in the big picture. For example, while only hierarchical societies built roads and invested heavily in ports, not all did so, and for the ones that did, it remains to be seen if they simply built over existing trails and paths or created novel networks.

21. Archaeologists have been trying to create better GIS models to account for the particularities of human movement (Llobera and Sluckin 2007), and transport relevant for interpreting archaeology, like travel by horse (Sunseri 2015).

22. Remote sensing is also giving us a new picture of life on the Silk Road, which in practice was more like a braided route than single road, and would have taken months, or a whole year, to traverse. Specifically, we can see the evolution of irrigated fields that would have been used to grow the surplus food that sustained travelers (Hu et al. 2017).

23. The occupation of Chaco Canyon, AD 850–1250, and the broader Chaco Phenomenon, has been discussed from a number of different perspectives (see Crown and Wills 2003; Earle 2001; Kantner and Vaughn 2012; Lekson 2015; VanDyke 2007).

24. Kantner anticipated the implications of the current ubiquity of geospatial technology in archaeology (Kantner 2008).

25. While the ORBIS project is based mainly on historical documents, rather than archaeology, archaeologists regularly record Roman roads and ports all over Europe. Doneus et al. (2015), for example, used airborne green lidar that returned usable results on land and in shallow water to map a Roman harbor in Croatia.

26. Economists excel at connecting the dots between seemingly unrelated phenomena. One recent study suggests that the way that Europe looks from space at night is down to the old Roman roads (Dalgaard et al. 2018). NOAA, the National Oceanic and Atmospheric Admiration, has a global map of "average visible, stable lights" going back to 1992. Economists like this as a proxy for economic activity, and it makes sense: rich and industrialized countries throw off a lot of light. On top of this data they placed a GIS layer of the Roman roads from Harvard's Digital Atlas of Roman and Medieval Civilizations (DARMC) (McCormick et al 2013). From that, they buffered five kilometers on either side of the road to work out how the old roadways correlated with modern prosperity.

27. The search algorithm is not preprogrammed with classification, but learns as it is used. So if you do a Google Image search for "idiot" you get pictures that people associate with that word, rather than a preprogrammed response.

28. Some of the pessimism about spatial analyses of sourced artifacts goes back, I think, to a misreading of classic works on the regional distribution of artifacts (Renfew 1972; Hodder and Orton 1976; Earle and Ericson 1977). Sourcing can show, for example, that people stayed more local than had been originally estimated based on other evidence (e.g., Duff et al. 2012). Intensive

studies within a day's walk of a natural source have shown how use changes over time (e.g., Tripcevich 2007). For a more balanced perspective on using archaeological evidence to infer social networks I recommend Matthew Peeples's (2018) book, *Connected Communities: Networks, Identity, and Social Change in the Ancient Cibola World.*

29. Puʻuwaʻawaʻa is the name of a 1.5-kilometer diameter volcanic hill on Hawaiʻi Island. It is in an out-of-the-way upcountry location and you would not casually walk by it unless you were hiking over the crest of the island. The only permanent houses recorded nearby date to the post-European era, when ranching made this a more attractive place to live.

Chapter 7: Food and Farms

1. This is why The Doctor can get away with saying that time is "like a big ball of wibbly-wobbly, timey-wimey stuff," and fly around in a big blue police box.

2. The United Nations predicts that the total number of hungry people will rise to two billion by 2050 (un.org/sustainabledevelopment/hunger/). The flipside of that truly appalling statistic is most people are not hungry, which is a great thing but not an excuse to ignore this pressing and growing problem.

3. The exception that proves the rule is in *The Hitchhikers Guide to the Galaxy* series. The restaurant at the end of the universe is not there because people are hungry; it was Douglas Adams's (1980) way of pointing out the absurdity of humanity's compulsion to put a restaurant next to every natural wonder we come across. I would also add that the author used entropy to great effect in *So Long and Thanks for All the Fish* (1984) when his character Marvin the Paranoid Android complains that all his time traveling has made him thirty-seven times older than the universe and nearly all his parts have been replaced at least fifty times.

4. This is a good study, but it stepped into two classic archaeological GIS traps. The first is the one where we keep discovering that people preferred to live near freshwater. The second is the one where our impressive total sample size gets watered down by creating time-slices with just a few data points spread over many, many years.

5. Geospatial technologies are at the forefront of several innovative approaches to counting populations over long periods of time, including using

drones to calculate the volume of abandoned villages as a proxy for total population (Duwe et al. 2016). The particular model described here, based on the CARD dataset, highlights, among other things, some of the challenges of creating spatially continuous data based on samples linked to geolocation through site records.

6. The highest-resolution picture we have of what happened when people settled down and started growing their food instead of chasing it is in Europe, where large and detailed GIS databases of radiocarbon dates have been used to detect booms and busts in populations.

7. The term "land use," it should be said, can refer to just about anything, but in most cases when archaeologists say it, we are referring to how people are getting food out of the environment.

8. This gets even more complex when you consider that some households will be a mix of people from different cultures, with different food preferences and food allergies.

9. When I started doing research for this book I was excited to discover that, in addition to *Grail Quest,* J.H. Brennan had written a book about time travel. That excitement quickly turned to disappointment when it turned out to be full of pseudoscience and New Age nonsense. I still recommend *Grail Quest* to young readers, as well as the *Magic Treehouse* series by Mary Pope Osborne.

10. Scholars have long speculated as to the social and political consequences of agriculture, which go beyond the obvious matter of how we feed ourselves. It is a big topic that I am not going to get into here, but I will recommend Michael J. Harrower's (2016) *Water Histories and Spatial Archaeology: Ancient Yemen and the American West* as a great example of a study grounded in real archaeology and sound scholarship.

11. This was during an annual event called the Hawaii Ecosystems Meeting, organized by Stanford University ecologist Peter Vitousek.

12. I loved playing *Sid Meier's Civilization* when it first came out. But I could fill a whole other book on how deeply problematic it is, especially in its promotion of a narrow, outdated view of how societies change over time. For a review written by archaeologists of the current version (Civ VI), see Mol, Politopoulos, and Ariese-Vandemeulebroucke (2017).

13. At Caracol, a good example of the kind of field survey-scale dataset that is possible can be seen in new research on the distribution and form of water reservoirs, households, and terraces. Adrian Chase of Arizona State University

has mapped more than fifteen hundred reservoirs and it turns out that "residential groups had access to a reservoir in their own group or in a neighboring group or terraced field in close proximity," thus making "elite control over these distributed water resources . . . difficult or impossible" (Chase 2016, 892).

Chapter 8: Living in the Past

1. The full quote is, "The past is a foreign country; they do things differently there," from the novel *The Go-Betweens* (Hartley 1953, 1).

2. While it is beyond the scope of this book, it is also worth noting that some archaeologists have argued that urbanism and the rise of the state must be intellectually decoupled, since we have examples of archaic state societies that arose without constructing cities (Jennings and Earle 2016).

3. There is broad agreement that archaeology has a speculation problem. For example, Stefano Campana (2018, 117), an archaeologist at the University of Siena, has pointed to limited material evidence having produced "little more than unsupported speculation." Barton (2013, 153) warns of the dangers of overconfidence, or indifference, in the ways archaeologists speculate, and makes the case for the value of telling fact from fiction to address real-world problems.

4. Michael E. Smith ties this to the way that ancient monument building is portrayed in *National Geographic*. He is not wrong; many of those reconstructions are cringe worthy.

5. A key variable that may account for this difference is domesticated mammals and their role in wealth, trade, and war in the Old World (Kohler et al. 2017).

6. For a recent summary, see Monica L. Smith's (2019) book *Cities: The First Six Thousand Years*.

7. Fun with flags: the main temple at Angkor Wat is featured on Cambodia's flag.

8. These studies have confirmed that Angkor Wat is not a series of temple-focused cities but one sprawling city.

9. It is called a "viewshed" because it is analogous to a natural watershed.

10. There are a number of creative ways to work around these limitations, too many to list here.

11. They call this a visibility graph analysis.

Chapter 9: Archaeology as Time Machine

1. Geography went digital over twenty years ago now (Goodchild 2000) and so has a more developed literature critiquing science and GIS (Pickles 1995), and GIS and spatial humanities (Bodenhamer, Corrigan, and Harris 2010).

2. Two points of clarification: First, there are both practical and ethical reason why excavations are kept small, mainly because when we dig we destroy that portion of the archaeological record, even if we preserve all the things we find there. Second, none of us are born with the ability to move under our own steam, and those of us who do grow to become mobile do not all get around with the same ease or capacity. So, while it is impossible for me to say how much of the planet a single person experienced in the past, it was certainly more than a standard one meter by one meter excavation.

3. I am again using the Maya as an example, but I could have picked any number of other places that I have talked about in this book, and still others I have not. For example, there is excellent geospatial archaeology being done elsewhere in Mesoamerica outside the Maya area using lidar (e.g., Rosenswig and López-Torrijos 2018).

4. Incredibly, that is only a small fraction of the Maya area; a back-of-the-envelope estimate based on the density reported suggests that with similar-quality lidar that covered the entire area, one could expect to map about nine million features.

5. Heather Richards-Rissetto, an archaeologist at the University of Nebraska, has used lidar data from Copan in a number of studies to create a realistic experience of the site (Richards-Rissetto 2017).

6. Art historian Erin Thompson of the John Jay College of Criminal Justice takes the position that copyrighting these is another form of the kind of collecting that the antiquarians did, in her words, "digital colonialism." A new initiative called the Open Heritage 3D Alliance (openheritage3d.org) provides a place to archive 3-D models and says it "will work to provide democratized access to primary heritage 3D data submitted from donors and organizations, and will help to facilitate an operation platform, archive, and organization of resources into the future."

7. The project's website, virtualrosewood.com, shows the evolution of the virtual reality version of Rosewood as well as a great deal of other information

that helps the visitor appreciate its place in "a particularly volatile moment in US history."

8. Our findings are consistent with the observation by Winter et al. (2018) that traditional sustainable management of ecosystems is better thought of as operating on the district *(moku)* scale rather than individual community *(ahupua'a)* scale.

9. Local knowledge, in this context, simply refers to information about places—things like stories and place-names—that may tell us about the distant past. It is especially important for groups with strong traditions of oral histories. These may, or may not, circulate outside of a residential group; they may, or may not, be written down or linked to maps; they may, or may not, be widely known within the community itself.

10. There is a growing literature on indigenous archaeology and community archaeology, and I recommend two books for anyone interested: Sonya Atalay's (2012) *Community-Based Archaeology: Research with, by, and for Indigenous and Local Communities,* and Kathleen L. Kawelu's (2015) *Kuleana and Commitment: Working toward a Collaborative Hawaiian Archaeology.*

11. Archaeologists do not regularly share all the data we collect in excavations but that may be changing. There are some experiments that take advantage of virtual cave environments to share rich geospatial data from excavations and foster collaborations (Levy and Jones 2018).

12. I have no knowledge of this case outside what is publicly available. I have, however, worked on and off in cultural resource management since I was seventeen years old, so I have a good idea how it works in practice.

13. To try and make the process more transparent, archaeologists in places like California and New Zealand (Aotearoa) will work with monitors who represent the local community.

14. Technically, since for more than sixty years we have been abandoning things in orbit around our planet, on the Moon, Mars, and far beyond (Gorman 2019), one could argue that our entire solar system is one big site.

References

Adams, Douglas. 1980. *The Restaurant at the End of the Universe*. London: Pan Books.

———. 1984. *So Long, and Thanks for All the Fish*. New York: Harmony Books.

Aimers, James J. 2007. "What Maya Collapse? Terminal Classic Variation in the Maya Lowlands." *Journal of Archaeological Research* 15 (4): 329–77.

Anderson, Atholl, John Chappell, Michael Gagan, and Richard Grove. 2006. "Prehistoric Maritime Migration in the Pacific Islands: An Hypothesis of ENSO Forcing." *Holocene* 16 (1): 1–6.

Anderson, David G., Thaddeus G. Bissett, and Stephen J. Yerka. 2013. "The Late Pleistocene Human Settlement of Interior North America: The Role of Physiography and Sea-Level Change." In *Paleoamerican Odyssey*, edited by Kelly E. Graf, Caroline V. Ketron, and Michael R. Waters, 235–55. College Station, TX: Texas A&M University Press.

Anderson, David G., Thaddeus G. Bissett, Stephen J. Yerka, Joshua J. Wells, Eric C. Kansa, Sarah W. Kansa, Kelsey Noack Myers, R. Carl DeMuth, and Devin A. White. 2017. "Sea-Level Rise and Archaeological Site Destruction: An Example from the Southeastern United States Using DINAA (Digital Index of North American Archaeology)." *PLoS One* 12 (11): e0188142.

Anderson, David G., and Christopher Gillam. 2000. "Paleoindian Colonization of the Americas: Implications from an Examination of Physiographic, Demographic, and Artifact Distributions." *American Antiquity* 65 (1): 43–66.

Anderson, David G., D. Shane Miller, Stephen J. Yerka, J. Christopher Gillam, Erik N. Johanson, Derek T. Anderson, Albert C. Goodyear, and Ashley M. Smallwood. 2010. "PIDBA (Paleoindian Database of the Americas) 2010: Current Status and Findings." *Archaeology of Eastern North America* 38: 63–90.

Andrefsky, William. 2008. "The Analysis of Stone Tool Procurement, Production, and Maintenance." *Journal of Archaeological Research* 17 (1): 65–103.

Asfaw, B., Y. Beyene, G. Suwa, R. Walter, T. White, Gabriel G. Wolde, and T. Yemane. 1992. "The Earliest Acheulean from Konso-Gardula." *Nature* 360 (6406): 732–35.

Atalay, Sonya. 2012. *Community-Based Archaeology: Research with, by, and for Indigenous and Local Communities.* Berkeley: University of California Press.

Bardolph, D. 2014. "A Critical Evaluation of Recent Gendered Publishing Trends in American Archaeology." *American Antiquity,* 79 (3): 522–40.

Barton, C. Michael. 2013. "Science of the Past or Science of the Future? Archaeology and Computational Social Science." In *Computational Approaches to Archaeological Spaces,* edited by Andrew Bevan and Mark Lake, 151–78. Walnut Creek, CA: Left Coast Press.

Barton, C. Michael, Isaac Ullah, and Helena Mitasova. 2010. "Computational Modeling and Neolithic Socioecological Dynamics: A Case Study from Southwest Asia." *American Antiquity* 75 (2): 364–86.

Bellamy, Edward. 1887. *Looking Backwards 2000–1887.* Boston: Ticknor and Co.

Benito-Calvo, Alfonso, Susana Carvalho, Adrian Arroyo, Tetsuro Matsuzawa, Ignacio de la Torre, and R. Sevcik. 2015. "First GIS Analysis of Modern Stone Tools Used by Wild Chimpanzees (*Pan troglodytes verus*) in Bossou, Guinea, West Africa." *PLoS One* 10 (3): e0121613.

Bennett, Matthew R., Sally Reynolds, Sarita Amy Morse, and Marcin Budka. 2016. "Laetoli's Lost Tracks: 3D-Generated Mean Shape and Missing Footprints." *Scientific Reports* 6: e21916.

Bevan, Andrew. 2011. "Computational Models for Understanding Movement and Territory." In *Tecnologías de Información Geográfica y Análisis Arqueológico del Territorio: Actas del V Simposio Internacional de Arqueología de Mérida,* edited by V. Mayoral Herrera and S. Celestino Pérez, 383–94. Madrid: Consejo Superior de Investigaciones Científicas.

———. 2015. "The Data Deluge." *Antiquity* 89: 1473–84.

Binford, Louis R. 1981. "Behavioral Archaeology and the 'Pompeii Premise.'" *Journal of Anthropological Research* 37 (3): 195–208.

———. 1992. "Seeing the Present and Interpreting the Past—and Keeping Things Straight." In *Space, Time, and Archaeological Landscapes,* edited by Jacqueline Rossignol and LuAnn Wandsnider, 43–64. New York: Plenum Press.

Blanton, Richard, and Lane Fargher. 2008. *Collective Action in the Formation of Pre-modern States.* New York: Springer.

Blom, Ronald G., Robert Crippen, Charles Elachi, Nicholas Clapp, George R. Hedges, and Juris Zarins. 2006. "Southern Arabia Desert Trade Routes, Frankincense, Myrrh, and the Ubar Legend." In *Remote Sensing in Archaeology,* edited by J. Wiseman and F. El-Baz, 71–87. New York: Springer.

Bodenhamer, David J., John Corrigan, and Trevor M. Harris., eds. 2010. *The Spatial Humanities: GIS and the Future of Humanities Scholarship.* Bloomington: Indiana University Press.

Bonsall, James, Robert Fry, Chris Gaffney, Ian Armit, Anthony Beckand Vince Gaffney. 2013. "Assessment of the CMD Mini-Explorer, a New Low-Frequency Multi-coil Electromagnetic Device, for Archaeological Investigations." *Archaeological Prospection* 20 (3): 219–31.

Bonsall, James, Chris Gaffney, and Ian Armit. 2014. "Back and Forth: Paving the Way Forward by Assessing Ten Years of Geophysical Surveys on Irish Road Schemes." In *Futures and Pasts: Archaeological science on Irish road schemes,* edited by B. Kelly, N. Roycroft, and M. Stanley, 1–13. Dublin: National Road Authority.

Borck, Lewis. 2018. "Constructing the Future History: Prefiguration as Historical Epistemology and the Chronopolitics of Archaeology." *Journal of Contemporary Archaeology* 5(2): 213–302.

Borck, Lewis, Barbara J. Mills, Matthew A. Peeples, and Jeffery J. Clark. 2015. "Are Social Networks Survival Networks? An Example from the Late Pre-Hispanic US Southwest." *Journal of Archaeological Method and Theory* 22 (1): 33–57.

Bove, Fredrick J. 1981. "Trend Surface Analysis and the Lowland Classic Maya Collapse." *American Antiquity* 46 (1): 93–112.

Brouwer Burg, Marieka. 2017. "It Must Be Right, GIS Told Me So! Questioning the Infallibility of GIS as a Methodological Tool." *Journal of Archaeological Science* 84: 115–20.

Brunn, Stanley D., and Martin Dodge. 2017. "What Is Where? The Role of Map Representations and Mapping Practices in Advancing Scholarship." In *Mapping Across the Academia,* edited by Stanley D. Brunn and Martin Dodge, 1–22. New York: Springer.

Butler, Octavia E. 1979. *Kindred.* New York: Doubleday.

Campana, Stefano R. L. 2011. "'Total Archaeology' to Reduce the Need for Rescue Archaeology: The BREBEMI Project." In *Remote Sensing for Archaeological Heritage Management,* edited by D. C. Cowley, 33–41. Brussels: Europae Archaeologia Consilium.

———. 2018. *Mapping the Archaeological Continuum: Filling "Empty" Mediterranean Landscapes.* New York: Springer.

Canuto, Marcello A., Francisco Estrada-Belli, Thomas G. Garrison, Stephen D. Houston, Mary Jane Acuña, Milan Kováč, Damien Marken, Philippe Nondédéo, Luke Auld-Thomas, Cyril Castanet, David Chatelain, Carlos R. Chiriboga, Thomáš Drápela, Tibor Lieskovský, Alexandre Tokovinine, Antolín Velasquez, Juan C. Fernández-Díaz, and Ramesh Shrestha. 2018. "Ancient Lowland Maya Complexity as Revealed by Airborne Laser scanning of Northern Guatemala." *Science* 361(6409): eaau0137.

Carballo, David M., and Thomas Pluckhahn. 2007. "Transportation Corridors and Political Evolution in Highland Mesoamerica: Settlement Analyses Incorporating GIS for Northern Tlaxcala, Mexico." *Journal of Anthropological Archaeology* 26 (4): 607–29.

Carter, Allison K., Piphal Heng, Miriam Stark, Rachna Chhay, and Damian Evans. 2018. "Urbanism and Residential Patterning in Angkor." *Journal of Field Archaeology* 43 (6): 492–506.

Casana, Jesse. 2014. "Regional-Scale Archaeological Remote Sensing in the Age of Big Data: Automated Site Discovery vs. Brute Force Methods." *Advances in Archaeological Practice* 2 (3): 222–33.

Casana, Jesse, and Jackson Cothren. 2013. "The CORONA Atlas Project: Orthorectification of CORONA Satellite Imagery and Regional-Scale Archaeological Exploration in the Near East." In *Mapping Archaeological Landscapes from Space,* edited by D. C. Comer and M. J. Harrower, 33–43. New York: Springer.

Chamberlin, Thomas C. 1965 [1890]. "The Method of Multiple Working Hypotheses." *Science* 148 (3671): 754–59.

Chaput, Michelle A., Björn Kriesche, Matthew Betts, Andrew Martindale, Rafal Kulik, Volker Schmidt, and Konrad Gajewski. 2015. Spatiotemporal distribution of Holocene populations in North America. *Proceedings of the National Academy of Sciences* 112 (39): 12127–32.

Chase, Adrian S. Z. 2016. "Beyond Elite Control: Residential Reservoirs at Caracol, Belize." *Wiley Interdisciplinary Reviews: Water* 3 (6): 885–97.

Chase, Arlen F., Diane Z. Chase, Jamie J. Awe, John F. Weishampel, Gyles Iannone, Holley Moyes, Jason Yaeger, and M. Katheryn Brown. The Use of LiDAR in Understanding the Ancient Maya Landscape: Caracol and Western Belize. *Advances in Archaeological Practice* 2 (3): 208–21.

Chase, Arlen F., Diane Z. Chase, Christopher T. Fisher, Stephen J. Leisz, and John F. Weishampel. 2012. "Geospatial Revolution and Remote Sensing LiDAR in Mesoamerican Archaeology." *Proceedings of the National Academy of Sciences* 109 (32): 12916–21.

Childe, V. Gordon. 1926. *The Aryans: A Study of Indo-European Origins.* London: Kegan Paul, Trench, Trubner, and Co.

———. 1936. *Man Makes Himself.* London: Watts and Co.

Ch'ng, Eugene. 2009. "Experiential Archaeology: Is Virtual Time Travel Possible?" *Journal of Cultural Heritage* 10: 458–70.

Cleal, R. M. J., K. E. Walker, and R. Montague. 1995. *Stonehenge in its Landscape: Twentieth-Century Excavations.* London: English Heritage.

Colwell, C., 2016. "How the Archaeological Review behind the Dakota Access Pipeline Went Wrong." *The Conversation,* November 20, 2016. https://theconversation.com/how-the-archaeological-review-behind-the-dakota-access-pipeline-went-wrong-67815.

Conolly, James, and Mark Lake. 2006. *Geographic Information Systems in Archaeology.* Cambridge: Cambridge University Press.

Conyers, Lawrence B. 2013. *Ground-Penetrating Radar for Archaeology.* 3rd ed. Landham, MD: Alta Mira Press.

Cooper, Anwen, and Chris Green. 2015. "Embracing the Complexities of 'Big Data' in Archaeology: The Case of the English Landscapes and Identities Project." *Journal of Archaeological Method and Theory* 23 (1): 271–304.

Cowley, David C. 2012. "In with the New, Out with the Old? Auto-extraction for Remote Sensing Archaeology." In *Remote Sensing of the Ocean, Sea Ice,*

Coastal Waters, and Large Water Regions: Proceedings of SPIE Conference 8532, edited by C. R. Bostater, S. P. Mertikas, X. Ney, C. Nicol, D. C. Cowley and J-P. Bruyant. Bellingham, WA: SPIE.

Cowley, David C., Charles Moriarty, George Geddes, Georgina L. Brown, Tom Wade, and Caroline J. Nichol. 2018. "UAVs in Context: Archaeological Airborne Recording in a National Body of Survey and Record." *Drones* 2 (1): 2.

Crown, Patricia L., and Wirt H. Wills. 2003. "Modifying Pottery and Kivas at Chaco: Pentimento, Restoration, or Renewal?" *American Antiquity* 68 (3): 511–32.

Crutchley, Simon, and Peter Crow. 2010. *The Light Fantastic: Using Airborne LiDAR in Archaeological Survey.* London: English Heritage.

———. 2018. *Using Airborne Lidar in Archaeological Survey: The Light Fantastic.* Swindon, UK: Historic England.

Dahlberg, Erik. 2016. "UAS Technology Tackles Rapa Nui." *Point of Beginning.* https://www.pobonline.com/articles/98008-uas-technology-tackles-rapa-nui.

Dalgaard, Carl-Johan, Nicolai Kaarsen, Ola Olsson, and Pablo Selaya. 2018. "Roman Roads to Prosperity: Public Good Provision." *CEPR Discussion Papers* 12745.

Darling, Andrew J. 2009. "O'odham Trails and the Archaeology of Space." In *Landscapes of Movement: Trails, paths, and roads in anthropological perspective,* edited by James E. Snead, Clark L. Erickson, and J. Andrew Darling, 61–83. Philadelphia: University of Pennsylvania Press.

Darwin, Charles. 1859. *On the Origins of Species.* London: John Murray.

de Camp, L. Sprague. 1939. *Lest Darkness Fall.* New York: Ballantine Books.

Dillehay, T. D., C. Ocampo, J. Saavedra, A. O. Sawakuchi, R. M. Vega, M. Pino, et al. 2015. "New Archaeological Evidence for an Early Human Presence at Monte Verde, Chile." *PLoS One* 10 (11): e0141923.

Doneus, M., I. Miholjek, G. Mandlburger, N. Doneus, G. Verhoeven, C. Briese, and M. Pregesbauer. 2015. "Airborne Laser Bathymetry for Documentation of Submerged Archaeological Sites in Shallow Water." *Conference Proceedings for The International Archives of the Photogrammetry, Remote Sensing and Spatial Information Sciences,* vol. XL-5/W5.

Duckers, Gary L. 2013. "Bridging the 'Geospatial Divide' in Archaeology: Community-Based Interpretation of LIDAR Data." *Internet Archaeology* 35: ia.35.10.

Duff, Andrew I., Jeremy M. Moss, Thomas C. Windes, John Kantner, and M. Steven Shackley. 2012. "Patterning in Procurement of Obsidian in Chaco Canyon and in Chaco-Era Communities in New Mexico Revealed by X-ray Fluorescence." *Journal of Archaeological Science* 39 (9): 2995-3007.

Dunnell, Robert C., and W. S. Dancey. 1983. "The Siteless Survey: A Regional-Scale Data Collection Strategy." In c*Advances in Archaeological Thought in America,* edited by M. B. Schiffer, 149-207. New York: Academic Press.

Duwe, Samuel, B. Sunday Eiselt, J. Andrew Darling, Mark D. Willis, and Chester Walker. 2016. "The Pueblo Decomposition Model: A Method for Quantifying Architectural Rubble to Estimate Population Size." *Journal of Archaeological Science* 65: 20-31.

Earle, Timothy K. 2001. "Economic Support of Chaco Canyon Society." *American Antiquity* 66 (1): 26-35.

———. 2009. "Routes through the Landscape: A Comparative Approach." In *Landscapes of Movement: Trails, paths, and roads in anthropological perspective,* edited by James E. Snead, Clark L. Erickson, and J. Andrew Darling, 253-70. Philadelphia: University of Pennsylvania Press.

Earle, Timothy K., and Jonathan E. Ericson, eds. 1977. *Exchange Systems in Prehistory.* New York: Academic Press.

Earley-Spadoni, Tiffany. 2017. "Spatial History, Deep Mapping and Digital Storytelling: Archaeology's Future Imagined through an Engagement with the Digital Humanities." *Journal of Archaeological Science* 84: 95-102.

Ebert, Claire, Keith M. Prufer, and Douglas J. Kennett. 2012. "Maya Monuments and Spatial Statistics: A GIS-Based Examination of the Terminal Classic Period Maya Collapse." *Research Reports in Belizean Archaeology* 9: 91-105.

Emerson, Charles W., Bryan Bommersbach, Brett Nachman, and Robert L. Anemone. 2015. "An Object-Oriented Approach to Extracting Productive Fossil Localities from Remotely Sensed Imagery." *Remote Sensing* 7 (12): 16555-70.

Erlandson, Jon M., and Todd J. Braje. 2015. "Coasting Out of Africa: The Potential Mangrove Forests and Marine Habitats to Facilitate Human

Coastal Expansion via the Southern Dispersal Route." *Quaternary International* 382 (24): 31–41.

Evangelidis, V., M-A. Tsompanas, G. C. Sirakoulis, and A. Adamatzky. 2015. "Slime Mould Imitates Development of Roman Roads in the Balkans." *Journal of Archaeological Science: Reports* 2: 264–81.

Evans, Damien. 2016. "Airborne Laser Scanning as a Method for Exploring Long-Term Socio-ecological Dynamics in Cambodia." *Journal of Archaeological Science* 74: 164–75.

Field, Julie S., Michael D. Petraglia, and Marta Mirazón Lahr. 2007. "The Southern Dispersal Hypothesis and the South Asian Archaeological Record: Examination of Dispersal Routes through GIS Analysis." *Journal of Anthropological Archaeology* 26 (1): 88–108.

Flannery, Kent, and Joyce Marcus. 2012. *The Creation of Inequality: How Our Prehistoric Ancestors Set the Stage for Monarchy, Slavery, and Empire.* Cambridge, MA: Harvard University Press.

Fleagle, J. G., D. T. Rasmussen, S. Yirga, T. M. Bown, and F. E. Grine. 1991. "New Hominid Fossils from Fejej, Southern Ethiopia." *Journal of Human Evolution* 21 (2): 145–52.

Franklin, Janet, A. J. Potts, E. C. Fisher, R. M. Cowling, and C. W. Marean. 2015. "Paleodistribution Modeling in Archaeology and Paleoanthropology." *Quaternary Science Reviews* 110: 1–14.

Freeland, Travis, Brandon Heung, David V. Burley, Geoffrey Clark, and Anders Knudby. 2016. "Automated Feature Extraction for Prospection and Analysis of Monumental Earthworks from Aerial LiDAR in the Kingdom of Tonga." *Journal of Archaeological Science* 69: 64–74.

Gaffney, Chris, and Vincent Gaffney. 2011. "Through an Imperfect Filter: Geophysical Techniques and the Management of Archaeological Heritage." In *Remote Sensing for Archaeological Heritage Management,* edited by D. C. Cowley, 117–27. Brussels: Europae Archaeologia Consilium.

Gaffney, Chris, Vince Gaffney, Wolfgang Neubauer, Eamonn Baldwin, Henry Chapman, Paul Garwood, Helen Moulden, Tom Sparrow, Richard Bates, Klaus Löcker, Alois Hinterleitner, Immo Trinks, Erich Nau, Thomas Zitz, Sebastian Floery, Geert Verhoeven, and Michael Doneus. 2012. "The Stonehenge Hidden Landscapes Project." *Archaeological Prospection* 19 (2): 147–55.

Gillings, Mark. 2015. "Mapping Invisibility: GIS Approaches to the Analysis of Hiding and Seclusion." *Journal of Archaeological Science* 62 (2015): 1–14.

———. 2017. "Mapping Liminality: Critical Frameworks for the GIS-Based Modeling of Visibility." *Journal of Archaeological Science* 84: 121–28.

Gleick, James. 2016. *Time Travel: A History.* New York: Pantheon Books.

González-Tennant, Edward. 2018. *The Rosewood Massacre: An Archaeology and History of Intersectional Violence.* Gainesville: University of Florida Press.

Goodchild, Michael F. 2000. "Communicating Geographic Information in a Digital Age." *Annals of the Association of American Geographers* 90 (2): 344–55.

———. 2013. "Prospects for a Space-Time GIS: Space-Time Integration in Geography and GIScience." *Annals of the Association of American Geographers* 103 (5): 1072–77.

Gorman, Alice. 2019. *Dr. Space Junk versus the Universe: Archaeology and the Future.* Cambridge, MA: MIT Press.

Guiducci, Dario, and Ariane Burke. 2016. "Reading the Landscape: Legible Environments and Hominin Dispersals." *Evolutionary Anthropology: Issues, News, and Reviews* 25 (3): 133–41.

Gupta, Neha. 2013. "What Do Spatial Approaches to the History of Archaeology Tell Us? Insights from Post-colonial India. *Complutum* 24 (2): 189–201.

Gupta, Neha, and Rodolphe Devillers. 2017. "Geographic Visualization in Archaeology." *Journal of Archaeological Method and Theory* 24 (3): 852–85.

Gustas, Robert, and Kisha Supernant. 2017. "Least Cost Path Analysis of Early Maritime Movement on the Pacific Northwest Coast." *Journal of Archaeological Science* 78: 40–56.

———. 2019. "Coastal Migration into the Americas and Least Cost Path Analysis." *Journal of Anthropological Archaeology* 54: 192–206.

Harris, Edward C. 1979. *Principles of Archaeological Stratigraphy.* London: Academic Press.

Harrower, Michael J. 2016. *Water Histories and Spatial Archaeology: Ancient Yemen and the American West.* Cambridge: Cambridge University Press.

Hartley, L. P. 1953. *The Go-Betweens.* London: Hamish Hamilton.

Henshilwood, Christopher S., Francesco d'Errico, Karen L. van Niekerk, Laure Dayet, Alain Queffelec, and Luca Pollarolo. 2018. "An Abstract Drawing from the 73,000-year-old Levels at Blombos Cave, South Africa." *Nature* 562: 115–18.

Hill, J. Brett. 2004. "Land Use and an Archaeological Perspective on Socio-natural studies in the Wadi Al-Hasa, West-Central Jordan." *American Antiquity* 69 (3): 389–412.

Hodder, Ian, and Clive Orton. 1976. *Spatial Analysis in Archaeology.* Cambridge: Cambridge University Press.

Holton, Graham E. L. 2010. "Heyerdahl's Kon Tiki Theory and the Denial of the Indigenous Past." *Anthropological Forum* 14 (2): 163–81.

Holtorf, Cornelius. 2016. "The Meaning of Time Travel." In *The Archaeology of Time Travel: Experiencing the Past in the Twenty-first Century,* edited by Bodil Petersson and Cornelius Holtorf, 1–24. Oxford: Archaeopress.

Horsburgh, K. Ann, Jayson Orton, and Richard G. Klein. 2016. "Beware the Springbok in Sheep's Clothing: How Secure are the Faunal Identifications upon Which We Built Our Models?" *African Archaeological Review* 33: 353–61.

Howey, Meghan C. L. 2011. "Multiple Pathways across Past Landscapes: Circuit Theory as a Complementary Geospatial Method to Least Cost Path for Modeling Past Movement." *Journal of Archaeological Science* 38 (10): 2523–35.

Howey, Meghan C. L., and Marieka Brouwer Burg. 2017. "Assessing the State of Archaeological GIS Research: Unbinding Analyses of Past Landscapes." *Journal of Archaeological Science* 84: 1–9.

Howey, Meghan C. L., Franklin B. Sullivan, Jason Tallant, Robert Vande Kopple, and Michael W. Palace. 2016. "Detecting Precontact Anthropogenic Microtopographic Features in a Forested Landscape with Lidar: A Case Study from the Upper Great Lakes Region, AD 1000–1600." *PLoS One* 11 (9): e0162062.

Hu, Ningke, Xin Li, Lei Luo, and Liwei Zhang. 2017. "Ancient Irrigation Canals Mapped from Corona Imagery and Their Implications in Juyan Oasis along the Silk Road." *Sustainability* 9: 1–14.

Huggett, Jeremy. 2015. "A Manifesto for an Introspective Digital Archaeology." *Open Archaeology* 1 (1): 86–95.

Hughes, Charles E., Michael J. Moshell, Dean Reed, Diane Z. Chase, and Arlen F. Chase. 2001. "The Caracol Time Travel Project." *The Journal of Visualization and Computer Simulation* 12 (4): 203–14.

Humphries, Nicolas E., Nuno Queiroz, Jennifer R. M. Dyer, Nicolas G. Pade, Michael K. Musyl, Kurt M. Schaefer, Daniel W. Fuller, Juerg M. Brunnschweiler, Thomas K. Doyle, Jonathan D. R. Houghton, Graeme C. Hays, Catherine S. Jones, Leslie R. Noble, Victoria J. Wearmouth, Emily J. Southall, and David W. Sims. 2010. "Environmental Context Explains Lévy and Brownian Movement Patterns of Marine Predators." *Nature* 465: 1066–69.

Irwin, Geoff. 1992. *The Prehistoric Exploration and Colonization of the Pacific*. Cambridge: Cambridge University Press.

Janmaat, Karline R. L., Simone D. Ban, and Christopher Boesch. 2013. "Chimpanzee Use of Long-term Spatial Memory to Monitor Large Fruit Trees and Remember Feeding Experiences across Seasons." *Animal Behaviour* 86 (6): 1183–1205.

Janmaat, Karline R. L., Christopher Boesch, Richard Byrne, Colin A. Chapman, Zoro B. Goné Bi, Josephine S. Head, Martha M. Robbins, Richard W. Wrangham, and Leo Polansky. 2016. "The Spatio-temporal Complexity of Chimpanzee Food: How Cognitive Adaptations Can Counteract the Ephemeral Nature of Ripe Fruit." *American Journal of Primatology* 78 (6): 626–45.

Jennings, Justin, and Timothy Earle. 2016. "Urbanization, State Formation, and Cooperation: A Reappraisal." *Current Anthropology* 57 (4): 474–93.

Jia, Xin, Yonggang Sun, Lin Wang, Wenfeng Sun, Zhijun Zhao, Harry F. Lee, Wenbo Huang, Shuangye Wu, and Huayu Lu. 2016. "The Transition of Human Subsistence Strategies in Relation to Climate Change during the Bronze Age in the West Liao River Basin, Northeast China." *Holocene* 26 (5): 781–89.

Kantner, John. 1997. "Ancient Roads, Modern Mapping: Evaluating Chaco Anasazi Roadways using GIS technology." *Expedition* 39 (3): 49–62.

———. 2008. "The Archaeology of Regions: From Discrete Analytical Toolkit to Ubiquitous Spatial Perspective." *Journal of Archaeological Research* 16 (1): 37–81.

Kantner, John, and Kevin J. Vaughn. 2012. "Pilgrimage as Costly Signal: Religiously Motivated Cooperation in Chaco and Nasca." *Journal of Anthropological Archaeology* 31 (1): 66–82.

Kawelu, Kathleen L. 2015. *Kuleana and Commitment: Working toward a Collaborative Hawaiian Archaeology*. Honolulu: University of Hawai'i Press.

Keller, Angela H. 2009. "A Road by Any Other Name: Trails, Paths, and Roads in Maya Language and Thought." In *Landscapes of Movement:*

Trails, paths, and roads in anthropological perspective, edited by James E. Snead, Clark L. Erickson, and J. Andrew Darling, 133–57. Philadelphia: University of Pennsylvania Press.

Kelly, Robert L. 1983. "Hunter-Gatherer Mobility Strategies." *Journal of Anthropological Research* 39 (3): 277–306.

———. 2016. *The Fifth Beginning: What Six Million Years of Human History Can Tell Us about Our Future*. Oakland: University of California Press.

Kirch, Patrick V. 1994. *The Wet and the Dry: Irrigation and Agricultural Intensification in Polynesia*. Chicago: University of Chicago Press.

Kobialka, Dawid. 2016. "A Cup of Decaf Past: An Archaeology of Time Travel, Cinema and Consumption." In *The Archaeology of Time Travel: Experiencing the Past in the Twenty-first Century*, edited by Bodil Petersson and Cornelius Holtorf, 213–28. Oxford: Archaeopress.

Kohler, Timothy A., Michael E. Smith, Amy Bogaard, Gary M. Feinman, Christian E. Peterson, Alleen Betzenhauser, Matthew Pailes, Elizabeth C. Stone, Anna Marie Prentiss, Timothy J. Dennehy, Laura J. Ellyson, Linda M. Nicholas, Ronald K. Faulseit, Amy Styring, Jade Whitlam, Mattia Fochesato, Thomas A. Foor, and Samuel Bowles. 2017. "Greater Post-Neolithic Wealth Disparities in Eurasia than in North America and Mesoamerica." *Nature* 551: 619–22.

Kokalj, Žiga, Klemen Zakšek, and Krištof Ošti. 2011. "Application of Sky-View Factor for the Visualization of Historic Landscape Features in Lidar-Derived Relief Models." *Antiquity* 85 (327): 263–73.

Kuhn, Steven, David A. Raichlen, and Amy E. Clark. 2016. "What Moves Us? How Mobility and Movement Are at the Center of Human Evolution." *Evolutionary Anthropology: Issues, News, and Reviews* 25 (3): 86–97.

Kuhn, Thomas. 1962. *The Structure of Scientific Revolutions*. Chicago: University of Chicago Press.

Kvamme, Kenneth. 1990. "Spatial Autocorrelation and the Classic Maya Collapse Revisited: Refined Techniques and New Conclusions." *Journal of Archaeological Science* 17 (2): 197–207.

———. 2003. "Geophysical Surveys as Landscape Archaeology." *American Antiquity* 68 (3): 435–57.

———. 2006. "There and Back Again: Revisiting Archaeological Locational Modeling." In *GIS and Archaeological Site Location Modeling*, edited by

Mark W. Mehrer and Konnie L. Wescott, 3–38. Boca Raton, FL: Taylor and Francis.

Ladefoged, Thegn N., Patrick V. Kirch, Samuel O. Gon, Oliver A. Chadwick, Anthony S. Hartshorn, and Peter M. Vitousek. 2009. "Opportunities and Constraints for Intensive Agriculture in the Hawaiian Archipelago prior to European Contact." *Journal of Archaeological Science* 36 (10): 2374–83.

Ladefoged, Thegn N., Mark D. McCoy, Gregory P. Asner, Patrick V. Kirch, Cedric O. Puleston, Oliver A. Cadwick, and Peter M. Vitousek. 2011. "Agricultural Potential and Actualized Development in Hawai'i: An Airborne LiDAR Survey of the Leeward Kohala Field System (Hawai'i Island)." *Journal of Archaeological Science* 38 (12): 3605–19.

Lander, Faye, and Thembi Russell. 2018. "The Archaeological Evidence for the Appearance of Pastoralism and Farming in Southern Africa." *PLoS One* 13 (6): e0198941.

Lasaponara, Rosa, and Nicola Masini, eds. 2012. *Satellite Remote Sensing: A New Tool for Archaeology.* New York: Springer.

Lekson, Stephen H. 2015. *Chaco Meridian: One Thousand Years of Political Power in the Ancient Southwest.* 2nd ed. Lanham, NY: Rowman and Littlefield.

Levison, Michael, R. Gerard Ward, and John W. Webb. 1973. *The Settlement of Polynesia: A Computer Simulation.* Minneapolis: University of Minnesota Press.

Levy, Thomas, and Ian Jones, eds. 2018. *Cyber-archaeology and Grand Narratives: Digital Technology and Deep-Time Perspective on Culture Change in the Middle East.* New York: Springer.

Limp, William (Fred), and Adam Barnes. 2014. "Solving the Grid-to-Ground Problem When Using High-Precision GNSS in Archaeological Mapping." *Advances in Archaeological Practice* 2 (2): 138–43.

Lin, Albert Yu-Min, Andrew Huynh, Gert Lanckriet, and Luke Barrington. 2014. "Crowdsourcing the Unknown: The Satellite Search for Genghis Khan." *PLoS One* 10 (3): e0121045.

Lipo, Carl P., and Terry L. Hunt. 2005. "Mapping Prehistoric Statue Roads on Easter Island." *Antiquity* 79 (303): 158–68.

Lipo, Carl P., Terry L. Hunt, and Sergio Rapu Haoa. 2013. "The 'Walking' Megalithic Statues *(Moai)* of Easter Island." *Journal of Archaeological Science* 40 (6): 2859–66.

Livarda, Alexandra, and Hector A. Orengo. 2015. "Reconstructing the Roman London Flavourscape: New Insights into the Exotic Food Plant Trade Using Network and Spatial Analyses." *Journal of Archaeological Science* 55: 244–52.

Llobera, Marcos, and Tim J. Sluckin. 2007. "Zigzagging: Theoretical Insights on Climbing Strategies." *Journal of Theoretical Biology* 249 (2): 206–17.

Lock, Gary, and John Pouncett. 2017. "Spatial Thinking in Archaeology: Is GIS the Answer?" *Journal of Archaeological Science* 84: 129–35.

Lucas, Gavin. 2005. *The Archaeology of Time.* New York: Routledge.

Mantha, Alexis. 2009. "Territoriality, Social Boundaries and Ancestor Veneration in the Central Andes of Peru." *Journal of Anthropological Archaeology* 28 (2): 158–76.

Martindale, Andrew, and Kisha Supernant. 2009. "Quantifying the Defensiveness of Defended Sites on the Northwest Coast of North America." *Journal of Anthropological Archaeology* 28(2): 191–204.

Marwick, Ben, and Suzanne E. Pilaar Birch. 2018. "A Standard for the Scholarly Citation of Archaeological Data as an Incentive to Data Sharing." *Advances in Archaeological Practice* 6 (2): 125–43.

Masao, Fidelis T., Elgidius B. Ichumbaki, Marco Cherin, Angelo Barili, Giovanni Boschian, Dawid A. Iurino, Sofia Menconero, Jacopo Moggi-Cecchi, and Giorgio Manzi. 2016. "New Footprints from Laetoli (Tanzania) Provide Evidence for Marked Body Size Variation in Early Hominins." *eLife* 5: e19568.

McCormick, M., G. Huang, G. Zambotti, and J. Lavash. 2013. "Roman Road Network (Version 2008)." *DARMC Scholarly Data Series*, no. 2013-5.

McCoy, Mark D. 2017. "Geospatial Big Data in Archaeology: Prospects and Problems Too Great to Ignore." *Journal of Archaeological Science* 84: 74–94.

McCoy, Mark D., Gregory P. Asner, and Michael W. Graves. 2011. "Airborne Lidar Survey of Irrigated Agricultural Landscapes: An Application of the Slope Contrast Method." *Journal of Archaeological Science* 38 (9): 2141–54.

McCoy, M. D., Ladefoged, T. N. 2009. "New Developments in the Use of Spatial Technology in Archaeology." *Journal of Archaeological Research* 17 (3): 263–95.

McCoy, Mark D., Peter R. Mills, Steven Lundlad, Timothy Rieth, Jennifer G. Kahn, and Rowan Gard. 2011. "A Cost Surface Model of Volcanic Glass

Quarrying and Exchange in Hawai'i." *Journal of Archaeological Science* 38
(10): 2547–60.

McKechnie, Iain, and Madonna L. Moss. 2016. "Meta-analysis in Zooarchaeology Expands Perspectives on Indigenous Fisheries of the Northwest Coast
of North America." *Journal of Archaeological Science: Reports* 8: 471–85.

Meldrum, Jeff, and Esteban Sarmiento. 2018. "Comments on Possible
Miocene Hominin Footprints." *Proceedings of the Geologists' Association* 129
(4): 577–80.

Menze, B., and Jason A. Ur. 2012. "Mapping Patterns of Long-Term Settlement in Northern Mesopotamia at Large Scale." *Proceedings of the
National Academy of Sciences* 109 (14): E778–87.

Milton, Katherine. 1988. "Foraging Behavior and the Evolution of Primate
Cognition." In *Machiavellian Intelligence: Social experience and the evolution
of intellect in monkeys, apes and humans,* edited by A. Whiten and R. Byrne,
285–305. Oxford: Oxford University Press.

Mol, Angus A. A., Aris Politopoulos, and Csilla E. Ariese-Vandemeulebroucke. 2017. "'From the Stone Age to the Information Age:' History and
Heritage in *Sid Meier's Civilization VI*." *Advances in Archaeological Practice*
5 (2): 214–19.

Montenegro, Álvaro, Richard T. Callaghan, and Scott M. Fitzpatrick. 2016.
"Using Seafaring Simulations and Shortest-Hop Trajectories to Model the
Prehistoric Colonization of Remote Oceania." *Proceedings of the National
Academy of Sciences* 45 (113): 12685–90.

Nash, David J., Sheila Coulson, Sigrid Staurset, J. Stewart Ullyott, Mosarwa
Babutsi, and Martin P. Smith. 2016. "Going the Distance: Mapping
Mobility in the Kalahari Desert during the Middle Stone Age though
Multisite Geochemical Provenancing of Silcrete Artefacts." *Journal of
Human Evolution* 96: 113–33.

Nathan, Ran. 2008. "An Emerging Movement Ecology Paradigm." *Proceedings of the National Academy of Sciences* 105 (49): 19050–51.

Neiman, F. D. 1997. "Conspicuous Consumption as Wasteful Advertising: A
Darwinian Perspective on Spatial Patterns in Classic Maya Terminal
Monument Dates." In *Rediscovering Darwin: Evolutionary Theory and
Archaeological Explanation,* edited by C. M. Barton, 267–90. Arlington, VA:
American Anthropological Association, .

Norambuena, Pablo, and Juan Sainz. 2016. "UAS Survey of Rapa Nui: Capturing 164 Square Kilometers of the World's Most Remote Inhabited Island." *GIM International,* June 29, 2016. Accessed December 19, 2018. https://www.gim-international.com/content/article/uas-survey-of-rapa-nui.

Opitz, Rachel, and Jason Herrman. 2018. "Recent Trends and Long-standing Problems in Archaeological Remote Sensing." *Journal of Computer Applications in Archaeology* 1 (1): 19–41.

Opitz, Rachel, and W. Fred Limp. 2015. "Recent Developments in High-Density Survey and Measurement (HDSM) for Archaeology: Implications for Practice and Theory." *Annual Review of Anthropology Volume* 44: 347–64.

O'Rourke, Michael J. E. 2018. "The Map Is Not the Territory: Applying Qualitative Geographic Information Systems in the Practice of Activist Archaeology." *Journal of Social Archaeology* 18 (2): 149–73.

Osborne, Anne H., Derek Vance, Eelco J. Rohling, Nick Barton, Mike Rogerson, and Nuri Fello. 2008. "A Humid Corridor across the Sahara for the Migration of Early Modern Humans Out of Africa 120,000 Years Ago." *Proceedings of the National Academy of Sciences* 105 (43): 16444–47.

Paliou, E., Wheatley, D., and G. P. Earl. 2011. "Three-Dimensional Visibility Analysis of Architectural Spaces: Iconography and Visibility of the Wall Paintings of Xeste 3 (Late Bronze Age Akrotiri)." *Journal of Archaeological Science* 38 (2): 375–86.

Parker Pearson, M., and Ramilisonina. 1998. "Stonehenge for the Ancestors: The Stones Pass on the Message." *Antiquity* 72 (276): 308–26.

Pedersen, Mikkel W., Anthony Ruter, Charles Schweger, Harvey Friebe, Richard A. Staff, Kristian K. Kjeldsen, Marie L. Z. Mendoza, Alwynne B. Beaudoin, Cynthia Zutter, Nicolaj K. Larsen, Ben A. Potter, Rasmus Nielsen, Rebecca A. Rainville, Ludovic Orlando, David J. Meltzer, Kurt H. Kjær, and Eske Willerslev. 2016. "Postglacial Viability and Colonization in North America's Ice-Free Corridor." *Nature* 537: 45–49.

Peeples, Matthew A. 2018. *Connected Communities: Networks, Identity, and Social Change in the Ancient Cibola World.* Tucson: University of Arizona Press.

Penny, Dan, Cameron Zacherson, Roland Fletcher, David Lau, Joseph T. Linier, Nicholas Fischer, Damian Evans, Christophe Pottier, and Mikhail Prokopenko. 2018. "The Demise of Angkor: Systematic Vulnerability of Urban Infrastructure to Climate Variations." *Science Advances* 4 (10): eaau4029.

Petersson, Bodil. 2016. "Waterworld: Travels in Time between Past and Future worlds." In *The Archaeology of Time Travel: Experiencing the Past in the Twenty-first Century,* edited by Bodil Petersson and Cornelius Holtorf, 201–12. Oxford: Archaeopress.

Petersson, Bodil, and Cornelius Holtorf, eds. 2016. *The Archaeology of Time Travel: Experiencing the Past in the Twenty-first Century.* Oxford: Archaeopress.

Phillips, Steven J., Robert P. Anderson, and Robert E. Schapire. 2006. "Maximum Entropy Modeling of Species Geographic Distributions." *Ecological Modelling* 190 (3–4): 231–59.

Pickels, John. 1995. "Representations in an Electronic Age: Geography, GIS, and Democracy." In *Ground Truth: The Social Implications of Geographic Information Systems,* edited by John Pickels, 1–30. New York: Guilford Press.

Pinhasi, Ron, Joaquim Fort, and Albert J. Ammerman. 2005. "Tracing the Origin and Spread of Agriculture in Europe." *PLoS Biol* 3(12): e410.

Premo, L. S. 2004. "Local Spatial Autocorrelation Statistics Quantify Multi-scale Patterns in Distributional Data: An Example from the Maya Lowlands." *Journal of Archaeological Science* 31 (7): 855–66.

Primeau, Kristy E., and David E. Witt. 2018. "Soundscapes in the Past: Investigating Sound at the Landscape Level." *Journal of Archaeological Science: Reports* 19: 875–85.

Quintus, Seth, Stephanie S. Day, and Nathan J. Smith. 2017. "The Efficacy and Analytical Importance of Manual Feature Extraction using Lidar Datasets." *Advances in Archaeological Practice* 5 (4): 351–64.

Raichlen, David A., B. M. Wood, A. D. Gordon, A. X. Mabulla, F. W. Marlowe, and H. Pontzer. 2014. "Evidence of Scale-Free Lévy Walk Foraging in Human Hunter-Gatherers." *Proceedings of the National Academy of Sciences* 111 (2): 728–33.

Reeder-Myers, L. A., and M. D. McCoy. 2019. "Preparing for the Future Impacts of Megastorms on Archaeological Sites: An Evaluation of Flooding from Hurricane Harvey, Houston, Texas." *American Antiquity* 84 (2): 292–301.

Reinhard, Andrew. 2018. *Archaeogaming: An Introduction to Archaeology in and of Video Games.* New York: Berghahn Books.

Renfew, Colin. 1972. "Trade and Culture Process in European Prehistory." *Current Anthropology* 10 (2/3): 151–69.

Richards-Rissetto, Heather. 2017. "What Can GIS + 3D Mean for Landscape Archaeology." *Journal of Archaeological Science* 84: 10–21.

Rockman, Marcy, and James Steele, eds. 2003. *Colonization of Unfamiliar Landscapes: The Archaeology of Adaptation.* London: Routledge.

Rosenswig, Robert M., and Ricardo López-Torrijos. 2018. "Lidar Reveals the Entire Kingdom of Izapa during the First Millennium BC." *Antiquity* 92 (365): 1292–1309.

Sadr, Karim. 2015a. "The Impact of Coder Reliability on Reconstructing Archaeological Settlement Patterns from Satellite Imagery: A Case Study from South Africa." *Archaeological Prospection* 23 (1): 45–54.

———. 2015b. "A Comparison of Accuracy and Precision in Remote Sensing Stone-Walled Structures with Google Earth, High Resolution Aerial Photography and LiDAR: A Case Study from the South African Iron Age." *Archaeological Prospection* 23 (2): 95–104.

Sadr, Karim, and Xavier Rodier. 2012. "Google Earth, GIS and Stone-Walled Structures in Southern Gauteng, South Africa." *Journal of Archaeological Science* 39 (4): 1034–42.

Schiffer, Michael B. 1972. "Archaeological Context and Systemic Context." *American Antiquity* 37 (2): 156–65.

———. 1976. *Behavioral Archaeology.* New York: Academic Press.

Schmidt, Gavin A., and Adam Frank. 2019. "The Silurian Hypothesis: Would It Be Possible to Detect an Industrial Civilization in the Geological Record?" *International Journal of Astrobiology.* 18 (2): 142–50.

Sevara, Christopher, Michael Pregesbauer, Michael Doneus, Geert Verhoeven, and Immo Trinks. 2016. "Pixel versus Object: A Comparison of Strategies for the Semi-automated Mapping of Archaeological Features Using Airborne Laser Scanning Data." *Journal of Archaeological Science: Reports* 5: 485–98.

Silva, Fabio, Chris J. Stevens, Alison Weisskopf, Cristina Castillo, Ling Qin, Andrew Bevan, and Dorian Q. Fuller. 2015. "Modelling the Geographic Origins of Rice Cultivation in Asia Using the Rice Archaeological Database." *PLoS One* 10 (9): e0137024.

Skonieczny, C., P. Paillou, A. Bory, G. Bayon, L. Biscara, X. Crosta, F. Eynaud, B. Malaize, M. Revel, N. Aleman, J.-P. Barusseau, R. Vernet, S. Lopez, and F. Grousset. 2015. "African Humid Periods Triggered the Reactivation of a Large River System in Western Sahara." *Nature Communications* 6: ncomms9751.

Smith, Michael E. 2009. "V. Gordon Childe and the Urban Revolution: A Historical Perspective on a Revolution in Urban Studies." *Town Planning Review* 80 (1): 1–29.

Smith, Michael E., Gary M. Feinman, Robert D. Drennan, Timothy Earle, and Ian Morris. 2012. "Archaeology as a Social Science." *Proceedings of the National Academy of Sciences* 109 (20): 7617–21.

Smith, Monica L. 2014. "The Archaeology of Urban Landscapes." *Annual Review of Anthropology* 43: 307–23.

———. 2019. *Cities: The First Six Thousand Years*. New York: Viking.

Stichelbaut, Birger, W. DeClerq, D. Herremans, and Jean Bourgeois. 2013. "First World War Aerial Photography and Medieval Landscapes: Moated Sites in Flanders." In *Archaeology from Historical Aerial and Satellite Archives*, edited by W. S. Hanson and I. A. Oltean, 69–85. New York: Springer.

Sullivan, Elaine. 2017. "Seeking a Better View: Using 3D to Investigate Visibility in Historic Landscapes." *Journal of Archaeological Method and Theory* 24 (4): 1227–55.

Sunseri, Jun Ueno. 2015. "A Horse-Travel Approach to Landscape Archaeology." *Historical Archaeology* 49 (2): 72–91.

Supernant, Kisha. 2017. "Modeling Métis Mobility? Evaluating Least Cost Paths and Indigenous Landscapes in the Canadian West." *Journal of Archaeological Science* 84: 63–73.

Surovell, Todd A., Jason L. Toohey, Adam D. Myers, Jason M. LaBelle, James C. M. Ahern, and Brian Reisig. 2017. "The End of Archaeological Discovery." *American Antiquity* 82 (2): 288–300.

Szymanowski, Rafal. 2016. "The Mobility Turn in the Social Sciences." In *Cultures of Motorway: Localities through Mobility as an Anthropological Issue*, edited by Agata Stanisz and Waldemar Kuligowski, 183–93. Wielichowo: TIPI.

Taylor, Candacy. 2016. "The Roots of Route 66." *The Atlantic*, November 3, 2016.

Thompson, Kenneth, Simon Fitch, and Vincent Gaffney, eds. 2007. *Mapping Doggerland: The Mesolithic Landscapes of the Southern North Sea.* Oxford: Archaeopress.

Tilley, Christopher. 2010. *Interpreting Landscapes.* Walnut Creek, CA: Left Coast Press.

Tomasso, Antonin, and Guillaume Porraz. 2016. "Hunter-Gatherer Mobility and Embedded Raw-Material Procurement Strategies in the Mediterranean Upper Paleolithic." *Evolutional Anthropology: Issues, News, and Reviews* 25 (3): 164–74.

Tripcevich, Nicholas. 2007. Quarries, Caravans, and Routes to Complexity: Prehispanic Obsidian in the South-Central Andes. PhD diss. University of California, Santa Barbara.

Trouillot, Michel-Rolph. 1995. *Silencing the Past: Power and the Production of History.* Boston: Beacon Press.

Tulving, Endel. 2002. "Chronesthesia: Conscious Awareness of Subjective Time." In *Principles of Frontal Lobe Function,* edited by D. T. Stuss and R. T. Knight, 311–25. New York: Oxford University Press.

Twain, Mark (Samuel Clemens). 1889. *A Connecticut Yankee in King Arthur's Court.* New York: Charles L. Webster and Co..

Ur, Jason A. 2003. "CORONA Satellite Photography and Ancient Road Networks: A Northern Mesopotamian Case Study." *Antiquity* 77 (295): 102–15.

———. 2010. *Urbanism and Cultural Landscapes in Northeastern Syria: The Tell Hamoukar Survey, 1999–2001.* Chicago: Oriental Institute of the University of Chicago.

VanDyke, Ruth. 2007. *The Chaco Experience: Landscape and Ideology at the Center Place.* Santa Fe: School for Advanced Research.

Vonnegut, Kurt. 1969. *Slaughterhouse-Five, or The Children's Crusade, a Duty-Dance with Death.* New York: Delacorte Press.

Wang, Lin, Yishi Yang, and Xin Jia. 2016. "Hydrogeomorphic Settings of Late Paleolithic and Early-mid Neolithic Sites in Relation to Subsistence Variation in Gansu and Qinghai Provinces, Northwestern China." *Quaternary International* 426: 18–25.

Wells, H. G. 1895. *The Time Machine.* London: Henry Holt and Co..

Wendorf, Fred, Angela E. Close, and Romuald Schild. 1987. "A Survey of the Egyptian Radar Channels: An Example of Applied Archaeology." *Journal of Field Archaeology* 14 (1): 43–63.

Wernke, Steven, Lauren E. Kohut, and Abel Traslaviña. 2017. "A GIS of Affordances: Movement and Visibility at a Planned Colonial Town in Highland Peru." *Journal of Archaeological Science* 84: 22–39.

Wheatley, David, and Mark Gillings. 2002. *Spatial Technology and Archaeology: The Archaeological Applications of GIS.* London: Taylor and Francis.

Whitley, D., and W. A. Clark. 1985. "Spatial Autocorrelation Tests and the Classic Maya Collapse: Methods and Inferences." *Journal of Archaeological Science* 12 (5): 377–95.

Whitley, Thomas G. 2017. "Geospatial Analysis as Experimental Archaeology." *Journal of Archaeological Science* 84: 103–14.

Wickstead, Helen. 2019. "Cults of the Distribution Map: Geography, Utopia and the Making of Modern Archaeology." In *Re-Mapping Archaeology: Critical Perspectives, Alternative Mappings,* edited by Mark Gillings, Piraye Hacıgüzeller, and Gary Lock, 37–72. London: Routledge.

Willey, Gordon. 1953. *Prehistoric Settlement Patterns in the Viru Valley, Peru.* Washington, DC: Smithsonian.

———. 1974. "The Viru Valley Settlement Pattern Study." In *Archaeological Researches in Retrospect,* edited by G. R. Willey, 149–78. Cambridge, MA: Winthrop.

Williams, Alan N., Sean Ulm, Chris S. M. Turney, David Rohde, and Gentry White. 2013. "Holocene Demographic Changes and the Emergence of Complex Societies in Prehistoric Australia." *PLoS One* 10 (6): e0128661.

Winter, Kawika B., Kamanamaikalani Beamer, Mehana Blaich Vaughan, Alan M. Friedlander, Mike H. Kido, A. Nāmaka Whitehead, Malia K. H. Akutagawa, Natalie Kurashima, Matthew Paul Lucas, and Ben Nyberg. 2018. "The *Moku* System: Managing Biocultural Resources for Abundance within Social-Ecological Regions in Hawai'i." *Sustainability* 10 (10): 3554.

Wittenberg, David. 2013. *Time Travel: The Popular Philosophy of Narrative.* New York: Fordham University Press.

Wylie, Alison. 2008. "Mapping Ignorance in Archaeology: The Advantages of Historical Hindsight." In *Agnotology: The Making and Unmaking of*

Ignorance, edited by R. Proctor and L. Londa Schiebinger, 183–205. Palo Alto, CA: Stanford University Press.

Xinqiao, Lu, Guo Huadong, and Shao Yun. 1997. "Detection of the Great Wall Using SIR-C Data in North-western China." *IEEE International Geoscience and Remote Sensing Symposium Proceedings,* 50–52.

Yates, Donna. 2018. "Crowdsourcing Antiquities Crime Fighting: A Review of GlobalXplorer." *Advances in Archaeological Practice* 6 (2): 173–78.

Zedar, Melinda A. 1997. "The American Archaeologist: Results of the 1994 SAA Census." *Society for American Archaeology Bulletin* 15 (2):12–17.